Computers in Linguistics

Computers in Linguistics

Christopher Butler

Basil Blackwell

First published 1985

Basil Blackwell Ltd
108 Cowley Road, Oxford OX4 1JF, UK

Basil Blackwell Inc.
432 Park Avenue South, Suite 1505,
New York, NY 10016, USA

British Library Cataloguing in Publication Data

Butler, Christopher, 1945–
Computers in linguistics.
1. Linguistics — Data processing
I. Title
410'.28'54 P98

ISBN 0–631–14266–5
ISBN 0–631–14267–3 Pbk

Library of Congress Cataloging in Publication Data

Butler, Christopher.
Computers in linguistics.

Bibliography: p.
Includes index.
1. Linguistics — Data processing. I. Title.
P98.B84 1985 410'.028'5 85–7540
ISBN 0–631–14266–5
ISBN 0–631–14267–3 (pbk.)

Typeset by Oxford Publishing Services
Printed in Great Britain by Billings Ltd, Worcester

Contents

Acknowledgements

I should like to express my gratitude to the copyright holder for permission to reproduce Sylvia Plath's poem 'Apprehensions' (From Sylvia Plath's *Crossing the Water*, London: Faber and Faber 1971, copyright Ted Hughes; and from *Winter Trees,* New York: Harper & Row, publishers) in a form suitable for input to the computer (chapter 14). My thanks are also due to Michael Stubbs, not only for permission to use a modified version of his lexical density program in chapter 14, but also for the valuable comments he made on early drafts of the book. I am also grateful to Peter Ford for his comments on chapter 1. Finally, my main debt is to the many students who, during the course of their efforts to assimilate the material presented here, have taught me a great deal about how to teach arts computing. For the many inadequacies which remain in the book I am, of course, solely responsible.

General introduction

It is probably not too much of an exaggeration to claim that the 'micro-processors' which are at the heart of computer systems are the single most important influence on our lives today, and will assume even greater importance in tomorrow's world. The sphere of influence of computers extends from space exploration to our everyday experience of computerised sales points in supermarkets, from the navigation of an aircraft to the booking of tickets by its passengers, from the control of electricity generation to the preparation of the bills which drop through our letter-boxes. The present generation of children are learning to accept such things as ordinary and are already, in their schools, gaining familiarity with the principles of computing. For many of us, however, the computer remains strange, powerful, even rather sinister. Yet, despite the slow emergence of so-called 'expert systems' mimicking human decision-making processes, computers are still very stupid beasts, incapable of action unless programmed by their human masters.

If properly understood, the computer can bring enormous benefit, not least in areas of academic interest which have hitherto been the traditional preserve of dedicated researchers spending long years on the often tedious manual analysis of their materials. The purpose of this book is to show how the computer can aid those who have a professional interest in the study of language. Such interests range over a wide field: one researcher may be engaged in isolating characteristics of the literary style of a particular author; another may wish to obtain information on the frequency and range of vocabulary items or syntactic constructions in technical texts in a foreign language; a third may wish to construct and test a model of the frequency distributions of words in a text; a fourth may have amassed a large body of data which he wishes to analyse for correlations between some linguistic parameter and factors such as age, social class or sex. In all these cases and many more, it is likely that computational methods will be of considerable value.

If computers are really rather stupid machines, needing much human effort before they can be made to do any job, then why, the reader may wonder, are they claimed to be of such value in such a rich variety of tasks? It is true that the machine is capable of only a few basic sorts of operation: as we shall see a little later, it can move items of information from one storage location to another, compare one item with another, and carry out arithmetical operations. The working section of a computer can be thought of as simply a multitude of tiny switches, each of which can be on or off, so that even such apparently simple operations as the comparison of two symbols, or the addition of two numbers, must in fact be broken down into a pattern of binary, on/off events. However, the operation of these 'switches' is electronic rather than mechanical, and herein lies the source of the computer's phenomenal powers. Electrical pulses travel at extremely high speeds, so that the computer works at rates many millions of times greater than those of a human operator. In order to appreciate the order of magnitude involved, let us consider one or two examples. Time yourself roughly in doing the following addition sum:

$$\begin{array}{r} 1582649816480149 82 \\ \underline{6421843307765159 98} \; + \\ \hline \end{array}$$

How long did you take? 15 seconds? 30 seconds? A powerful computer could carry out several million such additions in a single second. Consider a further example, this time from the area of language study. It took Ione Dodson Young about 25 years to produce a concordance (that is, a list of all the occurrences of each word, with context for each) for the complete poetic works of Byron, using traditional manual methods. In 1967, a computer generated a concordance of the complete works of Blake in about three hours (though this does not include the time taken to get the text into computer-readable form, a problem which we shall discuss briefly later). With the latest generation of computers, the time taken would be even less.

Not only is the computer incredibly fast, it is also extremely accurate. Mistakes can sometimes occur because of breakdown of the machine's internal mechanisms, but such cases are much rarer than mistakes due to errors by human programmers. Furthermore, the machine will be just as accurate when performing the millionth calculation or comparison as when performing the first: unlike human beings, it does not suffer from fatigue, boredom or lapses of memory. The mention of memory brings us to a further important point: a computer has, associated with its central processor, a certain amount of internal storage capacity or 'memory'. A small computer, such as the simplest micro-computers selling for around £40, may have only about 1 000 individual storage locations (in the jargon of computing, this would be referred to as 1K, where a K unit represents 1 024 storage locations), while a powerful computer may have several orders of magnitude more. However, this is not the limit of the computer's ability to store data since, as we shall see, additional ('secondary') storage capacity is usually available in the form of magnetic discs or tapes which can hold large amounts of data. This, then, is a further important factor: the computer and its secondary storage devices can hold a very large amount of data indeed (the Bible, or the complete works of Shakespeare, would present no problem whatever for a large machine), whereas the minds of human beings have much more humble capacities.

To sum up: the modern computer gains over the human researcher in its extremely high speed of operation, its relentless accuracy and its huge capacity for storing information. It is, however, capable of only a very few basic operations, so that considerable human ingenuity is needed to reduce complex problems to the machine's level of coding in terms of electrical impulses which are either 'on' or 'off'. It is with ways of inducing the computer to tackle problems in the study of language that the present book is concerned. Part I gives a brief introduction to the modern digital computer and surveys its applications in linguistic and literary studies. This part of the book includes an introduction to some 'pre-packaged' tools available for text analysis, for those who do not wish to learn a programming language. Part II offers a thorough introduction to the programming language SNOBOL4, which was specifically designed for the analysis of natural language texts.

Part I

Computers in linguistic and literary research

1 An introduction to the computer

1.1 Types of computer

When we use the term 'computer', we normally mean a 'digital' computer, which uses counting as its fundamental mechanism. There is another type, known as an 'analogue' computer, which works by measuring various quantities related to the phenomenon under investigation. Analogue machines are normally used only for rather specialised purposes, and we shall assume throughout this book that we are dealing with a digital computer.

Computers can also be classified according to their size and power. Nowadays, a wide range of 'micro-computers' is available for home use, as well as for restricted use in business and scientific applications. These are compact, desk-top machines with limited capacities, though the increasing availability of high-capacity 'secondary storage' devices (see p. 6) for such machines is making it possible for quite serious applications to be implemented on them. Rather larger and more powerful are the 'mini-computers' which are now to be found in even quite small businesses, as well as in industry and academic institutions. At the top end of the scale we have multi-user 'mainframe' computers, which may cost millions of pounds and are capable of handling complex tasks involving very large amounts of data. Because of its complexity and the large quantities of data often involved, linguistic and literary computing is usually carried out on the more powerful machines, and it is this level of work with which the present book is concerned. Some applications, however, can be implemented on less powerful computers, and with the very rapid pace of development in the micro-computer area it is likely that we shall soon be able to perform even quite sophisticated, large-scale analyses in our own homes.

In the following section the structure of a multi-user computer system will be described briefly; for further details readers should consult an elementary textbook on general computing, such as Hunt and Shelley (1983).

1.2 The fundamental components of a computer system

1.2.1 Computer hardware

The overall system The actual physical components of a computer system are often called the 'hardware'. The basic hardware components are shown diagrammatically in figure 1.1.

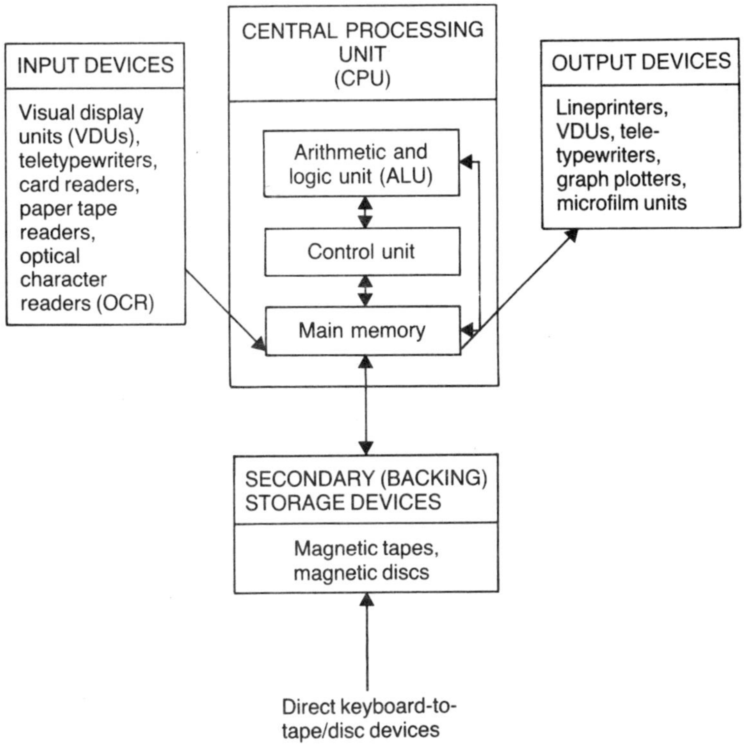

Figure 1.1 The basic hardware components of a computer system

Clearly, we need not only the central processing unit itself, but also some means of getting information into the computer, and some way of getting information out again after processing. Further, we may need secondary storage devices to supplement the limited storage capacity of the central processor itself. Input and output devices and secondary storage are often termed 'peripherals', since they are peripheral to the central processor, and may in fact be situated at some considerable distance from it. We shall now consider each of these principal hardware components in turn.

The central processing unit As shown in figure 1.1, the CPU consists of three parts. The heart of the machine, where the operations involved in comparison or calculation are carried out, is the arithmetic and logic unit (ALU). It will be remembered from the introductory chapter that the computer carries out all its arithmetical and logical operations in terms of a binary code representing 'on' and 'off' states of electrical circuits. In order to perform these operations, the ALU needs to know what tasks it is to perform, and on what data. This information is obtained from the main memory of the computer. Although the main memory may not be large enough to hold all the information relevant to the complete solution of a complex problem, it holds whatever information is relevant at a given point in the solving process. Conceptually, the main memory consists of a number of storage locations, each numbered to provide an 'address' so that the information in each location can be retrieved. Physically, the memory unit usually consists of a large number of microscopic electrical circuits embedded in a silicon chip. The third fundamental part of the CPU is the control unit, which supervises the flow of information between the main memory and the ALU, thus co-ordinating the various stages of processing.

Input devices Methods of getting information (data and instructions) into the computer have undergone important changes over the last few years. Until relatively recently, the usual method was to encode the information on punched cards. A typical card is divided into 12 rows, each with 80 columns. Each symbol which can be recognised by the computer (letters, numbers, punctuation marks, and so on) is represented by a unique combination of punched holes in any given column. The cards are prepared using a card punch, which has a keyboard very like a normal typewriter keyboard. Information punched on cards is usually checked, or 'verified', before it is passed to the computer: a second operator keys the information in again, but on a machine which checks for identity between the new input and the characters already punched. After verification, the cards can be fed into a card reader, which senses the pattern of holes and translates it into a representation of the characters in the computer. Cards can be read at an average rate of approximately 1 000 per minute, that is about 1 350 characters per second. Input by means of cards has a number of disadvantages: mistakes are slow to correct, since a mispunched card must be rejected and repunched; cards may become damaged; large card 'decks' require considerable storage space. Card input has now been largely superseded by other methods.

A second input method is to use paper tape. Like cards, paper tape has a number of rows, or 'channels' across it (often eight), and a pattern of punched holes represents a character. Tape is cheaper than cards, and requires less storage space, but is susceptible to tearing. Furthermore, the continuous nature of paper tape makes it rather difficult to insert or delete material. Paper tape readers work at a maximum rate of about 1 500 characters per second.

The most common method of input for a multi-user system now is the use of a terminal with a keyboard, like a typewriter keyboard, on which the required information can be typed. Increasingly often, this terminal is itself a micro-computer. Most terminals incorporate either a visual display unit (VDU), which displays the information on the screen as it is typed, or a teletypewriter (often abbreviated to 'teletype'), which prints the typed information on paper, so enabling the user to obtain hard copy. Such terminals are very flexible: they can be used for direct interaction with the central processor, or for storing information on secondary storage devices (see p. 6). Furthermore, the correction of errors and the alteration of previously stored information is generally quite simple, since most computer systems have powerful editing facilities for use with terminals. Terminals can be situated at some considerable distance from the central processor, so that an increasing number of users can interact with their local computer, or indeed with a network of computers in more remote locations, from terminals in their own offices.

All the methods of input outlined so far have the disadvantage of being very time-consuming and costly. This is an especially important problem for the linguistic and literary researcher, who often needs to use a large data base for his work. A relatively recent but increasingly available input technique, optical character recognition (OCR), overcomes this problem to a large extent. For some time now, computers have been used to sense highly standardised marks on, for example, multiple choice examination papers. Now, a refinement of this technique can be used to 'read' a wide variety of printed and typed materials, and to convert the data into a form which can be stored on magnetic tape or disc (see pp. 6–7). Typical of such devices is the Kurzweil Data Entry Machine (KDEM), which is able to recognise a number of standard type founts, and can be trained to read others. The machine matches the pattern of a given character, analysed as a matrix of dots, against a store of known character patterns, and accepts the character if it can be matched to within a certain degree of tolerance. If no such match can be made, the character is displayed on a screen for the user to check and enter the correct character. Given a cleanly printed copy on good paper, the KDEM can read at a rate of some 250–300 words per minute. There can be no doubt that as these machines become cheaper, OCR will be a standard input mechanism for linguistic and literary computing in the future.

Output devices The most common way of obtaining printed output from the computer is to use a lineprinter, consisting of rows of characters attached to a chain or drum. As the correct character is selected, a magnetically controlled hammer prints it in much the same way as a typewriter hammer. Usually, lineprinter output is printed on perforated and folded sheets of paper with a width of 120–36 (often 132) characters, though it is possible to print on smaller slips of paper, specially prepared forms, and so on. By the use of different character sets, output in non-Roman alphabets can be produced if required. Lineprinters can print at the rate of about 1 500 lines per minute. Other printers becoming commonly available include laser printers and smaller daisy wheel and dot matrix printers, the latter two often being attached to the terminal, so that the need to wait for centralised output is avoided.

In scientific applications, much use is made of plotters which can produce graphical output. Graph plotters are also of interest to the linguistic and literary researcher, since they can be adapted to plot the characters of non-Roman alphabets without the need for special lineprinter character sets.

Information can also be output to VDU and teletype terminals. VDUs are most suitable for cases where the output is simply to be inspected, but no hard copy is needed; if a printed copy is required, a teletype can be used.

A final output method of considerable interest to linguistic and literary researchers is computer output microfilm (COM), a device which takes information on magnetic tape (see below) and converts it, at high speeds, into a highly reduced photographic image on microfilm, which may be in roll form or as individual 'microfiches'. Since the output from a linguistic or literary analysis can often be voluminous, microfilm offers a cheap and compact way of storing results. The only disadvantage is that a special reader is needed to magnify the image to normal size for inspection. Hard copy is easily generated by means of a printing attachment.

Secondary ('backing') storage We have seen that the central memory capacity of a computer is limited (although large mainframe machines can contain very large internal memories), so that it may not be able to hold, at any one time, all the information necessary for the solving of a problem. This is often the case, for example, where the processing of large amounts of text is being undertaken. Thus secondary, or 'backing', storage is often needed to supplement the main memory. Information stored on secondary devices can be transferred to and from the CPU as required. Secondary storage can be used not only as temporary holding devices, but also as permanent stores for information which will be required repeatedly for processing. There are two main types of secondary storage, magnetic tapes and magnetic discs, each with their own advantages and limitations.

Magnetic tape is available in reels up to 2 400 feet long, and is similar to that used on domestic tape recorders, except that it is rather stronger and wider. Across the width of the tape are a number of tracks (usually nine) containing spots which can be either magnetised or unmagnetised. The pattern of spots across the tape at any one point represents a character, just as does the pattern of holes punched on paper tape or cards. Information is written to the tape, and read from it, by means of read/write heads, one per track. Magnetic tape is a 'serial' storage device, that is, the information can be read only in the order in which it was encoded on tape. This means that the entire tape may need to be scanned in order to retrieve certain items, so that access to information is relatively slow. However, magnetic tape is cheap and easily stored, and a 2 400-foot tape can hold up to 30 million characters, which can be transferred to the main memory at a rate of up to 800 000 characters per second. The information on a tape can, of course, be erased when no longer required, and replaced by fresh information. For these reasons, magnetic tape is widely used, especially for applications where serial searching is not disadvantageous.

Magnetic discs are rather like gramophone records, arranged in packs mounted on a central rotating shaft. As on tapes, information is stored as patterns of magnetised and unmagnetised spots in tracks. In most disc units there is, for each surface, a head which moves across the tracks to write information to the disc or read from it; some disc units have a number of fixed read/write heads. Unlike the head of a magnetic tape unit, that of a disc unit can access any item of information without having to scan all the previous information; that is, it is a 'direct access' system. This greatly decreases the search time for information, as compared with a magnetic tape: the average search time for a large disc unit would be about 10 milliseconds (i.e. 0.01 sec.). Transfer rates to the CPU are also very high, up to about 1.2 million characters per second. The capacity of a large disc is extremely high, up to about 1 280 million characters. Thus discs offer considerable advantages over tapes; disc cartridges are, however, very much more expensive than magnetic tapes. As with tapes, information on discs can be erased and replaced as required. Mention should also be made of the small flexible 'floppy discs' which are becoming increasingly important, especially for micro- and mini-computer systems. These discs are loaded in cartridge form, and typically hold up to 500 000 characters.

Whatever the type of storage device used, information is organised into what are called 'files', each of which consists of a number of 'records', which may correspond to a punched card, a line on a VDU screen, or whatever. We might, for instance, set up a data file containing a particular poetic text, each record encoding one line of verse. The instructions to the computer to do a particular job may also be retained in files (see section 1.4).

1.2.2 Computer software

So far, we have concentrated on computer 'hardware', the actual machinery which constitutes the CPU and peripheral devices. However, this sophisticated machinery can do nothing unless it is given instructions, these instructions being referred to as the 'software'. The present book is concerned principally with the kinds of software which are of especial usefulness in solving problems connected with language study. It should be realised, however, that a large amount of software, written by computer manufacturers and by systems designers, is involved in the control and integration of the various components of a computer installation. When such an installation is running smoothly, the average user can, of course, remain blissfully unaware of the complex flow of information regulating not only the running of his own job, but also its interaction with jobs being run by other users.

1.3 What can the computer do?

This whole book is, of course, concerned with what computers can do in the field of linguistic and literary research. Here, we shall merely suggest a general classification of the kinds of task for which the computer is suited.

Firstly, the computer may be used as a *sorting* device. It can compare two items stored in its memory, on the basis of their numerical value or their position in an alphabetical sequence. This function of the computer is probably more important in the social and psychological sciences than in the physical sciences, and is the basis of many applications to language study, from the analysis of questionnaire data to the production, from textual data, of word lists in alphabetical or frequency ordering.

Secondly, the computer may be used as a very sophisticated *counting* device, able to perform complex calculations at a very high speed. This function is of paramount importance in the physical sciences, where the processing of large amounts of numerical experimental data (often referred to as 'number-crunching'!) is often required. The calculating function is also important, however, in many other areas, including the study of language. As we saw in the introductory chapter, many linguistic studies require the collection and statistical processing of quantitative data, and this processing is a task for which the computer is very well suited.

These two functions, of sorting and counting, are the basis of those linguistic applications of computing concerned with the analysis of textual data, data from tests, and the like. These are the applications on which we shall be focusing here. There are, however, other types of application, which we shall mention only in passing in chapter 2, and which involve the use of the computer as a *model-testing* device or as a *simulating* device. Both of these functions are ultimately derived from the sorting and counting functions, but perhaps require a few words of separate explanation.

Many of those interested in the study of language for various purposes spend much of their time constructing models of the phenomena they are studying. The purpose of a model is to provide a simplified representation of a restricted range of phenomena, which can be tested and modified. Models may be concrete (for example a hardware model of the human vocal tract) or abstract (for instance a mathematical model of the vocabulary distribution in a text, or a set of linguistic rules modelling part of the native speaker's grammar). Computers are useful in testing the extent to which the model is an accurate reflection of the phenomena it purports to represent. We might, for example, use a computer to generate all the sentences allowed by a certain set of linguistic rules, and then compare these with the grammaticality judgements of native speakers. Or we might test the degree to which a mathematical model of the vocabulary distribution of a text accounts for a set of observed data.

Finally, we turn briefly to the use of computers to simulate the activities of human beings. Considerable advances are being made in the computer simulation of human speech production, and, to a lesser extent, speech recognition. We might also mention here the creative use of computers, for instance in the writing of 'concrete poetry', an activity parallel to the use of sound synthesisers in the construction of musical works, or the production of works of computer art.

1.4 Computer programming: some fundamental concepts

Earlier, we made a distinction between physical 'hardware' and the 'software' needed to make the machinery do the jobs required of it. The software consists of *programs* (the American spelling of the word is in standard use), containing ordered sequences of instructions to the machine.

In order to write a program of instructions in some form which is (directly or indirectly – see below) intelligible to the computer, we must first break down the problem we wish to solve, into elementary steps to be performed in a certain order; this sequence of steps is known as an *algorithm*. The process of deciding on the logic of a program can be conducted in ordinary English, being essentially independent of the 'language' in which the instructions will finally be expressed (though, as we shall see, different computer languages tend to be particularly suitable for different types of task). The steps which will eventually be translated into a program are often displayed diagrammatically in the form of a *flowchart*. Consider the process of reading lines of text from a data file, testing each for whether or not it contains a question mark, and printing out those lines which do have a question mark, together with the number of such lines (see figure 1.2).

Certain symbols are conventionally used to indicate particular types of step within a flowchart:

beginning or end of process

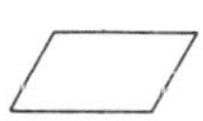
input of data or output of results

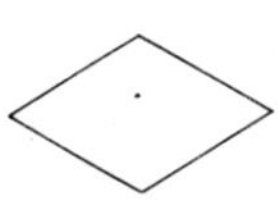
decision point, with yes or no answer

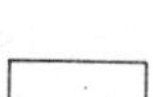
action

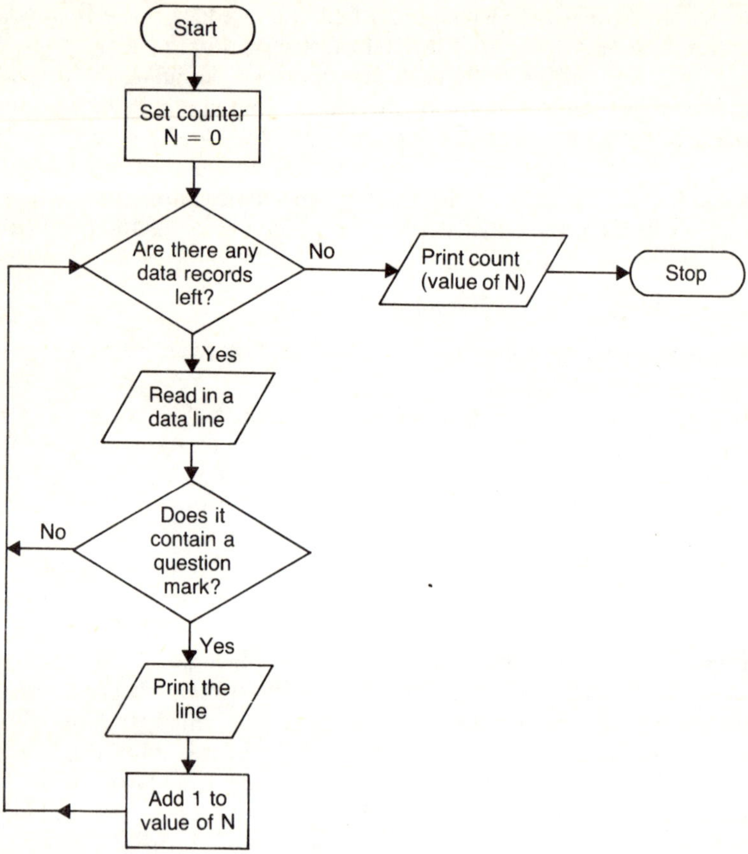

Figure 1.2 Flowchart for printing all text lines containing a question mark. (See text)

It cannot be too strongly emphasised that in the construction of an algorithm nothing must be taken for granted or left to chance: the computer will need very precise and absolutely explicit instructions if it is to carry out its allotted task. When we have decided on a suitable algorithm for the task in hand (whether by drawing a flowchart or in some less formal manner) we are in a position to encode the instructions in a form intelligible to the computer; that is, we can write a program.

It will be remembered from the introductory chapter that the computer operates in terms of a binary code representing the state of electrical impulses. The only 'language' it understands directly is its own *machine code*, a representation of these binary elements. Programming in machine code is useful for certain purposes (machine code programs are fast, because the machine understands the instructions directly), but extremely tedious, and is best left to experts in computer services and home micro-computer owners wishing to run fast games programs and the like. To overcome some of the tedium of machine code programming, many systems have a so-called *assembly language*, which allows the use of mnemonics standing for combinations of machine code operations, and is translated into machine code by a special program called an assembler.

For the average user, by far the most important method of giving instructions to the computer is to use a *high-level language* such as BASIC, FORTRAN, ALGOL, PASCAL, COBOL or SNOBOL, the last of these being the language we shall describe in detail in Part II of this book. There are many other high-level languages, some of general use, some specific to certain types of application. Each instruction in a high-level language may represent a number of machine operations, so that programming is more economical and less tedious than in machine code or even an assembly language. High-level languages have their own 'vocabulary' of terms, and a 'syntax' specifying the ways in which these terms may be used. Violation of the rules may produce errors which are fatal and cause termination of the program, or which produce wrong results. As with an assembly language, instructions in a high-level language (the so-called 'source program') must be translated into a form which the computer can easily use (the 'object program'), by a special program built into the system. In the case of high-level languages, this translation program is called a *compiler*. Clearly, the machine must have a compiler for each high-level language which can be used on it. For most high-level languages, including such common ones as FORTRAN and PASCAL, compilers are available which convert the source program directly into an object program in machine code, which can be stored and used again without the need to recompile each time. However, many implementations of the less common languages, including SNOBOL, are normally run using 'interpreters', which translate the source program statement by statement during the actual running or 'execution' of the instructions. Yet other compiling systems, such as the one to be discussed in chapter 13, convert all the source program into a more compact intermediate form, which is then interpreted.

Learning a high-level language obviously requires effort and time, though we shall see later that it is effort well spent. Potential computer users who wish to do just one particular job (say, the production of word lists for a series of texts) may not be willing to learn to write their own programs. For such users, 'package programs' may provide at least some of the answers to their problems. These are designed to carry out particular types of analysis in response to reasonably simple instructions, given in something approaching English, so that the user needs to know very little about how the program works. The user's instructions drive a program, or set of programs, written in a high-level language, which in turn can be translated into machine code by the appropriate compiler. We shall discuss some package programs for text analysis in chapter 3. Meanwhile, in chapter 2, we shall examine the scope of linguistic and literary computing.

2 The scope of linguistic and literary computing

2.1 Introduction

In this chapter we shall survey the kinds of application to which computers have been put in the study of language. Most of the chapter will be devoted to the use of the computer in the processing of textual material, and the uses to which such processing may be put. There then follows a brief note on the use of computers in the processing of numerical data from linguistic research.

2.2 What kinds of linguistic unit can we sort and count?

The computer can recognise only those symbols which are part of its own character set: letters, punctuation marks, spaces, numbers, various other symbols such as %, + and so on. A text in machine-readable form is simply a sequence of such characters encoded in a standard way on magnetic tape, disc, or whatever. Sorting and counting must be reduced, ultimately, to operations on such sequences. It follows that analyses at the graphological level (the level at which letters combine to form orthographic words, and words to form phrases and sentences delimited by punctuation) are relatively easy to carry out, while the ease of obtaining information on units at other levels depends on the extent to which rules can be specified for the deduction of categories at these levels from sequences of graphological units. We shall consider below the levels of graphology, phonology (the sound system), lexis (vocabulary), syntax (the combination of words in grammatical constructions) and semantics (meaning).

2.2.1 Graphological analyses

It is a simple matter to obtain counts of individual letters and punctuation marks appearing in a text. The production of lists of word-forms for a text is also an easy task, as is the counting of such forms. The definition of a word-form can be determined by the user: for example, we may take only spaces and punctuation marks to be word delimiters (in which case hyphenated forms and forms with apostrophes will be considered as single words), or we could include hyphens and apostrophes as word separators, so that *tea-pot* will be analysed as two words, *tea* and *pot*, and *John's* also as two words, *John* and *s*. Word lists can be sorted by the computer in various ways: in order of ascending or descending frequency, in alphabetical order, or in alphabetical order of the reverse of the word (that is, starting from the end of the word rather than the beginning – useful for studies of rhyme, word structure, and so on).

Moving up the scale of analytical sophistication, we may produce an *index* of some or all of the word-forms in a text, giving a reference location for each occurrence of each word selected. The reference given may be determined by the user: for a prose text the chapter and line number would probably suffice; for a set of poems the poem title, stanza and line number; for a play perhaps the act, scene, character speaking, and line number.

For some purposes, an index provides insufficient information, because there is no indication of the actual context for each occurrence of a word-form. In such cases a *concordance* may be produced. This gives, in addition to a reference location for each citation, a certain amount of context (for instance a line, a sentence, a certain number of printed characters), again determined by the user. Concordances can be arranged in various ways: a particularly useful format is that in which the 'keyword' is arranged centrally on the page, with context on either side. The contexts themselves can also be sorted in various ways: for example by alphabetical order of the context on the right or left of the keyword (the former allowing the user to pick out recurrent phrases), or in order of occurrence in the text. Concordances, while giving more information than indexes, are very much bulkier, and hence costlier to produce. Because of this, the producer of a concordance may well have to make compromises which reduce the volume of the output. Clearly, a large amount of context for each citation will improve the usefulness of the concordance for some purposes, but shorter contexts will reduce considerably the size of the finished product. Similarly, the inclusion of even very high-frequency grammatical words (such as *the, and, in* for English) may be useful for those who wish to study certain aspects of syntax, but will produce many pages of output, so that we may decide on a compromise solution, such as producing an index, rather than a concordance, for all words over a certain frequency limit. For discussion of these and other problems involved in concordance making, see Oakman (1973), Spevack (1973), Ingram (1974), Dixon (1978), Burton (1981a, b, c, 1982). Examples of output from concordance-generating programs will be given in chapter 3.

In addition to word-lists, indexes and concordances, we may produce statistical information giving, for example, the numbers of words occurring once, twice, three times, and so on (that is, a 'frequency profile' for the words in the text), or the 'type/token ratio' (the number of different words as a ratio of the total number of running words). We may also obtain easily information on the length of graphological units, for instance the distribution of word lengths in terms of letters, or of sentence lengths in terms of words.

Because of the ease of producing analyses at the level of letters and word-forms, and the availability of package programs for this type of analysis (see chapter 3), most computational work on texts has relied on analysis at this level.

2.2.2 Lexical analyses

We have seen that the output of normal word-lists, indexes and concordances is based on word-*forms*, since these are what can be easily recognised by the computer. In studies of the vocabulary of a text, however, we are often more interested in the frequency of particular *lexemes*, which can often be represented by a number of separate word-forms. Take the lexeme LOVE, for example: this could appear in a text as *love, loves, loved, loving*; the lexeme BE has no fewer than eight forms: *be, is, am, are, was, were, been, being*. In highly inflected languages such as Finnish, or even German, the number of word-forms corresponding to a given lexeme may be even greater. For instance, the German verb AUFNEHMEN could appear in a text in any of over 30 forms, and the Finnish verb OTTAA in about 60 forms. In a word-list or concordance, all these forms would normally be listed separately. In some cases, as with LOVE, the forms would not be too widely separated in the list or concordance, but this would not be true of all cases (for instance, BE). Furthermore, even when the different forms have been located, their frequencies have to be summed to give an overall value for the lexeme. This process of grouping the forms of a lexeme, or 'lemma', is called *lemmatisation*.

Unfortunately, lemmatisation is difficult to automate, because the rules for recognising a form as an instance of a particular lemma are complex and have not been specified in a completely explicit way for any one language. Progress has, however, been made in the lemmatisation of English (Dawson, 1974), Old English (Venezky, 1973a), French (Meunier, Boisvert and Denis, 1976; Maegaard, 1976), German (Hann, 1975; Krause and Willée, 1981), Swedish (Hellberg, 1972), Arabic (Bathurst, 1971), Hebrew (Price, 1969), Russian (Sågvall, 1973), Serbo-Croatian (Spraycar, 1980), Dutch (Boot, 1980) and Latin (Wolfart, 1979).

2.2.3 Syntactic analyses

Syntactic analysis of a text requires the recognition of clause and phrase boundaries, and the classification of clauses (as main or subordinate, for instance), phrases (as nominal, verbal, prepositional, and so on) and individual words (as nouns, verbs, adjectives, or other parts of speech). Additionally, we may require to know the grammatical functions of the phrases, for instance as subject, object, adjunct, or whatever. In an automatic analysis, the computer must be able to deduce this information simply from the sequence of letters, spaces and punctuation marks. This is clearly an extremely difficult task, and it is not surprising that automatic parsing systems are often considerably less than 100 per cent accurate. In order to obtain some idea of the problems involved, let us consider briefly how we might attempt to isolate English clauses, and within these, just one kind of phrase, the prepositional phrase.

One possible clue to clause boundaries is punctuation: colons and semicolons most often separate clauses (as in the present sentence); commas may also act as clause separators, though they have other functions as well. A further useful feature is that subordinate clauses are often introduced by subordinating conjunctions (such as *because, if, although*), which form a fairly small finite set of items easily stored as a 'dictionary' inside the computer. Even this recognition device has its complications: for example, some subordinating conjunctions have the same form as words acting as other parts of speech (for instance, *when* and *where* can be interrogative adverbs, *as* can be a preposition). Co-ordinating conjunctions (such as *and, but, or*) can also be useful, though again there are serious complications, since these can join units other than clauses (as in '*John and Mary* arrived', 'The *intelligent but dull* boy got a PhD', 'Have you *seen or heard* the postman?'.

The first stage in isolating a prepositional phrase is to recognise the preposition itself, and this is easily done by reference to a dictionary of prepositions stored in the machine. A rather more difficult task is to recognise where the prepositional phrase ends. Here, it is useful to ask what items could *not* normally be found in a prepositional phrase. If the computer scans along the text from a preposition and finds, for example, an auxiliary verb (such as *have, can, may* and so on – again a small finite list which can be stored as a dictionary), a punctuation mark other than a comma, or another preposition, it is likely that the prepositional phrase has already ended. Double preposition constructions such as *because of, up to*, are a complicating factor for the last criterion, but the computer can be instructed to treat these as part of a single phrase. Having isolated the phrase, we might attempt to assign classes to its component words by considering the likely structures of phrases of different lengths. A two-word prepositional phrase, for instance, will consist of just preposition + noun (as in *to London, in cities*). A three-word phrase is likely to consist of either preposition + determiner + noun (for example, *in the city, for this reason, by my mother*) or preposition + adjective + noun (*in large cities, for good reasons*); these two possibilities can be differentiated by reference to a dictionary of determiners, since these again constitute a fairly small finite set of items. A four-word prepositional phrase will normally be either preposition + determiner + adjective + noun (as in *in a large city*) or preposition + adjective + adjective + noun (*in large dirty cities*); again, we can decide between the two possibilities by reference to a dictionary of determiners.

Techniques similar to those outlined above in fact form part of the strategy used by a package program for syntactic analysis, EYEBALL. We shall discuss this program further in a later section in this chapter and the use of a more recent version of the program, OXEYE, will be described in chapter 3. It is hoped that this very brief treatment of some issues in the parsing of clauses and prepositional phrases will have given some idea of the multitude of problems faced by the designer of an automatic syntactic analyser. These difficulties have caused many researchers to resort to the precoding of their texts by insertion of markers indicating the grammatical classification of the words and phrases. The computer would then be used simply to sort and count the patterns revealed (see also section 2.4).

2.2.4 Phonological analyses

The degree to which raw text can be successfully processed to yield information about the use of the sound system of a language depends on the extent to which the phonological properties of the language can be derived from the graphological properties by explicit rules. For a language such as Spanish or Czech, in which there is a close and consistent relationship between letters and sound units, we could assume, as a first approximation, that a given letter represents the same sound unit wherever it occurs. If this is done for a language such as English or French, however, problems arise due to the complex correspondences between letters and sound units. Consider the English letter *i*, which can be pronounced in a number of ways (as in l*i*st, mach*i*ne, *i*ce, not to mention its occurrence in combinations such as *ie, ei, ai, oi*), or the letter *c*, which is pronounced like an *s* before *e* or *i*, but like a *k* before *a, o, u* or a consonant, or at the end of a word. 'Silent' letters such as *k* in Modern English *knight, w* in *wren*, or *nt* in French *aiment*, are a further problem. Of course, if these complex letter/sound relationships can be worked out in the form of absolutely explicit rules, they can be converted into a form which will allow the computer to determine the phonological value of each letter or letter combination in a text. The complexity of such a task has, however, caused some investigators to regard automatic phonological analysis as unrealistic at present, and to recode their texts in the form of sound unit representations before feeding them into the computer. In such analyses, as with syntactically precoded texts, the machine is being used merely to sort and count the occurrences of various classes of unit.

Some success has been achieved in the automatic metrical analysis of poetry, especially in Latin and Greek, where syllable lengths can often be assigned by a consideration of the spelling. For example, in Latin verse, any vowel letter which is followed by two consonant letters (with certain specifiable exceptions) must be in a long syllable.

2.2.5 *Semantic analyses*

We have seen that syntactic analysis by computer presents grave problems; we might expect the difficulties of a semantic analysis to be even greater, since meaning is even more abstract than linguistic form. One approach is to study the 'collocations' of individual items, that is, the way they associate with other items. Some items show highly regular, predictable collocations (for example, *rancid* with *butter, addled* with *egg*); however, if large amounts of textual data are analysed, larger scale patterns of statistical association can be discerned. By comparison of the collocates of a large number of items, 'sets' of lexically related words within semantic 'fields' can be isolated. A second approach is to produce word-lists, and analyse them automatically by means of a thesaurus held within the computer system, to isolate predominant themes in the text.

A much simpler and more frequently used technique is for the investigator to start with an intuitive conception of a particular semantic field (say of colour, or parts of the body), and to prepare a word-list for the text, which he can then scan for items within his chosen field. He can then produce concordances of those items in which he is interested.

2.3 Uses of analyses at the various levels

In this section, we shall present a brief review of the major uses to which computational techniques of text analysis have been put, with the intention of giving the reader an overview of the computer's potential in this area, in the hope that he may be stimulated into consulting original work in fields which interest him.

2.3.1 *Computational stylistics*

Style as a quantitative phenomenon Literary critics and linguists alike have long puzzled over the question 'What is style?', and even a cursory glance at the literature reveals a bewildering variety of definitions. The following attempt, by Nils Enkvist, highlights the essentially quantitative nature of the phenomenon: 'The style of a text is a function of the aggregate of the ratios between the frequencies of its phonological, grammatical and lexical items, and the frequencies of the corresponding items in a contextually related norm' (Enkvist, 1964: 28).

This type of approach to style encourages us to think that the computer may be of considerable usefulness in stylistic studies, if we can program it to recognise and count the phonological, grammatical and lexical features involved. Literary critics have sometimes been rather sceptical of statistical studies of texts, feeling that 'mere counting' can never reveal the essence of literature as the product of creative acts. It is indeed true that the ease with which the computer can handle large amounts of textual data and produce statistical analyses of whatever it counts in the text can lead (and has led) to investigations in which the identification and counting of linguistic features appears to be an end in itself. In any study which professes to be stylistic, rather than simply using literary texts as a convenient source of linguistic material, it is important that the quantitative properties of texts should be related to literary interpretation. Provided that we bear this in mind, and recognise the difficulties of isolating linguistic features at other than the graphological level, automatic analysis can be a very useful tool in stylistics, helping to obtain objective quantitative evidence for the stylistician's subjective hunches, and even bringing out patterns which the investigator had not suspected were present. Space does not permit detailed discussion here of the problems inherent in a quantitative approach to style; for a balanced treatment of the issues, see Leech and Short (1981).

We may recognise two broad areas within the domain of computational stylistics. Firstly, computers have been used to study the stylistic characteristics of particular texts, authors, genres, periods, and so on: we could call this 'pure' computational stylistics. In some cases this involves examining just one body of texts; in others, two or more sets of texts are compared. Secondly, isolation of stylistic 'fingerprints' by computer has been used to help solve problems concerned with disputed authorship, chronology and integrity of texts. This area constitutes what we might think of as 'applied' computational stylistics. We shall look briefly at each area in turn, giving examples of studies focusing on the various levels of linguistic analysis discussed in section 2.2.

'Pure' computational stylistics A large number of studies have used word-lists, indexes or concordances, with or without lemmatisation. Raben (Raben, 1964; Raben and Lieberman, 1976) used automatically produced indexes to study vocabulary similarity in Milton's *Paradise Lost* and Shelley's *Prometheus Unbound*; Burton (1968, 1973) found an automatically generated concordance of grammatical words (articles, conjunctions, prepositions, and the like) useful in comparing the styles of two Shakespeare plays, *Antony and Cleopatra* and *Richard II*; Crosland (1975) used a concordance to study the symbolic devices employed in Fitzgerald's *The Great Gatsby*, and was able to show that the impressionistic statements found in much of the critical literature on the work should be regarded with caution. Duggan (1973) found concordances helpful in his study of oral formulaic style in the medieval French *Chanson de Roland*: Adamson (1977, 1979) used an index and concordance to study colour terms in Camus's *L'Étranger*, drawing parallels between colour and psychological phenomena; Ariew's (1978) work on Breton's surrealist prose poem 'Poisson Soluble' employed a word-index to show periodic patterns of fire and water images.

Word-lists have also been used to study vocabulary richness (that is, the extent of the author's tendency to use many different words rather than repeating the same vocabulary items over and over again) as a stylistic feature. The simplest measure of vocabulary richness is the *type/token ratio*, which is the ratio of the number of different words to the total number of running words. Unfortunately the type/token ratio is dependent on text length, as well as on the author's style, so that this simple measure can be validly used only to compare texts of approximately equal length. Techniques are available, however, to compensate for the effect of text length (see, for example, Martin, 1974; Honoré, 1979). For examples of studies using vocabulary richness as a stylistic indicator, see the work of Martin (1973, 1974) on Dutch poetry and prose, and Butler (1979) on the poetry of Sylvia Plath.

Word length and sentence length, which, as we have seen, are easily measured by means of a computer, have also been used as stylistic indicators. Tallentire (1976) used computational analysis to confirm his intuitions about word and sentence length differences in the work of Virginia Woolf and Katherine Mansfield. English (1977), studying the short stories of the Russian writer Leskov, in which a story narrated by one of the characters is embedded within the authorial narrative, showed that the authorial and character narratives differed significantly in both word and sentence length. Butler (1979) showed that word and sentence length distributions in the poetry of Sylvia Plath exhibited variations consistent with a strong overall trend towards formally simpler language in the later poems than in the earlier ones.

Punctuation counts can also be useful in stylistic studies, though it is important to be aware of the possible complicating effects of editorial changes in this area. For an example, see again Butler's (1979) work, showing a greater proportion of run-on lines, and of 'formal' punctuation marks such as the colon and semicolon, in the earlier poetry of Sylvia Plath than in the later work (see also chapter 14 of the present book, where some of the programs used in this work are discussed).

Let us turn now to phonological analyses. Both alliteration and metrical patterning have been studied by means of the computer. Wright (1974) assumed that letter frequencies would give a rough guide to alliterative patterning in Shakespeare sonnets. We saw earlier that the complexity of the relations between sound units and letters in English makes this a somewhat vain hope, and indeed Wright's results are disappointing; for instance, *w* appeared in one line in the words *ow'st, wandrest, when* and *grow'st*, and one would clearly not want to call these instances of alliteration on the sound unit /w/. The same problem arose in Kliman's (1973) work on the Scots poet Barbour, in which a simple program was written to print all lines containing initial alliteration, as judged by letter repetition. Kliman's solution to the problem of non-one-to-one correspondence was to instruct the computer to print asterisks below lines with problematic letters such as *c* in initial position in more than one word. This pinpoints instances of false alliteration (for example between *c* and *ch*), but misses true alliteration between, for instance, *c* (followed by *e* or *i*) and *s*. Rather more successful was Dilligan's study of Robert Bridges' experiments in 'quantitative verse' (Dilligan, 1972). Dilligan programmed the computer to produce rather broad phonetic transcriptions of the texts, from which patterns of assonance and alliteration were tabulated. However, in later, more sophisticated analyses (Dilligan and Bender, 1973) it was found that the automatically produced transcription was too broad to be useful, and a more accurate transcription was supplied manually for each word type in the text. The results of the analyses are impressive, including not only counts of vowels, consonant clusters, and patterns of assonance and alliteration, but also information on metrical patterning. In work by Logan (1982), a phonemic dictionary was built up gradually as successive texts were processed, and the dictionary was used to provide a partial transcription of further texts, which acted as a basis for automatic scansion.

Metrical phenomena in Latin and Greek verse have been studied computationally by Waite (1973, 1977). A common metrical pattern in such verse is the dactylic hexameter, which has a regular basic structure with specifiable variations. The spelling is, in many cases, a good guide to the length of syllables: for example, as we saw earlier, in Latin, a vowel followed by two consonants must normally be in a long syllable. Thus quite a number of syllable lengths in each line can be determined automatically, and the resulting partial analysis checked against the possible scansion patterns. In over 90 per cent of cases, only one scansion fits the observed pattern. Unfortunately, not all types of metre are as amenable to automatic scansion as the dactylic hexameter. For example, the iambic senarius, much used by Plautus, has 7 776 possible scansions. Even here, however, the computer can help. Manual allocation of syllable quantities to each word as the investigator comes to it in a text would be wasteful, since many of the words are repeated. It is much more efficient to produce a word-list first, assign syllable quantities to each word on the list, then get the computer to assign these quantities to each occurrence of each word in the texts. There are some complications, due to the fact that some words may have more than one possilbe scansion; these are overcome by printing out problem lines for manual allocation of quantities. Elision also produces complications, but again the machine can be instructed to print out all lines where elision is possible.

Computational work on the syntax of literary texts falls into two broad categories: those investigations where the texts are manually precoded for syntactic categories, and those in which the computer itself is used to perform the syntactic analysis. In the former category come several studies based on the work of Milic (1967), who provided manual codings for texts by Swift and four of his contemporaries. Milic then used the computer to determine the percentages of various word classes, the percentage of sentences beginning with each word class, and the distribution of patterns of groups consisting of three words. In this way, stylistic markers for Swift were isolated. Among the studies using modified versions of Milic's categories are the analysis of 'Golden' Elizabethan verse by Cherubini (1975) and Cluett's (1976) stylistic study of a wide range of English prose texts.

Among studies which have used the computer as a syntactic parser for stylistic purposes, particular mention should be made of a number of investigations using the EYEBALL package mentioned earlier, developed by Ross and Rasche in the USA (see Ross and Rasche, 1972; Ross, 1973, 1981). Such studies include Ross's (1974) work on Blake's *Songs of Innocence and Experience*, showing the remarkable syntactic similarity of the two sets of texts, and Pringle and Ross's (1977) study of Joyce's *Ulysses*, demonstrating syntactic differences between dialogue and narrative mode. Other automatic parsing programs have been used for stylistic analysis (see, for example, Oakman's (1975) study of Carlyle's syntax), but EYEBALL and its later version OXEYE seem to be the most promising tools in this area.

We saw earlier that a number of investigations have used word indexes and concordances in the study of 'themes' (such as that of colour) in literary texts. An approach which makes greater use of the computer in performing these essentially semantic tasks is to use a built-in dictionary or thesaurus, which allows word-lists to be sorted into semantic groupings. Examples include Dengler's (1974) work on Roman Catholic catechisms, Spolsky's (1970, 1974) semantic analyses of poetry, Sedelow's (1970) programs for the thematic analysis of English text, and Fortier and McConnell's (1973, 1976) package of programs for isolating themes in French texts.

'Applied' computational stylistics Computational stylistics offers powerful (though easily abused) techniques for the obtaining of objective quantitative data which may aid in the solution of problems of disputed authorship or chronological placement of texts. The general strategy is to use the computer to examine a large number of linguistic features, in the hope of isolating a set of stylistic markers or 'fingerprints', uniquely characterising a particular author, period, or whatever. Extreme care must be exercised in such work, for an author's style may be influenced by many and varied factors in addition to his own individuality. The language used by an author in an early short story may well differ considerably from that used by the same author in a mature novel. The aim in characterising the work of a particular author is therefore to examine as wide a range of work as possible, in order to search for stylistic parameters which are constant across different genres and periods of the author's output, and whose values for the writer in question differ significantly from the values for other authors with whom he is to be compared.

Two pioneering studies of authorship began by looking at sentence length, but found that certain aspects of vocabulary were better discriminators. Ellegård's (1962a and b) work on a set of eighteenth-century letters written under the pseudonym Junius used the computer simply to produce tables and perform statistical calculations on manual counts, in a variety of samples from eighteenth-century writers, of words judged by Ellegård to be of higher relative frequency in the Junius letters than in his samples as a whole. It is unfortunate that at the time of Ellegård's work (less than 25 years ago!) memory storage was too limited to allow automatic word counting on large corpora. Mosteller and Wallace (1964) worked on a rather simpler problem: which of two writers, Alexander Hamilton or James Madison, had written a set of 12 disputed papers out of 88 propaganda documents, collectively called the Federalist papers, produced in 1787–8. Sentence length having proved similar in authentic samples from the two writers, Mosteller and Wallace went on to produce computerised word counts, which revealed that Hamilton used quite frequently certain words (such as *enough, while* as opposed to *whilst, upon*), which were rare or non-existent in Madison's work. These stylistic fingerprints showed a very high degree of probability in favour of Madison as the author of the disputed papers.

Austin (1970), in his work on the disputed authorship of a sixteenth-century English manuscript, the *Groatsworth of Wit*, also relied on the large differences in relative frequency of certain words in the writing of two authors, in this case Robert Greene and Henry Chettle. Austin developed quantitative criteria for isolating such marker words and, using automated concordances of the disputed work and authentic works by the two authors, was able to deduce that the text was likely to be by Chettle.

Much the same technique was used in research by Kenny (1977, 1978), intended to solve a slightly different kind of problem. Classical scholars are agreed that two ethical treatises, the Nicomachean Ethics and the Eudemean Ethics, are attributable to Aristotle. Three books, however, appear in both sets of Ethics, and Kenny set out to discover which set they properly belonged to stylistically, or if indeed they were a patchwork of sections from both sets. Kenny used word counts generated by the COCOA package (a forerunner of the Oxford Concordance Program to be discussed in chapter 3), to compare the frequencies of certain high-frequency classes of words (particles, connectives, prepositions, pronouns, demonstratives, the definite article, some adverbs) in the two sets of Ethics and the disputed books, testing the differences for statistical significance. The evidence was strongly in favour of grouping the disputed books with the Eudemean set. This was confirmed by looking at words which were especially favoured in one of the two sets: in almost all cases the disputed books followed the Eudemean rather than the Nicomachean pattern. This study serves as an excellent example of how simple word counts, combined with statistical tests, can aid in text attribution. For a similar study of Aristotle's *Metaphysics*, see Kenny (1979).

Graphological and lexical criteria have also been used in the controversial work of the Revd A.Q. Morton on Classical and New Testament Greek (see Morton, 1965, 1978; Michaelson and Morton, 1972, 1973,

1976). In a paper read to the Royal Statistical Society, Morton (1965) presented the results of analyses of a variety of Greek authors. He studied sentence length distributions, and also the frequencies of common words such as καί (*and*) and δέ (*but*), as in Kenny's work discussed earlier, the idea being that such items are less subject to the writer's conscious control than lower frequency 'lexical' words. Morton claimed that his measures reflected habits which are constant over time and over different subject matters, for a given author and literary genre. He also discussed a number of exceptions to the general pattern, explaining them away in literary terms. Finally, he used his measures to claim that Paul probably wrote only 4 of the 14 'Pauline' epistles, and that the others came from at least 6 different authors. Morton's work has given rise to severe criticism: it has been pointed out that it is difficult to know what constitutes a sentence in Greek prose, where the original punctuation is not available; that sentence length often differs so much within a given author's work that it is suspect as an authorship discriminator; that Morton explains away exceptions by means of those subjective techniques which he himself criticises; and that the application of his techniques to certain groupings of texts gives rise to conclusions about authorship which are contrary to all the historical and theological evidence. Despite this and later criticism, Morton has continued to publish further analyses of the Pauline epistles, based largely on the distribution of frequent items within the sentence (Michaelson and Morton, 1973) and the word class of the last item in the sentence (Michaelson and Morton, 1972). More recently, Morton has attracted yet further publicity by applying stylometric techniques to statements allegedly made by defendants in legal trials, but claimed, by the defendants, to have been written by the police (see Morton, 1978). In this work he has made extensive use of words occurring in adjacent positions (for instance, *of course, as if, that it*).

We turn now to an extensive and very careful authorship study (Kjetsaa, 1976, 1977, 1979) which has utilised both graphological/lexical and syntactic analyses. This is concerned with the Russian novel *The Quiet Don*, the question being whether it was written entirely by Mikhail Sholokhov, or whether Sholokhov in fact plagiarised the work of a minor novelist, Fyodor Kryukov, as had been claimed by an anonymous Russian critic. Kjetsaa has examined large samples from known works by Sholokhov and Kryukov, as well as the disputed work, using a wide range of measures: grouping sentence lengths into classes; the overall distribution of parts of speech; their distribution in the first two and last three positions in the sentence; the type/token ratio and vocabulary frequency profile. All Kjetsaa's measures strongly suggested that Sholokhov wrote his own work, rather than plagiarising Kryukov's. Kjetsaa (1981) has also studied authorship problems connected with Dostoevsky's work.

The syntactic classification developed by Milic, discussed earlier, has been used by Köster (1971) in the investigation of the authorship of a Tory propaganda pamphlet, *The Story of the St Albans Ghost*, written at the time of Swift. Köster compared the pamphlet with known samples from Swift and other writers of the period. Her results were, however, disappointing, since they did not provide compelling evidence for or against any particular authors. Köster, like Milic, used the computer merely to sort and count patterns and perform statistical calculations. Baillie (1974), on the other hand, used the EYEBALL package for automatic syntactic analysis in his investigation of the authorship of *Henry VIII*, claimed to have been written at least partly by Fletcher rather than by Shakespeare. In the preliminary work reported in the paper, certain groupings and ratios of word class and function categories derived from EYEBALL analyses were able to distinguish reliably between samples from Shakespeare's *Cymbeline* and *The Winter's Tale*, on the one hand, and Fletcher's *Valentinian* and *The Woman's Prize*, on the other. The range of variability among different scenes and characters in a given play, and between plays by the same author, was not sufficient to preclude the use of these stylistic identifiers, which were to be used later in the study of the disputed text.

Few studies of disputed authorship have used phonological criteria. One example of such a study is Greenblatt's (1973) work on 'The Expostulation', a poem which has been attributed to both Donne and Jonson. Greenblatt analysed manually the metrical patterns of authentic samples of the two poets, and used the computer to compare these with the patterns for the disputed text, concluding that although Jonson may have been the author, Donne almost certainly was not.

Finally, we should mention studies on the dating of literary works by a given author. Much the same types of technique are appropriate here as for authorship studies. Mansell (1974), for instance, coded syntactic classes manually for Hemingway's *The Old Man and the Sea* and for four other texts written by Hemingway over a period of nearly 20 years. By examining a number of syntactic properties, Mansell was able to conclude that *The Old Man and the Sea* resembled the earlier rather than the later texts, and so was probably composed long before its publication in 1952. More recently, Brainerd (1980) has studied statistically the chronology of Shakespeare's plays. He took a set of 19 plays whose dates were not in question, and isolated a set of factors (frequency of certain lemmas, relative frequency of split lines of verse, percentage of contractions involving pronouns, average length of verse lines) which showed a strong covariation with date. He then used these markers to predict the dates of certain plays for which the year of composition was in dispute.

2.3.2 Lexicography

The production of a dictionary, especially one which purports to be representative of the many varieties of a language, is a dauntingly large and complex task, which may involve a team of lexicographers and the expenditure of considerable sums of money. Since an important part of the lexicographer's work is concerned with the gathering and sorting of large amounts of textual data, it is not surprising that most modern dictionary projects have turned to the computer for help. We shall see, however, that although the computer is indeed invaluable in dictionary-making, the skills of the human lexicographer are irreplaceable at certain stages of the process.

In order to assess the value of the computer in this area, let us first examine the stages in the traditional manual production of a dictionary. The range of coverage must first be decided: for instance, whether the dictionary is to be representative of non-standard as well as standard forms of the language, what weighting is to be given to spoken and written media, and so on. It must also be decided how much information is to be given: for example, the degree of detail of syntactic classification, or indications of the variety of language to which the word belongs. A body of textual material will then be collected and converted to a form in which it can be used to extract examples of the usage of individual words. In the traditional manual process, a slip of paper would be prepared for each occurrence of each word to be considered for inclusion in the dictionary. On these slips, which would be sorted into alphabetical order, would be written the word-form and the context in which it appears, together with the lemma or headword to which it belongs. This process obviously involves the lexicographer in performing manual lemmatisation of the word-forms, and in distinguishing homographs (words which are spelled the same, but have different meanings, such as *bark*, used of a dog or a tree). The distinction between the two meanings of *bark* is a fairly clear case of homography, but it is not always obvious whether we are dealing with two separate vocabulary items, or with multiple but related meanings of a single item (known as polysemy). Take, for example, the word *head* in its various uses as a noun: the head of the human body, the head of a school or firm, the head of a river, and so on. These all have a common semantic feature (being at the 'top' of something), so should we perhaps treat them as a range of meanings of a single item? In deciding questions of this kind, the lexicographer may rely on a combination of criteria, including the degree of relatedness of meaning, also the etymology of the items (the two items *bark* have different etymologies, but the various uses of *head* have the same historical origin). After sorting and arranging the various senses for polysemous words, and choosing appropriate citations for each use of every word he wishes to include, the lexicographer is ready for the final stage, the preparation of the dictionary for printing. This will involve decisions about layout, the use of typographical devices for indicating headwords, syntactic classification, and so on.

We may now assess the extent to which the computer may lighten the lexicographer's burden at each stage. Clearly, at the stage of excerpting the textual material, the computer is extremely useful. With the development of sophisticated OCR techniques (see p. 5), the preparation of large textual corpora in machine-readable form no longer presents such a major problem. The computer can then produce word counts, indexes and concordances as required. Concordance citations can be produced on individual slips of paper if desired. Decisions will, of course, have to be made about the extent of excerption of the texts: it is likely that for very common words only a portion of the corpus will need to be fully excerpted, although the lexicographer must keep a watch for rare uses of common items. Problems may also arise in deciding on the optimum size and type of context for each citation. Mechanically selected contexts, such as a line of text or a certain number of characters either side of the headword, often prove unsuitable, especially for prose, since they usually correspond to no particular syntactic unit. Various possible solutions to the problem are discussed by de Tollenaere (1973): more flexible contexts can be obtained by pre-editing the texts to indicate mini-contexts ending at sensible points (a method suitable only for small corpora), or by an automatic procedure based on a hierarchy of punctuation marks, designed to give a syntactic unit of context wherever possible.

The computer is rather less useful in the tasks of lemmatisation and homograph separation. As we saw earlier, lemmatisation is quite difficult to accomplish automatically, although progress is being made. Automatic homograph separation is also extremely problematic, since the computer has no internal representation of the meaning of the items. A number of dictionary projects have used a combination of manual and automatic procedures for dealing with these problems. One technique, used in the production of the *Dictionary of Old English* in Toronto (see Bratley and Lusignan, 1976; Cameron 1977), is to lemmatise one text manually, using the interactive facilities of a computer terminal, and storing in the computer a 'machine dictionary' giving the lemma for each word-form which occurs in the text. This machine dictionary can then be used to lemmatise any of the word-forms which recur in a second text. At this stage, the results are checked, homographs separated, and any new lemmas added for word-forms not previously encountered. In this way, the machine dictionary becomes ever more complete, and the lemmatisation of further texts increasingly efficient. When all the texts have been lemmatised, the computer is used to generate a concordance with all the word-forms sorted by lemma. A second technique, used in the production of a historical dictionary of Italian at the Accademia della Crusca in Florence, is to allocate a number to each successive word-form in the texts, and tell the computer which numbered words to assign to a given lemma (see Aitken, 1971). A third possibility, used in the preparation of the *Trésor de la langue française (TLF)* at Nancy, is to provide to the computer a look-up list of commonly occurring forms, with their lemmas. A technique of potential use in sorting out homographs is the analysis of collocations into which lexical items enter. For instance, *bark*, in one of its meanings, might be expected to occur quite frequently in the company of items such as *dog, loud,* and so on, while in its other meaning it might occur with *tree, branch* and similarly related words. However, we do not yet have enough detailed information about collocations in any one language for this to be a generally useful tool at present, though some use has been made of the technique in the *TLF* project.

The computer is unfortunately of very little help at the stage of editing the various citations for potential dictionary entries. It is at present not possible to give the machine the kind of information needed to decide between homography and polysemy, so that the lexicographer himself must still undertake the task of deciding on entries and sorting words into their senses. However, the computer may be of some use in presenting citations, for example on a VDU screen, for perusal by the lexicographer.

The final stage, of arranging headwords, citations and additional information, and printing them out, is one at which the computer can offer considerable benefits. The lexicographer may type, on a terminal keyboard, abbreviated references to quotations, codes for different typefaces and layouts, and so on, and the computer may be programmed to produce the required output. The quality of the best computer-generated output is now so high that automatic photocomposition is frequently used as a method of printing the final product.

Less than 15 years ago, Aitken (1971: 15) wrote: 'In the end, perhaps, the essentially selective aims (so far as concerns particular occurrences of words) of the conventional historical dictionary and the computer's lack of discrimination remain fundamentally incompatible.' In the 1980s, it remains true that the lexicographer's role is indispensable; however, the computer has proved an extremely valuable adjunct to these essential human skills. For details of computer-aided dictionary projects, readers are referred to Aitken's (1971) work on the *Dictionary of the Older Scottish Tongue*, Bailey and Robinson's project concerned with a dictionary of Early Modern English (Bailey and Robinson, 1968; Robinson and Bailey 1973), Henderson's (1975) work on a dictionary of American English dialectal forms, Lara's (1976) work on a dictionary of Mexican Spanish, and the accounts by Spevack of work on a dictionary of Shakespeare's writing (Spevack, Neuhaus and Finkenstaedt, 1974; Spevack and Neuhaus, 1977). Further discussion of a more general nature can be found in Alford (1973), Venezky (1973b) and Allén (1977).

2.3.3 Textual editing

Like the production of a dictionary, the preparation of a critical edition of a literary text can be broken down into a number of stages, some of which can benefit considerably from the aid of the computer, while others involve operations requiring the skill and knowledge of the human editor.

The first stage is the collection of the variant texts on which the final edition will be based. The texts must then be examined in order to isolate the places where they vary. From the list of variants, the editor attempts to decide on the 'stemmatic' relationship between the texts, often expressed in the form of a family tree, showing the putatively original text at the top, with various groups of related versions descending from it. In this process, the editor may be guided by various criteria, such as dates of production (if known), and which readings are supported by the largest number of occurrences. The next stage is the reconstruction of the text using selected readings from the variants, and the compilation of an 'apparatus criticus' giving the most significant variant readings, usually printed at the bottom of each page of the reconstructed text. The final stage is the printing of the finished edition.

The stage of locating the texts for comparison will be made easier as more and more bibliographical data bases become available in machine-readable form. This computerisation is already under way for the catalogues of some libraries of worldwide importance.

The task of isolating variants is one which would seem ideally suited to the computer's ability for rapid sorting, and this is indeed the stage which has been most extensively investigated in terms of computerisation. There are, however, some difficult problems. Firstly, it is not always clear what should be taken as constituting a variant. Most projects on automatic collation of texts have considered any variation, including omissions and additions of words, variant spellings, even capitalisation and punctuation differences, as significant. Others (for example Silva and Love, 1969) have ignored punctuation, capitalisation, and certain other differences which were considered non-significant. Yet others (for example Petty and Gibson, 1970) have adopted statistical measures of similarity between blocks of words in the texts under comparison.

A second problem is detecting the end of a variant. It is very simple for the human eye to scan quite large sections and rapidly find where the texts come back into alignment. For the computer, this is a time-consuming process, for which fully explicit rules must be given. The projects which have examined the feasibility of computerised collation have adopted a number of different approaches to this problem, and several have built-in facilities for levels of scanning of various degrees of fineness, first looking for small local variations, then, if the variant is more extensive, examining successively larger blocks of text until a match is found (for examples see Froger, 1967; Cabaniss, 1970; Gilbert, 1973, 1976).

It is important that the variants should be printed out in a form which allows easy inspection by the editor. Perhaps the best plan is to print in full each line from a text chosen as a base, together with a list of variants below it, showing only those parts of the line which differ from the base text. This system is adopted in, for instance, Widmann's (1971, 1973) work on Shakespeare's *A Midsummer Night's Dream*.

The establishment of stemmatic relations between texts is another area where the computer shows great potential, since it requires the comparison of large numbers of variants, often for quite large numbers of texts, in an attempt to determine the degree of relatedness of the texts. Methods of stemmatisation may be based on mathematical models which can be formalised in computational terms (see, for example, Zarri, 1973, 1976,

1977; Griffith, 1968, 1969). For a review of the usefulness and limitations of the computer in this area see Poole (1974).

The reconstruction of the original text and selection of significant variants for the apparatus criticus, at the very heart of the editing task, is an area where the skill and interpretive judgement of the human editor cannot be replaced by a machine. Nevertheless, the computer can still provide some help, for instance in producing concordances of variant readings which can be of considerable value in enabling the editor to decide on the forms to be selected for the final edition.

The final stage, printing of the text and apparatus, like the corresponding stage in dictionary production, is one where the computer is extremely useful. The machine can be used as an interactive text editor, and the final product typeset by photocomposition.

For excellent reviews of computational text editing, the relevant chapters of the books by Oakman (1980) and Hockey (1980) are to be recommended. Further references to work in this area can be found there, and also in the bibliography by Ott (1974).

2.3.4 Language teaching and learning

In recent years there has been a growing interest in the potential of computers as an aid in the teaching and learning of languages. We may divide studies in this area into two types: those in which automatic analysis of texts has been used as an aid to course design, and those in which the computer is used in the presentation of teaching materials to the student.

The analysis of texts can provide lexical and syntactic information which is highly relevant to decisions about the content and ordering of course materials. The production of lemmatised word counts for a range of texts will provide measures of the frequency and range of occurrence of lexical items, both important factors in deciding on the vocabulary content of teaching materials (see, for instance, the work of Burnett-Hall and Stupples (1971) on the construction of a Russian course for schools, and that of Kanocz and Wolff (1971) on the selection of lexical items for a German course run by the British Broadcasting Corporation). Word-lists will also provide information on the frequency of words with primarily syntactic function, such as articles, pronouns, conjunctions, and so on. Lists sorted on the endings of words may be useful in determining the frequency and range of morphological markers of tense, gender, concord relations, and the like (see, for example, Dudrap and Emery's (1971) work on morphological markers of gender in French).

The gathering of information of all these kinds is particularly important in the planning of courses in languages for special purposes, where a maximum of information relevant to specialist users must often be taught in a short time. Automated text analysis was found to be extremely useful in the design of a short course in German for chemistry students, designed at the University of Nottingham (see Butler, 1974). A corpus of some

83 000 words, consisting of articles from German chemistry journals, was prepared in machine-readable form by an early version of the OCR technique, and word-lists and concordances produced by means of the COCOA package program. Word counts were valuable in demonstrating, for example, the quantitative importance of certain pronouns, prepositions, subordinating conjunctions and modal verbs, and the relative unimportance of others. Reverse alphabetical word-lists aided in the investigation of inflected forms of verbs, nouns and adjectives. Concordances were useful in enabling the course writer to find examples of particular classes of item (for instance pronouns, conjunctions and participles) for inclusion in course examples.

The use of computers in the presentation of materials for language learning is an important instance of the computer-assisted learning (CAL) techniques which are increasingly used in our schools and institutions of higher education. A well-designed system can allow the learner a choice of tasks, present the material in a visually interesting manner, provide feedback and reinforcement, and keep scores on tests. The learner can obtain instruction whenever he has access to the computer, and can work at his own pace. There is evidence that computer-assisted language learning is popular with users, often maintaining their interest rather better than a language laboratory course. There are, however, some drawbacks: the production of the software demands considerable expenditure of time and effort; much ingenuity will be needed if computers are to be used to teach languages beyond the stage of drilling vocabulary, morphological forms, and the like; given the rather rudimentary state of speech analysis techniques (see the next section), the computer cannot yet accept spoken input in a flexible manner, so that the improvement of oral fluency is beyond the range of present CAL techniques. For examples of CAL projects in language teaching, see Decker (1976), Holmes (1980) on French, Last (1979) on German and Dutch, Ahmad, Colenso and Corbett (1978) on Russian, Packard (1975) and Gear (1981) on Ancient Greek, Peckett (1975) and Vellios, Erickson and Gulino (1981) on Latin, Brookman, Hockfield and Patton (1981) on Sumerian, and Decker et al. (1981) on Ancient Egyptian hieroglyphics. For reviews of the area, see Higgins (1983), Higgins and Johns (1984), Kenning and Kenning (1983) and Wyatt (1984).

2.3.5 The use of computers in the simulation of human language processing

As our knowledge of human language increases, and as the power and storage capacity of computers becomes ever greater and the cost per unit of power and storage ever smaller, an increasing amount of effort is being put into the construction of systems which will simulate human linguistic activity. These studies are enormously important in both practical and theoretical terms. Practically, they lead to the development of systems for the translation of one human language into another, the rapid interrogation of large data bases giving information on a wide range of subjects, the training of human beings in specialised tasks by means of a dialogue between man and machine, and so on. At a theoretical level, such studies will tell us more about language and its processing by human beings.

We may recognise a number of variables in these studies. Some focus on the ability of the computer to *understand* human languages, others on its ability to *produce* output which is a good approximation to human language; yet others combine these two features. A further variable is whether the input and/or output is to be in the written or the spoken medium. And in cases where the machine is being used both receptively and productively, a further variable is whether the source and target language are the same or different.

It is obviously much simpler for the machine to operate, receptively and productively, with written rather than spoken language. As we have seen, the computer recognises characters corresponding to written English, and can be programmed to recognise transliterations of non-Roman alphabets, and even to recognise and produce non-Roman characters. In a system using the computer for both recognition and production of written language, the task is clearly easiest when the language for input and output is the same. Examples of uses to which such a system could be put include the interrogation of data bases; the understanding and abstracting of written documents such as scientific papers; the production of technical manuals, at various levels of sophistication, from a set of data stored in the machine; and so on. For a relatively non-technical review of such applications, see Hendrix and Sacerdoti (1981).

Studies of the kind mentioned above are essentially applications of the insights gained in the theoretical field of Artificial Intelligence, where important advances have been made in simulating human discourse, taking into account not only the sentence structures and vocabulary of the language, but also discourse connectedness. For studies of this kind, see the work of Winograd (1972) on communication based on a micro-world of coloured blocks of different shapes and sizes, Davey's (1978) program for the generation of text describing a game of noughts and crosses, also the work of McDonald (1980) on natural language production seen as decision making under constraints, McKeown's (1982) work on the generation of text in relation to questions about a data base, and the work of Mann and Matthiessen (see, for instance, Mann and Matthiessen, 1983) on a grammar for automatic text generation based on Halliday's systemic functional grammar. Further discussion can be found in Brady and Berwick (1983).

An additional complication is introduced when the language of input differs from that of the text to be output. The idea that computers could be used to translate from one language to another was suggested in 1946, soon after the first digital machines were constructed. Early enthusiasm gave way to pessimism, as the enormous problems of fully automatic high-quality translation became apparent, and in 1967 funding for work on machine translation was seriously cut by a decision of the National Science Foundation in the USA not to continue their support. Nevertheless, there has been renewed interest in machine translation in recent years, in response to the need to make available the ever-growing quantity of information which emerges from publishing houses, business corporations, government institutions, and so on.

It is generally agreed that fully automatic translation of high quality, accepting any kind of text as input, is an ideal which will not be achieved in the immediate future. Progress towards this ideal is limited by the extent of our knowledge about human languages. In particular, the semantic analysis of language, which is arguably the most important area for machine translation, is still at a rudimentary stage, even for English. Because of these limitations, many experts in machine translation have decided to focus on much more modest aims.

Most of the systems which have been developed operate on specific types of text, for whose translation there is a practical need, and whose range of linguistic properties is more limited than in the language as a whole. Probably the greatest need is for translation of scientific and technical texts, and this is the aim of, for example, the Georgetown Automatic Translation project (see Macdonald, 1979), the CULT project based at the Chinese University of Hong Kong (Loh, 1976; Loh and Kong, 1978; Loh, Hing-Sum and Kong, 1979), the SYSTRAN project (Toma, 1976a and b, 1978), and the project at the University of Montreal designed to translate weather reports (METEO – see TAUM, 1973). The evolution of multilingual bureaucracies such as the European Economic Community creates the need for translation of legal and administrative documents: this is the aim of a large-scale project, EUROTRA, being implemented collaboratively in the EEC countries (see Rolling, 1978; King and Perschke, 1982).

A second way in which the task of designing a machine translation system may be simplified is to concentrate on just one source and one target language. For instance, the CULT system translates between Chinese and English, and SYSTRAN was originally developed for translating Russian scientific journals into English, although it has since been extended to allow translation of other language pairs. For some purposes, however, dual language translation is not appropriate: for instance, the EUROTRA system must ultimately be capable of translating from any of the EEC's official languages into any other.

A third method of simplifying the task of designing a machine translation system is to relax the requirement of full automation, allowing the human user either to pre-edit the input text, or to post-edit the output. The CULT project has adopted the former expedient: complex sentences are broken down into simpler ones before the text is input to the machine. SYSTRAN, on the other hand, uses raw text as input, but relies on post-editing the output. With the increasing availability of OCR techniques for input, it is likely that pre-editing will be seen as undesirable. Post-editing can cause misleading results if done by someone with a good knowledge of the language, but a poorer grasp of the field to which the text refers.

As far as the techniques of machine translation are concerned, two general approaches can be distinguished, whose characteristics are clearly summarised by Macdonald (1979). The *empirical* approach sets out to design a system which will work for a particular type of text for which translation is required, and which is oriented towards the human user rather than towards the demands of the machine. The *theoretical* approach, on the other hand, begins with a model of linguistic description, and formulates, on the basis of this model, rules of strictly controlled types, geared to the goals of computational efficiency. Empirical systems usually operate in a series of stages based on linguistic levels: first, morphological analysis of the source text, then segmentation into syntactic units, insertion and deletion of material according to syntactic constraints, lexical choice, and recombination of the target language items in an appropriate order. Such systems normally allow 'shunting' back and forth in the text, so that problems can be tackled in a particular order, and some problems solved in more than one step. Theoretical systems, on the other hand, tend to integrate the various levels of analysis into a single super-grammar, and are based on sequential, left-to-right processing of the text. Macdonald claims that empirical systems have produced considerably more promising results than theoretical systems, and that a sensible plan might be to develop empirical systems further, then attempt to build in the computational elegance of theoretical systems without sacrificing linguistic efficiency. For other reviews of problems and techniques in machine translation, see Hutchins (1978), CEC (1978), Snell (1979) and Zachary (1979).

It is clear that even when written language is used as input and output for an automatic recognition and/or production system, there are very great difficulties to be overcome. The problems are compounded if spoken input or output is required. Considerable advances are being made in the field of speech synthesis, using computer-controlled electronic hardware models of the human vocal tract, although much remains to be accomplished. For relatively non-technical accounts of this area, see Atmar (1977), Rice (1977), Cater (1983) and Sclater (1983). The recognition of human speech is an even more difficult task, since the vocal apparatus shows such a wide range of individual variation, which is superimposed on differences due to sex, age and accent. We may, however, hope that eventually we shall be able to engage in spoken dialogue with computers. The potential implications of such a development are truly overwhelming.

We shall say nothing here about the artistic use of computers, for instance in the generation of concrete poetry.

2.3.6 Corpus-based descriptive linguistics

Several corpora of English are now available in machine-readable form, and are being used in various areas of description. The first such body of texts was the Brown Corpus, consisting of approximately one million words of written American English made up of 500 texts from material published in 1961. A wide range of material is represented, including newspaper articles, religious writing, scientific publications, fiction of various kinds, and so on. Kučera and Francis (1967) contains alphabetical and rank order frequency lists, also studies of word distribution and sentence length in the corpus.

A corpus of British English parallel to the Brown Corpus, the Lancaster–Oslo–Bergen (LOB) Corpus, has also been assembled. It consists of 500 texts of about 2 000 words each, from British written material published in 1961. The distribution among text categories is very similar to that of the Brown Corpus. Work on the grammatical tagging of the LOB corpus is at an advanced stage (see Leech, Garside and Atwell, 1983; Atwell, 1983).

A third major collection of material, the London–Lund Corpus, consists of spoken educated British English, and is based on the Survey of English Usage, directed by Randolph Quirk at University College London, and prepared for the computer by a team led by Jan Svartvik at the University of Lund. It consists of 87 samples of about 5 000 words each, with detailed prosodic marking. The material includes spontaneous surreptitiously recorded conversations, also non-surreptitious public and private conversations and telephone talk, spontaneous sports and non-sports commentary, speeches in court, political speeches, sermons, lectures, and so on.

The three corpora discussed above, also a grammatically tagged version of the Brown Corpus, are available on magnetic tape, as are complete concordances for the Brown and LOB corpora (the latter incorporating also the words and frequencies from the Brown Corpus, so that comparisons can readily be made), and two concordances for the London–Lund Corpus, one based on spontaneous surreptitiously recorded conversation, the other on the remaining material. The Brown Corpus, also the concordances for the Brown and LOB materials, are also available on microfiche.* A printed version of 34 surreptitiously recorded conversational texts from the London–Lund Corpus can be found in Svartvik and Quirk (1980).

Research based on these corpora is reported in several books (see Johansson, 1982; Hofland and Johansson, 1982; Svartvik et al., 1982; Coates 1982). Numerous articles have also appeared, for example on complementation (Elsness, 1982), relative clauses (de Haan, 1984), modal expressions (Hermerén, 1978; Coates and Leech, 1980; Leech and Coates,

---

*Anyone interested in obtaining the Brown, LOB or London–Lund materials should contact the Norwegian Computing Centre for the Humanities, PO Box 53, N-5014 Bergen-University, Norway. *ICAME News* (the newsletter of the International Computer Archive of Modern English) can also be obtained from this address.

1980; Krogvig, 1981; Krogvig and Johansson, 1981), discourse particles (Svartvik, 1980), topicalisation (Gustafsson, 1982) and verb–particle combinations (Akkerman, 1984).

2.4 The computational analysis of non-textual data

The computer is of use, not only in the analysis of textual material, but also in the manipulation of all kinds of data derived from linguistic observation and experimentation. In the majority of such cases, the manipulations will be of a statistical nature. For instance, we may wish to study the occurrence of certain linguistic variables in the speech of informants from a particular area, classified by age, sex and class, with a view to demonstrating correlations between linguistic and social variables. Or we may be interested in comparing the achievements, on a proficiency test, of two groups of language learners taught by different methods. In such cases, the computer is not involved in the generation of the quantitative data (as it is in, for example, automated parsing or word-frequency listing), but is used, for instance, to prepare tables showing cross-classifications in the data, and to carry out tests for the statistical significance of differences between groups. An understanding of such uses of the computer obviously requires prior knowledge of the statistical principles involved, and the reader is referred to Butler (1985) for details of the techniques and their computational implementation. A brief review of two statistical packages is included in chapter 3 of the present book.

2.5 Conclusion

We have seen, in this chapter, that the computer is of great actual or potential use in a wide range of applications involving human languages, including stylistic studies, lexicography, textual editing, the preparation and presentation of language teaching materials, and the simulation of human linguistic processing tasks such as translation, as well as in descriptive linguistics and in the manipulation of all kinds of data from linguistic observation and experiments, not necessarily involving the automatic analysis of texts. Progress in these areas is limited largely by the extent of our knowledge about human language, and our ability to formulate linguistic problems in ways suitable for solution in computer terms.

In the next chapter, we shall discuss some of the package programs which have been developed to aid the researcher in the solution of the problems reviewed here.

3 Some useful package programs

3.1 Introduction

At the end of chapter 1 it was mentioned that because of the understandable reluctance of many 'occasional' computer users to learn a high-level programming language, various 'package' programs have been written, to allow the inexperienced user to perform certain specific tasks by means of simple English-like instructions. In the present chapter, after an initial discussion of the preparation of textual materials for computer analysis, we shall examine three packages which are especially useful in text processing, and two widely available packages for the statistical manipulation of data.

3.2 The preparation of textual materials

In what follows, it will be assumed that the text is being prepared manually (for example, typed at a terminal) rather than read directly from the printed page by OCR techniques (see p. 5). At the end of this section, a little will be said about OCR-prepared texts.

Clearly, all the information in a text which we wish to include must be represented in terms of the character set of the computer on which the analysis will be run. It cannot be too strongly emphasised that it is advisable to include as much information as is practically convenient when coding the text. Capitalisation (probably of different kinds, such as at the beginning of a sentence, at the beginning of a poetic line, for proper names), changes of typeface, punctuation and layout are likely to be important even for modern texts. With older texts, all kinds of additional information may be required, such as indicators of missing or illegible segments, reconstructed forms, and so on. Some texts may include words in foreign languages, which should be separately marked. For dramatic texts, stage directions need to be distinguished from the text proper. To mark these various features, we can use characters which are not present in the text itself, for instance ↑ , #, $, = and probably %.

For a researcher who is interested just, say, in the occurrence of words pertaining to courtship in the plays of a particular dramatist, it may not be obvious why he should spend time and trouble on the inclusion of all the seemingly irrelevant material suggested above. It should be remembered, however, not only that the same researcher may well wish to pursue different lines of enquiry on the same textual corpus at some later date, but also that his text may be of use to others working on related problems, whose interests in the text may require different information from that which he himself needs. It is always possible to delete unwanted information, but information which has not been coded may be very difficult to recover. Because the preparation of text *is* such a laborious task, the scholar has a responsibility to make sure that his material is of use to as many people as possible. After all, he may himself benefit from similar concern by others.

A further important point concerns the inclusion of text references. In many cases, the processing of a text will involve the production of indexes or concordances which give the location of a word in the text. We must therefore provide, in the coded text, all the information which might be required. For a prose text, the title, author, chapter numbers and page numbers might suffice. For a poetic text, title, author and stanza number (where applicable) might be appropriate. For a dramatic text, we should probably wish to include not only title, author, act and scene numbers, but also an indication of the character who is speaking at a given point. Further information, such as the date of publication and the edition, may also be useful. It is advisable to code text references in a consistent and distinctive format. The safest course is probably to adopt the reference format specified in the COCOA package (word COunt and COncordance on Atlas), which was the forerunner of the Oxford Concordance Program (OCP) to be described in section 3.3. We shall see that the packages reviewed in this chapter accept the COCOA format very readily. The reference is enclosed in angle brackets, and consists of a one-letter identifier of category (for instance, we could choose A for author, T for title, S for stanza, and so on), followed by a space, and then by the actual identification. Examples are given below.

<A Shakespeare>	to indicate Shakespeare as author,
<T Catch 22>	to indicate the title of the novel,
<S 3>	to indicate the third stanza of a poem.

Such references need to be inserted only where there is a change of identification: a new S reference before each stanza of a poem, a new T reference where there is a change of title, and so on. If more than one reference is needed at a particular point, it is best to place each on a separate line.

We are now in a position to code a short piece of simple English text in a form suitable for computational processing. Until quite recently, many computers (and package programs) recognised only 64 different characters, which meant that only upper case letters, numbers, punctuation marks and certain other symbols could be used. Many texts which have been prepared in machine-readable form are therefore in upper case only. In figure 3.1 is a coded representation of the first paragraph of Hardy's *Tess of the d'Urbervilles* (Macmillan edition, 1902) in upper case. There are no complications here, except that initial capitalisation has been indicated by placing a ♯ sign in front of the words concerned (the symbol being, of course, quite arbitrarily chosen).

```
<A HARDY>
<T TESS OF THE D'URBERVILLES>
<C 1>
     #ON AN EVENING IN THE LATTER PART OF #MAY A MIDDLE-AGED
MAN WAS WALKING HOMEWARD FROM #SHASTON TO THE VILLAGE OF
#MARLOTT, IN THE ADJOINING #VALE OF #BLAKEMORE OR
#BLACKMOOR.  #THE PAIR OF LEGS THAT CARRIED HIM WERE RICKETY,
AND THERE WAS A BIAS IN HIS GAIT WHICH INCLINED HIM SOMEWHAT
TO THE LEFT OF A STRAIGHT LINE.  #HE OCCASIONALLY GAVE A SMART
NOD, AS IF IN CONFIRMATION OF SOME OPINION, THOUGH HE WAS NOT
THINKING OF ANYTHING IN PARTICULAR.  #AN EMPTY EGG-BASKET
WAS SLUNG UPON HIS ARM, THE NAP OF HIS HAT WAS RUFFLED, A
PATCH BEING QUITE WORN AWAY AT ITS BRIM WHERE HIS THUMB CAME
IN TAKING IT OFF.  #PRESENTLY HE WAS MET BY AN ELDERLY
PARSON ASTRIDE ON A GRAY MARE, WHO, AS HE RODE, HUMMED A
WANDERING TUNE.
```

Figure 3.1 Coded representation of the opening of Hardy's *Tess of the d'Urbervilles*

Many computers now have up to 256 characters in the character set, and so are able to distinguish between upper and lower case letters. We shall assume that this is so for our next example. Note, however, that it is still advisable to include a marker for proper nouns and related items, so that the machine can distinguish between, for instance, the two occurrences of *Sale* in the sentences below.

Sale of these goods without a licence is prohibited.

%Sale is a town in Cheshire, England.

Here, % has been used as an indicator of proper-name status. In figure 3.2 is shown the text of Oscar Wilde's poem *San Miniato* (Collins edition, 1956) as coded for computer processing. Note that since many computers do not have the long dash in their character set, we have used the equals sign to represent this. The % sign has been used before capitalised proper names.

Now let us consider something rather more complicated. Let us suppose that we wish to prepare the text of Marlowe's play *The Jew of Malta*, in the Penguin edition of 1980. Part of Act 2, Scene 1 is coded in figure 3.3. Here, we have used $ to indicate capitalisation at the beginning of a line, % to indicate capitalisation of proper names, & for any other capitalisation, ♯ for all Spanish words in the text, @ before all italicised words, and (( )) to

```
<A Wilde>
<P San Miniato>
<S 1>
See, I have climbed the mountain side
Up to this holy house of %God
Where once that %Angel-%Painter trod
Who saw the heavens opened wide,
<S 2>
And throned upon the crescent moon
The %Virginal white %Queen of %Grace,=
%Mary! could I but see thy face
Death could not come at all too soon.
<S 3>
O crowned by %God with thorns and pain!
Mother of %Christ! O mystic wife!
My heart is weary of this life
And over-sad to sing again.
<S 4>
O crowned by %God with love and flame!
O crowned by %Christ the %Holy %One!
O listen ere the searching sun
Show to the world my sin and shame.
```

Figure 3.2 Coded representation of Wilde's 'San Miniato'

enclose stage directions. A little more needs to be said about the coding of foreign words and italicised items. If the text contains fairly long stretches of foreign material, or of material in a different typeface, it may be more convenient simply to place a marker at the beginning and end of such a section, rather than before every word. This may indeed be sufficient for some analyses: for instance, we shall see that the OCP package allows material between specified delimiters to be selected on its own, or excluded from the analysis. For certain purposes, however (for instance if we require to list all the words in the text, but with all the foreign words at the end of the list), it may be necessary to convert the more simply coded version into one in which the marker is present before each word. This is easily done by means of a simple supplementary program written in the SNOBOL language described in Part II of this book.

We now turn to the problem of coding languages other than English. Some languages use the Roman script, but have symbol combinations which count as single letters. As examples, the Spanish and Welsh alphabets are given below.

Spanish:	A B C CH D E F G H I J K L LL M N Ñ O P Q R S T U V X Y Z
Welsh:	A B C CH D DD E F FF G NG H I J L LL M N O P PH R RH S SI T TH U W Y

Such combinations give little difficulty in most analyses using text processing packages, since these usually allow the user to specify the alphabet, including any letter combinations which may occur. Multiple characters may, however, increase the difficulty of writing one's own programs to analyse texts. It is therefore worth considering the use of a single character in the coding of combinations: for instance, we could code

```
<A MARLOWE>
<T THE JEW OF MALTA>
<Z 2>
<S 1>
<C ABIGAIL>
$NOW THAT MY FATHER'S FORTUNE WERE SO GOOD
$AS BUT TO BE ABOUT THIS HAPPY PLACE!
$'TIS NOT SO HAPPY: YET, WHEN WE PARTED LAST,
$HE SAID HE WOULD ATTEND ME IN THE MORN.
$THEN, GENTLE %SLEEP, WHERE'ER HIS BODY RESTS,
$GIVE CHARGE TO %MORPHEUS THAT HE MAY DREAM
$A GOLDEN DREAM, AND OF THE SUDDEN WALK,
$COME AND RECEIVE THE TREASURE &I HAVE FOUND.
<C BARABAS>
#@BUENO #@PARA #@TODOS #@MI #@GANADO #@NO #@ERA:
$AS GOOD GO ON, AS SIT SO SADLY THUS.
$BUT STAY: WHAT STAR SHINES YONDER IN THE EAST?
$THE LOADSTAR OF MY LIFE, IF %ABIGAIL.
$WHO'S THERE?
<C ABIGAIL>
$WHO'S THAT?
<C BARABAS>
$PEACE, %ABIGAIL! 'TIS &I.
<C ABIGAIL>
$THEN, FATHER, HERE RECEIVE THY HAPPINESS.
<C BARABAS>
$HAST THOU'T?
<C ABIGAIL>
$HERE,  ((@&THROWS @DOWN @BAGS.))  &HAST THOU'T?
$THERE'S MORE, AND MORE, AND MORE.
<C BARABAS>
$&O MY GIRL!
$MY GOLD, MY FORTUNE, MY FELICITY,
$STRENGTH TO MY SOUL, DEATH TO MINE ENEMY!
$WELCOME THE FIRST BEGINNER OF MY BLISS!
$&O %ABIGAIL, %ABIGAIL, THAT &I HAD THEE HERE TOO!
$THEN MY DESIRES WERE FULLY SATISFIED:
$BUT &I WILL PRACTISE THY ENLARGEMENT THENCE:
$&O GIRL! &O GOLD! &O BEAUTY! &O MY BLISS!
((@&HUGS @THE @BAGS.))
<C ABIGAIL>
$FATHER, IT DRAWETH TOWARDS MIDNIGHT NOW,
$AND 'BOUT THIS TIME THE NUNS BEGIN TO WAKE.
$TO SHUN SUSPICION, THEREFORE, LET US PART.
<C BARABAS>
$FAREWELL, MY JOY, AND BY MY FINGERS TAKE
$A KISS FROM HIM THAT SENDS IT FROM HIS SOUL.
((@&EXIT %ABIGAIL @ABOVE))
$NOW, %PHOEBUS, OPE THE EYE-LIDS OF THE DAY,
$AND, FOR THE RAVEN, WAKE THE MORNING LARK,
$THAT &I MAY HOVER WITH HER IN THE AIR,
$SINGING O'ER THESE, AS SHE DOES O'ER HER YOUNG.
#$HERMOSO #PLACER #DE #LOS #DINEROS.
((@&EXIT))
```

Figure 3.3 Coded representation of part of Marlowe's *The Jew of Malta*

CH as, say, ♯, LL as £, N as @. This system does, however, have the disadvantage of making the printout rather more difficult to read.

The tilde (˜) in Spanish is an example of a 'diacritic' which modifies the value of the symbol. In some cases, such as Spanish Ñ, the modified symbol is regarded as a separate letter of the alphabet. In other cases, such as accents over vowels in French, Spanish and Italian, the modified symbol is not regarded as a separate letter. We must, however, code such diacritics, since we shall want to distinguish between, for example, French *aime (loves)* and *aimé* (the past participle, *loved*), or Spanish *entro* (I enter) and *entró* (he/she/it entered). A convenient method of coding is to use numbers, in combination with the basic letters, to indicate diacritics.

We might, for instance, distinguish the following types of diacritic in French:

acute accent (´)	1
grave accent (`)	2
circumflex accent (ˆ)	3
diaresis (¨)	4
cedilla (¸)	5

It does not matter whether the distinguishing number comes before or after the letter, thus: e2 or 2e, c5 or 5c. In figure 3.4 is shown a coding of the opening of Part 2 of Proust's *Du Côté de Chez Swann* (volume 1 of *A la Recherche du Temps Perdu*) in the Gallimard edition of 1954, in upper and lower case, with diacritics marked.

```
<A Proust>
<T Du cote de chez Swann>
<S 2>
<P 225>
   Pour faire partie du "petit noyau", du "petit groupe", du "petit
clan" des %Verdurin, une condition e1tait suffisante mais elle e1tait
ne1cessaire: il fallait adhe1rer tacitement a2 un Credo dont un des
articles e1tait que le jeune pianiste, prote1ge1 par %Mme %Verdurin
cette anne1e-la2 et dont elle disait: "C5a ne devrait pas e3tre permis
de savoir jouer %Wagner comme c5a!", "enfonc5ait" a3 la fois %Plante1
et %Rubinstein et que le docteur %Cottard avait plus de diagnostic
que %Potain.
```

Figure 3.4 Coded representation of part of Proust's *Du Côté de Chez Swann*

We must now consider the preparation of texts written in non-Roman scripts. These must, of course, be transliterated into a form using only the resources of the computer's character set. Wherever possible, it is best, for the reasons given earlier, to use only a single character for each symbol in the foreign script. However, for a language such as Russian, which has 33 letters in its alphabet, it may be more convenient, in the interests of legibility of the output, to use two or even more characters per letter of the original alphabet. One possible transliteration scheme for Russian is shown below.

А	Б	В	Г	Д	Е	Ё	Ж	З	И	Й	К	Л	М	Н	О	П	Р	С	Т	У	Ф	Х
A	B	V	G	D	YE	YO	ZH	Z	I	I*	K	L	M	N	O	P	R	S	T	U	F	KH

Ц	Ч	Ш	Щ	Ъ	Ы	Ь	Э	Ю	Я
TS	CH	SH	SHCH	**	Y	*	E	YU	YA

In figure 3.5 this scheme has been used to code a sentence from Chekhov's *Papa*.

```
TONKAYA, KAK GOLLANDSKAYA SEL*D*, MAMASHA VOSHLA V KABINET

K TOLSTOMU I KRUGLOMU, KAK ZHUK, PAPASHE I KASHLYANULA.
```

Figure 3.5 Coding of a sentence from Chekhov's *Papa*

Finally, we must consider the adequacy, for computational processing, of texts prepared by OCR methods. The KDEM machine discussed briefly earlier (p. 5) recognises distinct shapes on the printed page, and will therefore distinguish between upper and lower case letters in any typeface it has been trained to read. It will allow up to six different typefaces in any given text, and will insert numerical codings in the text to indicate any changes in typeface. It will also insert end of page markers. For many analyses, then, a text prepared by OCR methods is quite adequate, except that references to author, title, and so on, will have to be added. This task is, however, easily accomplished by the use of the interactive editing facilities offered by most computer systems.

3.3 The Oxford Concordance Program

3.3.1 General features

The Oxford Concordance Program (OCP) is an extremely comprehensive and flexible package, designed at the University of Oxford, which allows the user to obtain word counts, indexes, concordances and statistical information from texts in English or any other language which can be coded into a form compatible with the computer's character set. The program itself is written in the ubiquitous high-level language FORTRAN (though the user, of course, does not need to know anything about this language), and so can be implemented on a wide range of computers. Only an outline of the facilities offered by OCP can be presented here: for further details, readers should consult the OCP *Users' Manual* (Hockey and Marriott, 1980a), available from the Oxford University Computing Service. A description of the main features of the program can also be found in a series of four articles (Hockey and Marriott, 1979a, b, c, 1980b). In what follows, only the instructions to the OCP package itself will be considered: potential users should consult their own computer centres for information on how to run the package on their local machine.

3.3.2 An outline of the facilities available in the OCP package

OCP instructions are grouped into four sections, according to their function. Each section has a heading, which begins with an asterisk, and must occupy a separate line, with the heading starting in position 1.

*INPUT	defines the format of the input text, and specifies which parts of it are to be analysed.

*WORDS	defines what letters can make up words, and what order of letters the computer is to use for sorting words.
*ACTION	defines the analysis to be performed (word-list, index, concordance), and gives details of how the items are to be selected and sorted.
*FORMAT	defines the format of the output: for instance, how many columns in a word-list, how many lines per page, whether headwords in a concordance are to be centrally aligned, whether titles are to be printed.

Each section can contain a number of instructions after the heading, each of which must end with a full stop. Each instruction has an in-built 'default': that is, if the user does not include any particular instruction, OCP will make assumptions about what is required. If the defaults are required for *all* instructions in a particular section, the whole section, including the heading, may be omitted. Let us now look at each section in rather more detail.

The *INPUT section has three possible types of instruction: TEXT, REFERENCES and SELECT. TEXT defines the position of the text on the input records. The default is to assume that the text does not extend beyond position 80, and that there are no words hyphenated at the ends of lines. REFERENCES defines the format of any text references to author, title, chapter, and so on (see section 3.2). If the text contains only COCOA-style references, using angle brackets as delimiters, the following instruction may be used:

```
REFERENCES COCOA.
```

The default is for the text to contain no references. SELECT allows parts of a text to be selected for processing: for instance, between certain line numbers, or only those parts corresponding to a particular reference category. If all the text is to be processed, the SELECT instruction may be omitted.

The *WORDS section can contain any or all of seven instructions: ALPHABET, DIACRITICS, PADDING, PUNCTUATION, IGNORE, COMPRESS, MAXIMUM WORD. ALPHABET defines those characters which can occur in words, and are to be used to form the alphabetical order for sorting. It allows letters to be treated as equal for sorting purposes. If upper and lower case letters are used, they should be declared as equal. The default is the English alphabet, preceded by the apostrophe. DIACRITICS allows the declaration of codings for such marks as accents in French, and so on, as discussed in section 3.2. The default is for just the hyphen to be treated as a diacritic. Words containing diacritics will be listed separately from, but immediately after, the corresponding words without diacritics (for instance, *tea-pot* after *teapot*, or French *aimé* after *aime*, if they were encoded as, say, *aime1* and *aime* respectively, and 1 were declared as a diacritic). PADDING letters are those which the user does not wish to have any effect on sorting. Round brackets, and any letters which have not been declared, but are not in the default of any other instructions, are treated as padding characters in the default option. PUNCTUATION defines those characters which are to be treated as word separators. The default is for . , ! ? : and ; to be treated as punctuation. The space is always treated as a word separator. IGNORE specifies any letters the user wants completely removed from the text for purposes of the analysis, the default being for no characters to be ignored. COMPRESS specifies any characters for which multiple occurrences are to be compressed to a single occurrence. The default is for multiple spaces to be compressed. MAXIMUM WORD specifies the longest word length which will be recognised by OCP. The default of 20 letters is sufficient for most English texts.

The *ACTION section has seven possible instructions: DO, PICK, STOP, SORT KEYS BY, SORT CONTEXT BY, REFERENCES and MAXIMUM CONTEXT. DO specifies the task to be performed. The default is a word index, but a word-list or concordance can also be requested, with or without vocabulary statistics (the number of running words, the number of different words, the type/token ratio, and a frequency profile showing the number of forms occurring once, twice, three times, and so on). PICK selects particular items for listing, or for use as headwords in a concordance. The user can specify a list of words for inclusion in, or exclusion from, the analysis (for instance, picking just *and* and *or*, or all the words except *in, on, at, by*). Alternatively, words can be selected, for inclusion or exclusion, by alphabetic range (for instance, all words beginning with A to M), by frequency in the text, or by length in letters. OCP also allows the selection of phrases, collocations (pairs of words occurring within a particular distance), or word samples of specified sizes. It can also search for word patterns (for instance, all words ending in *ing*, or all words beginning with *re*). Combinations of options are possible: indeed, the criteria are extremely flexible. The default is to pick every word found in the text.

The STOP instruction allows the user to stop the OCP run either before the sorting phase, or after sorting but before formatting of the output. This enables the user to combine OCP with his own programs for sorting and formatting. The SORT KEYS BY instruction defines the order in which words are to be listed: by forward or reverse alphabetical order, ascending or descending frequency, ascending or descending length, or any sensible combination of these. The default is to sort by forward alphabetical order, as defined by the ALPHABET instruction. The SORT CONTEXT BY instruction specifies the ordering of occurrences of the same word in a concordance or index. For instance, we might find the following occurrences of *blue* in a text:

She bought two blue sweaters.
She was feeling blue that day.

The user may have the occurrences sorted by alphabetical order of what is on the right of the keyword (that is, in the order given above, since *sweaters* comes before *that* alphabetically), by alphabetical order of what is to the left (that is, in the reverse order to that above, since the final letter of *feeling* precedes that of *two*), by reference categories (for instance, all occurrences in one chapter of a text listed before all those in another), by order of occurrence in the text, or by a combination of these. The default is to list in text order.

Still within the *ACTION section, the REFERENCES instruction defines which reference categories should be given for the entries in an index or concordance, how many characters of each reference are to be printed, and what format the references should take. If, for example, we had references to act and scene numbers in a play text, we could ask for act (one character), scene (one character) and line number (up to 3 characters). OCP automatically counts line numbers for any text, and the default is for just these to be given as references. The MAXIMUM CONTEXT instruction gives the maximum amount of context to be selected for each occurrence of a word in a concordance. The context width can be specified in words or letters, to left or right or both, and in certain more refined ways within these limits (for instance, up to some particular punctuation mark). The default context is one text line.

The *FORMAT section has six possible instructions: LAYOUT, HEADWORDS, CONTEXT, REFERENCES, PRINT and TITLES. LAYOUT specifies the number and width of columns, the number of lines on a page, the width of margins, the number of blank lines to be left below entries for each headword, and so forth. The default for a word index would be 30-character columns, 60 lines per page, with no margin. HEADWORDS defines the position of headwords and frequencies in the output, for instance whether they are to be centred on the page, or placed to the left or right. CONTEXT defines how the context will appear in a concordance, or the list of references for each word in an index. The context can be aligned to the right or left of the page, or so that the keywords are centrally positioned. The default for a concordance is for a single line of context to be printed with central alignment of the keywords. REFERENCES allows the references to be placed on the right or left of the contexts in a concordance, or defines the justification of lines of references for an index. The default is for references to be printed on the left for a concordance, or left-justified for an index. PRINT allows the user to omit or change characters at the stage of printing the output. TITLES allows titles to be printed as headings or footings on each page, with or without page numbering, and with or without an indication of the range of headwords on each page. The default is for no titles, page numbers or headword ranges to be printed.

Every set of OCP instructions must be terminated by a line containing just the instruction *GO. If defaults are required for all options in all sections, this line is all that is needed.

3.3.3 Examples of OCP analyses

In this section, some of the kinds of output which can be obtained from the OCP package, as run on an ICL 2977 computer, will be illustrated. The texts analysed will be those from Hardy, Wilde, Marlowe and Proust, for which appropriate codings were discussed in section 3.2.

The output in figure 3.6 illustrates the generation of a word index for the excerpt from Hardy's *Tess of the d'Urbervilles*. All the default options have been used except that the form of the text references has been specified as the COCOA type. Note that a warning has been issued, to the effect that the ♯ symbol has not been declared as a letter. This is because none of the defaults for the ALPHABET, DIACRITICS or PUNCTUATION commands contains ♯. The program is simply warning the user that the undeclared character has been detected, and will be treated as a padding character.

```
*INPUT
REFERENCES COCOA.
*GO

A 1, 5, 6, 6, 9, 12, 12       HIM 4, 5                     PARSON 12

ADJOINING 3                   HIS 5, 9, 9, 10              PART 1

AN 1, 8, 11                   HOMEWARD 2                   PARTICULAR 8

AND 5                         HUMMED 12                    PATCH 10

ANYTHING 8                    IF 7                         PRESENTLY 11

ARM 9                         IN 1, 3, 5, 7, 8, 11         QUITE 10

AS 7, 12                      INCLINED 5                   RICKETY 4

ASTRIDE 12                    IT 11                        RODE 12

AT 10                         ITS 10                       RUFFLED 9

AWAY 10                       LATTER 1                     SHASTON 2

BEING 10                      LEFT 6                       SLUNG 9

BIAS 5                        LEGS 4                       SMART 6

BLACKMOOR 4                   LINE 6                       SOME 7

BLAKEMORE 3                   MAN 2                        SOMEWHAT 5

BRIM 10                       MARE 12                      STRAIGHT 6

BY 11                         MARLOTT 3                    TAKING 11


CAME 10                       MAY 1                        THAT 4

CARRIED 4                     MET 11                       THE 1, 2, 3, 4, 6, 9

CONFIRMATION 7                MIDDLE-AGED 1                THERE 5
```

```
EGG-BASKET 8
ELDERLY 11
EMPTY 8
EVENING 1
FROM 2
GAIT 5
GAVE 6
GRAY 12
HAT 9
HE 6, 7, 11, 12
NAP 9
NOD 7
NOT 7
OCCASIONALLY 6
OF 1, 2, 3, 4, 6, 7, 8, 9
OFF 11
ON 1, 12
OPINION 7
OR 3
PAIR 4
THINKING 8
THOUGH 7
THUMB 10
TO 2, 6
TUNE 13
UPON 9
VALE 3
VILLAGE 2
WALKING 2
WANDERING 13
WAS 2, 5, 7, 9, 9, 11
WERE 4
WHERE 10
WHICH 5
WHO 12
WORN 10

TOTAL WORDS READ      =  133
TOTAL WORDS SELECTED  =  133
TOTAL WORDS PICKED    =  133
TOTAL VOCABULARY      =   93
```

Figure 3.6 Word index for the Hardy text

A slightly more complex case, using the Wilde text, is shown in figure 3.7. Note that the % sign, used to indicate proper noun capitalisation, has been declared as a diacritic. Note also that in declaring the equals sign (used for a dash) as punctuation, it must be preceded by an 'escape

```
*INPUT
REFERENCES COCOA.
*WORDS
DIACRITICS "%".
PADDING "-".
PUNCTUATION ". , := !".
*ACTION
DO WORDLIST.
SORT KEYS BY END.
*GO
mystic                         1     that                        1
oversad                        1     crescent                    1
climbed                        1     not                         1
```

```
opened                  1      heart       1
throned                 1      %Christ     2
crowned                 3      but         1
world                   1      saw         1
could                   2      Show        1
And                     5      by          3
%God                    3      thy         1
trod                    1      holy        1
face                    1      %Holy       1
%Grace                  1      My          2
once                    1      weary       1
side                    1      %Mary       1
wide                    1
See                     2
life                    1
wife                    1
the                     7
shame                   1
flame                   1
come                    1
%One                    1
ere                     1
where                   1
house                   1
white                   1
have                    1
love                    1
of                      4
searching               1
sing                    1
Death                   1
with                    2
I                       2
%Virginal               1
all                     1
%Queen                  1
listen                  1
again                   1
pain                    1
mountain                1
sin                     1
moon                    1
soon                    1
upon                    1
sun                     1
O                       5
who                     1
too                     1
to                      3
Up                      1
Mother                  1
%Angel%Painter          1
is                      1
this                    2
heavens                 1
thorns                  1
at                      1
TOTAL WORDS READ     =  107
TOTAL WORDS SELECTED =  107
TOTAL WORDS PICKED   =  107
TOTAL VOCABULARY     =   75
```

Figure 3.7 Reverse alphabetical word-list for the Wilde text

character', which for most implementations of OCP is a colon. This is because the equals sign has a special function in OCP (to equate, for example, upper and lower case letters), and so an escape character is needed to indicate that the symbol has its ordinary, literal value. The instruction SORT KEYS BY END indicates that the word-list is to be given in alphabetical order from the end of the words, so that, for instance,

```
*INPUT
REFERENCES COCOA.
*WORDS
DIACRITICS "%".
PADDING "-".
PUNCTUATION ". , := !'.
*ACTION
DO INDEX AND STATS.
REFERENCES S = 1, L = 2.
*GO
```

```
again 3 12
all 2 8
And 2 5, 3 9, 3 12, 4 13, 4 16
%Angel%Painter 1 3
at 2 8
but 2 7
by 3 9, 4 13, 4 14
%Christ 3 10, 4 14
climbed 1 1
come 2 8
could 2 7, 2 8
crescent 2 5
crowned 3 9, 4 13, 4 14
Death 2 8
ere 4 15
face 2 7
flame 4 13
love 4 13
%Mary 2 7
moon 2 5
Mother 3 10
mountain 1 1
My 3 11, 4 16
mystic 3 10
not 2 8
O 3 9, 3 10, 4 13, 4 14, 4 15
of 1 2, 2 6, 3 10, 3 11
once 1 3
%One 4 14
opened 1 4
oversad 3 12
pain 3 9
%Queen 2 6
saw 1 4
thorns 3 9
throned 2 5
thy 2 7
to 1 2, 3 12, 4 16
too 2 8
trod 1 3
Up 1 2
upon 2 5
%Virginal 2 6
weary 3 11
Where 1 3
white 2 6
Who 1 4
wide 1 4
wife 3 10
with 3 9, 4 13
world 4 16
```

```
%God 1 2, 3 9, 4 13              searching 4 15
%Grace 2 6                       See 1 1, 2 7
have 1 1                         shame 4 16
heart 3 11                       Show 4 16
heavens 1 4                      side 1 1
holy 1 2                         sin 4 16
%Holy 4 14                       sing 3 12
house 1 2                        soon 2 8
I 1 1, 2 7                       sun 4 15
is 3 11                          that 1 3
life 3 11                        the 1 1, 1 4, 2 5, 2 6, 4 14,
                                 4 15, 4 16
listen 4 15                      this 1 2, 3 11
```

FREQUENCY	NUMBER SUCH	WORDS IN FREQUENCY	VOCAB TOTAL	WORD TOTAL	PERC. OF VOCABULARY	PERC. OF WORDS	PERC. OF WORDS IN FREQUENCY
1	60	60	60	60	80.00	56.07	56.07
2	7	14	67	74	89.33	69.16	13.08
3	4	12	71	86	94.67	80.37	11.21
4	1	4	72	90	96.00	84.11	3.74
5	2	10	74	100	98.67	93.46	9.35
7	1	7	75	107	100.00	100.00	6.54

```
TYPE/TOKEN RATIO = 0.701
TOTAL WORDS READ       =   107
TOTAL WORDS SELECTED   =   107
TOTAL WORDS PICKED     =   107
TOTAL VOCABULARY       =    75
```

Figure 3.8 Word index and statistics for the Wilde text

```
*Input
References Cocoa.
*Words
Diacritics "1 2 3 5 %".
Punctuation ', . ! :: "'.
Padding "-".
*Action
Do concordance.
Pick words "*AIT".
References P = 3, L = 2.
*Go
                                                           avait  1

225  7       et %Rubinstein et que le docteur %Cottard avait plus de diagnostic

                                                           devrait  1

225  5 cette anne1e-la2 et dont elle disait: "C5a ne devrait pas e3tre permis

                                                           disait  1

225  5                   cette anne1e-la2 et dont elle disait: "C5a ne devrait pas e3tre permis

                                                           enfonc5ait  1

225  6          de savoir jouer %Wagner comme c5a!", "enfonc5ait" a3 la fois %Plante1

                                                           e1tait  3

225  2                clan" des %Verdurin, une condition e1tait suffisante mais elle e1tait
225  2       une condition e1tait suffisante mais elle e1tait
225  4                                           articles e1tait que le jeune pianiste, prote1ge1 par %Mme %Verdurin

                                                           fallait  1

225  3                                 ne1cessaire: il fallait adhe1rer tacitement a2 un Credo dont un des
```

Figure 3.9 Concordance of words ending in *ait* in the Proust text

```
*INPUT
REFERENCES COCOA.
SELECT EXCEPT BETWEEN "((" TO "))".
*WORDS
ALPHABET "A B C D E F G H I J K L M N O P Q R S T U V W X Y Z #".
PADDING "$ & @ - '".
DIACRITICS "%".
*ACTION
DO WORDLIST.
*GO
```

A	2	IT	2	THESE	1
%ABIGAIL	4	JOY	1	THIS	2
ABOUT	1	KISS	1	THOUT	2
AIR	1	LARK	1	THUS	1
AND	7	LAST	1	THY	2
AS	4	LET	1	TIME	1
ATTEND	1	LIFE	1	TIS	2
BE	1	LOADSTAR	1	TO	6
BEAUTY	1	MAY	2	TOO	1
BEGIN	1	ME	1	TOWARDS	1
BEGINNER	1	MIDNIGHT	1	TREASURE	1
BLISS	2	MINE	1	US	1
BODY	1	MORE	3	WAKE	2
BOUT	1	MORN	1	WALK	1
BUT	3	MORNING	1	WE	1
BY	1	%MORPHEUS	1	WELCOME	1
CHARGE	1	MY	12	WERE	2
COME	1	NOT	1	WHAT	1
DAY	1	NOW	3	WHEN	1
DEATH	1	NUNS	1	WHEREER	1
DESIRES	1	O	6	WHOS	2
DOES	1	OER	2	WILL	1
DRAWETH	1	OF	4	WITH	1
DREAM	2	ON	1	WOULD	1
EAST	1	OPE	1	YET	1
ENEMY	1	PART	1	YONDER	1
ENLARGEMENT	1	PARTED	1	YOUNG	1
EYELIDS	1	PEACE	1	#BUENO	1
FAREWELL	1	%PHOEBUS	1	#DE	1
FATHER	2	PLACE	1	#DINEROS	1
FATHERS	1	PRACTISE	1	#ERA	1
FELICITY	1	RAVEN	1	#GANADO	1

```
FINGERS                          1    RECEIVE          2    #HERMOSO        1
FIRST                            1    RESTS            1    #LOS            1
FOR                              1    SADLY            1    #MI             1
FORTUNE                          2    SAID             1    #NO             1
FOUND                            1    SATISFIED        1    #PARA           1
FROM                             2    SENDS            1    #PLACER         1
FULLY                            1    SHE              1    #TODOS          1
GENTLE                           1    SHINES           1
GIRL                             2    SHUN             1
GIVE                             1    SINGING          1
GO                               1    SIT              1
GOLD                             2    %SLEEP           1
GOLDEN                           1    SO               3
GOOD                             2    SOUL             2
HAD                              1    STAR             1
HAPPINESS                        1    STAY             1
HAPPY                            2    STRENGTH         1
HAST                             2    SUDDEN           1
HAVE                             1    SUSPICION        1
HE                               3    TAKE             1
HER                              2    THAT             6
HERE                             3    THE             12
HIM                              1    THEE             1
HIS                              2    THEN             3
HOVER                            1    THENCE           1
I                                5    THERE            1
IF                               1    THEREFORE        1
IN                               3    THERES           1
TOTAL WORDS READ        =      256
TOTAL WORDS SELECTED    =      256
TOTAL WORDS PICKED      =      256
TOTAL VOCABULARY        =      159
```

Figure 3.10 Word-list for the Marlowe text, excluding stage directions

```
*INPUT
REFERENCES COCOA.
SELECT WHERE C = "ABIGAIL" EXCEPT BETWEEN "((" TO "))".
*WORDS
ALPHABET "A B C D E F G H I J K L M N O P Q R S T U V W X Y Z #".
PUNCTUATION ". , ! ? :: ( )".
PADDING "$ & @ - '".
DIACRITICS "%".
*ACTION
DO CONCORDANCE.
PICK FREQUENCY GT 1 AND EXCEPT WORDS "I IT AND".
REFERENCES T = 7, Z = 1, S = 1, L = 2.
*GO

                                                     DREAM  2

THE JEW 2 1  6  $GIVE CHARGE TO %MORPHEUS THAT HE MAY DREAM
THE JEW 2 1  7                              $A GOLDEN DREAM, AND OF THE SUDDEN WALK

                                                     FATHER  2

THE JEW 2 1 16                                 $THEN, FATHER, HERE RECEIVE THY HAPPINESS
THE JEW 2 1 29                                       $FATHER, IT DRAWETH TOWARDS MIDNIGHT NOW

                                                     HAPPY  2

THE JEW 2 1  2                $AS BUT TO BE ABOUT THIS HAPPY PLACE
THE JEW 2 1  3                             $'TIS NOT SO HAPPY: YET, WHEN WE PARTED LAST

                                                     HE  3

THE JEW 2 1  4                                       $HE SAID HE WOULD ATTEND ME IN THE MORN
THE JEW 2 1  4                               $HE SAID HE WOULD ATTEND ME IN THE MORN
THE JEW 2 1  6         $GIVE CHARGE TO %MORPHEUS THAT HE MAY DREAM

                                                     HERE  2

THE JEW 2 1 16                        $THEN, FATHER, HERE RECEIVE THY HAPPINESS
THE JEW 2 1 18                                       $HERE. ((@&THROWS @DOWN @BAGS.)) &HAST THOU'T?

                                                     MORE  3

THE JEW 2 1 19                               $THERE'S MORE, AND MORE, AND MORE
THE JEW 2 1 19                     $THERE'S MORE, AND MORE, AND MORE
THE JEW 2 1 19          $THERE'S MORE, AND MORE, AND MORE

                                                     NOW  2

THE JEW 2 1  1                                       $NOW THAT MY FATHER'S FORTUNE WERE SO GOOD
THE JEW 2 1 29    $FATHER, IT DRAWETH TOWARDS MIDNIGHT NOW
```

```
                                                          RECEIVE  2

THE JEW 2 1  8                              $COME AND RECEIVE THE TREASURE &I HAVE FOUND
THE JEW 2 1 16                        $THEN, FATHER, HERE RECEIVE THY HAPPINESS

                                                          SO  2

THE JEW 2 1  1      $NOW THAT MY FATHER'S FORTUNE WERE SO GOOD
THE JEW 2 1  3                              $'TIS NOT SO HAPPY: YET, WHEN WE PARTED LAST

                                                          THAT  3

THE JEW 2 1  1                                   $NOW THAT MY FATHER'S FORTUNE WERE SO GOOD
THE JEW 2 1  6                 $GIVE CHARGE TO %MORPHEUS THAT HE MAY DREAM
THE JEW 2 1 14                                 $WHO'S THAT?

                                                          THE  4

THE JEW 2 1  4        $HE SAID HE WOULD ATTEND ME IN THE MORN
THE JEW 2 1  7             $A GOLDEN DREAM, AND OF THE SUDDEN WALK
THE JEW 2 1  8                 $COME AND RECEIVE THE TREASURE &I HAVE FOUND
THE JEW 2 1 30               $AND 'BOUT THIS TIME THE NUNS BEGIN TO WAKE

                                                          THEN  2

THE JEW 2 1  5                                           $THEN, GENTLE %SLEEP, WHERE'ER HIS BODY RESTS
THE JEW 2 1 16                                           $THEN, FATHER, HERE RECEIVE THY HAPPINESS

                                                          THIS  2

THE JEW 2 1  2                $AS BUT TO BE ABOUT THIS HAPPY PLACE
THE JEW 2 1 30                             $AND 'BOUT THIS TIME THE NUNS BEGIN TO WAKE

                                                          TO  4

THE JEW 2 1  2                                    $AS BUT TO BE ABOUT THIS HAPPY PLACE
THE JEW 2 1  6                              $GIVE CHARGE TO %MORPHEUS THAT HE MAY DREAM
THE JEW 2 1 30     $AND 'BOUT THIS TIME THE NUNS BEGIN TO WAKE
THE JEW 2 1 31                                           $TO SHUN SUSPICION, THEREFORE, LET US PART


TOTAL WORDS READ     =    107
TOTAL WORDS SELECTED =    107
TOTAL WORDS PICKED   =     35
TOTAL VOCABULARY     =     14
```

Figure 3.11 Concordance of words, except I, IT, AND, of frequency greater than 1, in the Marlowe text

rhyming words with identically spelt endings (such as *flame* and *shame*) are adjacent.

Our third example, shown in figure 3.8, again uses the Wilde text. This time, an index is produced, giving, for each occurrence of each word, a reference consisting of one character representing the stanza number and two for the line number. In addition, a frequency profile and the type/token ratio are requested by means of the STATS command.

Figure 3.9 shows a concordance derived from the Proust text. The numerals 1, 2, 3, 5, representing accents and the cedilla, are declared as diacritics, as is the capitalisation marker % which appears before proper names. This example illustrates the use of the PICK command, in this case to pick for the concordance all words ending in *ait*. A three-figure page reference and a line number of up to two figures are requested.

Figure 3.10 shows a word-list for the excerpt from Marlowe's *The Jew of Malta*. The SELECT instruction is used to exclude any material occurring between ((and)), the delimiters used in the text for stage directions. The ♯ sign, which prefixes all Spanish words in the text, is declared at the end of the alphabet, so that all Spanish words will be output at the end of the word-list.

Our final example (figure 3.11) again uses the Marlowe text. All Abigail's speeches (except the stage directions embedded in them) are selected, and the PICK instruction is used to pick out all words occurring more than once, except I, IT and AND. The references for each concordance entry are to title, act, scene and line.

Many examples illustrating the full flexibility of the OCP package are given in the OCP *Users' Manual*.

3.4 The CLOC package

3.4.1 A brief comparison with OCP

CLOC is a package, written at the University of Birmingham, which, like OCP, produces word-lists, indexes and concordances from machine-readable texts. It suffers from some disadvantages when compared with OCP: it does not have such flexibility in the formatting of the output, and is not at present implementable on such a wide range of computers. Its main advantage over OCP is that it has rather better facilities for the study of collocations, that is the co-occurrences of words in texts. A further advantage is that after the text has been separated into words, CLOC allows the user to store the resulting word file in a form which can be used repeatedly in later analyses, without having to go through the word-separation stage each time. For more detailed descriptions of the package than that given here, see Reed (1977, 1982, 1984), Reed and Schonfelder (1979), and for a review see Burnard (1980).

3.4.2 A summary of the facilities offered by CLOC

The instructions to the CLOC package are given in the form of a sequence of 'control statements', each consisting of two 'fields'. The *control field* occupies positions 1 to 15 in the line, and presents information such as the type of analysis to be performed. The *specification field*, occupying positions 16 to 80, gives more detailed information to the package. For instance, a request to produce an alphabetical word-list would be presented as

```
WORDLIST       ALPHA
```

If the user does not wish to employ the fixed format, he may terminate the control field with a left-facing bracket, and then continue with the contents of the specification field, thus:

```
WORDLIST)ALPHA
```

The latest version of CLOC accepts upper and lower case letters both in the control instructions and in the text to be analysed. Some control statements have subsidiary commands after them, each of which must begin with an asterisk. There are six main types of command: not all of these need be present in every CLOC run, since each command has a default which will be used if no instruction is given to the contrary. Since the command types are quite similar to those of OCP, they will be described only very briefly.

The INPUT DETAILS command allows the user to specify the maximum width of text lines, the form of any text references, any delimiters of material which is to be ignored in the analysis, and any symbols indicating continuation lines or the insertion of an extra line boundary.

As with OCP, the CLOC package allows the user to define what is to be taken as a word. The command

```
ITEMIZE USING  CLOC
```

requests the itemisation of the text into words, and has a number of subsidiary commands which define letter characters, padding characters which are to be ignored when putting words into vocabulary tables, 'deferred' letters which are to be ignored for sorting purposes but will appear in vocabulary tables, and characters which are to be taken as word separators, also any which are to be totally ignored in the analysis. CLOC automatically prints the total number of words, the number of different words, and the maximum word length found, after itemising the text.

A third section of commands allows the user to save the itemised text in a named file, and then to retrieve this file for use in later analyses.

The OUTPUT DETAILS command allows the specification of the maximum line width for word-lists, indexes or concordances, in accordance with the properties of the lineprinter or terminal being used.

The word selection section of commands allows the user to specify that all the words in the text are to be taken for analysis, or to select words by frequency, by an explicit list, or by a pattern (for instance, all words ending in *ing*, or all words of five letters ending in *e*). These criteria can be combined, and can be used either to specify words for inclusion in the analysis, or to exclude unwanted items. As with OCP, then, the selection criteria are very flexible.

There follows a section of commands specifying the task which is to be performed. This may be to produce a word-list, an index, a concordance, a list of co-occurrences of specified pairs of words, or a list of collocations of the items selected. For word-lists, indexes, concordances and collocations, the words may be sorted by ascending or descending alphabetical order from the beginning or end of the word, by ascending or descending frequency, by ascending or descending length, or by order of first or last appearance in the text. The alignment of keywords and contexts in a concordance can be chosen. The amount of context can be specified as a number of words on each side of the keyword, or in terms of delimiters such as punctuation marks. The CO-OCCURRENCE command may be used to isolate whole phrases, or occurrences of two or more specified words separated by any range of numbers of words (for instance, the phrase *men and women*, or the words *men* and *women* separated by just one word, or by up to three words). The COLLOCATIONS command allows the concordancing of all collocates of the selected words, up to a distance (the 'span') specified by the user, and within certain limits of frequency of occurrence (for instance all words occurring at least three times within five words of the chosen items). Because such an analysis can produce very large quantities of output, even for a small text, there is an extremely useful option which produces a condensed list of collocations, each entry consisting simply of the keyword, its collocate, and the frequency of occurrence of the two items individually, and as a pair. Specific items may be rejected for collocational analysis, and the context width in a full list of co-occurrences or collocations may be specified by the user.

Every set of CLOC control statements must terminate with a line containing just the word FINISH.

```
<A Hardy>
<T Tess of the D'Urbervilles>
<C 1>
     On an evening in the latter part of #May a middle-aged
man was walking homeward from #Shaston to the village of
#Marlott, in the adjoining #Vale of #Blakemore or
#Blackmoor.  The pair of legs that carried him were rickety,
and there was a bias in his gait which inclined him somewhat
to the left of a straight line.  He occasionally gave a smart
nod, as if in confirmation of some opinion, though he was not
thinking of anything in particular.  An empty egg-basket
was slung upon his arm, the nap of his hat was ruffled, a
patch being quite worn away at its brim where his thumb came
in taking it off.  Presently he was met by an elderly
parson astride on a grey mare, who, as he rode, hummed a
wandering tune.
```

Figure 3.12 The Hardy text in upper and lower case

```
CLOC mark 2e run on  5 Dec 1983 at 13.53.12 (copyright(C) Alan Reed,1982)
                         listing of control statements

                         Input details   Refs<>
                         Itemise using   CLOC
                         *Letters        ABCDEFGHIJKLMNOPQRSTUVWXYZ-#
                         *Deferred       -#
default                  *separators     !"$%&'()*+,./0123456789:;=?@[\]^_`{|}~
the text contains :
     133  running words
      93  distinct words
and the maximum word length is 12 characters

                         Save text       HARDYCLOC
text file HARDYCLOC saved on  5 Dec 1983 at 13.53.19
default                  output details width120
                         Every word
                         Wordlist        Alpha
                         Finish


output from CLOC mark 2e run on  5 Dec 1983 at 13.53.19
-------------------------------------------------------
table of 93 words in ascending alphabetic order
-----------------------------------------------
    7 a                 1 adjoining      3 an             1 and               1 anything         1 arm
    2 as                1 astride        1 at             1 away              1 being            1 bias
    1 #blackmoor        1 #blakemore     1 brim           1 by                1 came             1 carried
    1 confirmation      1 egg-basket     1 elderly        1 empty             1 evening          1 from
    1 gait              1 gave           1 grey           1 hat               4 he               2 him
    4 his               1 homeward       1 hummed         1 if                6 in               1 inclined
    1 it                1 its            1 latter         1 left              1 legs             1 line
    1 man               1 mare           1 #marlott       1 #may              1 met              1 middle-aged
    1 nap               1 nod            1 not            1 occasionally      8 of               1 off
    2 on                1 opinion        1 or             1 pair              1 parson           1 part
    1 particular        1 patch          1 presently      1 quite             1 rickety          1 rode
    1 ruffled           1 #shaston       1 slung          1 smart             1 some             1 somewhat
    1 straight          1 taking         1 that           6 the               1 there            1 thinking
    1 though            1 thumb          2 to             1 tune              1 upon             1 #vale
    1 village           1 walking        1 wandering      6 was               1 were             1 where
    1 which             1 who            1 worn

end of output from CLOC mark 2e run on  5 Dec 1983 13.53.21
-----------------------------------------------------------
```

Figure 3.13 Alphabetical word-list produced by CLOC

```
CLOC mark 2e run on  5 Dec 1983 13.53.22 (copyright(C) Alan Reed,1982)
                      listing of control statements

                      Get text        HARDYCLOC
text file HARDYCLOC accessed. (saved on  5 Dec 1983 at 13.53.19)
the text contains :
     133  running words
      93  distinct words
and the maximum word length is 12 characters

default               output details width120
                      Select words
                      *Pattern        *ING *ED *LY
                      Concordance     Alpha,Cite from.to.exclusive,Refs L2
                      Finish


output from CLOC mark 2e run on  5 Dec 1983 at 13.53.26
-------------------------------------------------------
concordance of 16 nodes
======================
node  adjoining  occurs 1 times
 3 homeward from #Shaston to the village of #Marlott, in the adjoining #Vale of #Blakemore or #Blackmoor

node  anything  occurs 1 times
 8            of some opinion, though he was not thinking of anything in particular

node  being  occurs 1 times
10     upon his arm, the nap of his hat was ruffled, a patch being quite worn away at its brim where his thumb came in

node  carried  occurs 1 times
 4                                The pair of legs that carried him were rickety, and there was a bias in his gait

node  elderly  occurs 1 times
11                             Presently he was met by an elderly parson astride on a grey mare, who, as he rode,

node  evening  occurs 1 times
 1                                          On an evening in the latter part of #May a middle-aged man was

node  hummed  occurs 1 times
12   elderly parson astride on a grey mare, who, as he rode, hummed a wandering tune

node  inclined  occurs 1 times
 5  him were rickety, and there was a bias in his gait which inclined him somewhat to the left of a straight line

node  middle-aged  occurs 1 times
 1                 On an evening in the latter part of #May a middle-aged man was walking homeward from #Shaston to the

node  occasionally  occurs 1 times
 6                                            He occasionally gave a smart nod, as if in confirmation of

node  presently  occurs 1 times
11                                             Presently he was met by an elderly parson astride on a

node  ruffled  occurs 1 times
 9 egg-basket was slung upon his arm, the nap of his hat was ruffled, a patch being quite worn away at its brim where

node  taking  occurs 1 times
11 being quite worn away at its brim where his thumb came in taking it off

node  thinking  occurs 1 times
 8  as if in confirmation of some opinion, though he was not thinking of anything in particular

node  walking  occurs 1 times
 2  evening in the latter part of #May a middle-aged man was walking homeward from #Shaston to the village of #Marlott

node  wandering  occurs 1 times
13  parson astride on a grey mare, who, as he rode, hummed a wandering tune

end of output from CLOC mark 2e run on  5 Dec 1983 at 13.53.29
-------------------------------------------------------------
```

Figure 3.14 Concordance produced by CLOC

```
CLOC mark 2e run on  5 Dec 1983 at 13.53.30 (copyright(C) Alan Reed,1982)
                       listing of control statements

                       Get text       HARDYCLOC
text file HARDYCLOC accessed. (saved on  5 Dec 1983 at 13.53.19)
the text contains :
     133 running words
      93 distinct words
and the maximum word length is 12 characters

default                output details width120
                       Every word
                       Collocations   Condensed
default                *span          4 by 4
default                *frequency     >1
                       Select words
                       *Pattern       *ING
                       Collocations   Cite 6 by 6
                       *Span          5 by 5
default                *frequency     >1
                       Finish


output from CLOC mark 2e run on  5 Dec 1983 at 13.53.33
-------------------------------------------------------
condensed collocation analysis of 93 nodes
==========================================
    node             collocate        pair
    ----             ---------        ----
    7 a                8 of             2
    7 a                6 was            3
    7 a                4 his            2
    7 a                1 line           2
    7 a                4 he             3
    7 a                1 occasionally   2
    7 a                2 as             3
    1 adjoining        8 of             2
    3 an               2 on             2
    3 an               6 in             2
    3 an               6 was            2
    1 arm              4 his            2
    2 as               7 a              3
    1 #blackmoor       8 of             2
    1 #blakemore       6 the            2
    4 he               8 of             3
    4 he               7 a              3
    4 he               6 was            2
    4 his              6 was            3
    4 his              7 a              2
    4 his              6 in             2
    4 his              1 arm            2
    4 his              6 the            2
```

```
4 his               1 nap            2
4 his               8 of             2
6 in                3 an             2
6 in                6 the            3
6 in                8 of             5
6 in                4 his            2
1 line              7 a              2
1 #marlott          6 the            2
1 nap               4 his            2
1 occasionally      7 a              2
8 of                6 in             5
8 of                6 the            8
8 of                7 a              2
8 of                2 to             2
8 of                1 adjoining      2
8 of                1 or             2
8 of                1 #blackmoor     2
8 of                4 he             3
8 of                6 was            2
8 of                4 his            2
2 on                3 an             2
1 or                8 of             2
6 the               6 in             3
6 the               8 of             8
6 the               2 to             2
6 the               1 village        2
6 the               1 #marlott       2
6 the               1 #blakemore     2
6 the               4 his            2
2 to                6 the            2
2 to                8 of             2
1 village           6 the            2
6 was               7 a              3
6 was               4 his            3
6 was               4 he             2
6 was               8 of             2
6 was               3 an             2

collocation analysis of 8 nodes (cited about node)
==================================================
node  adjoining  occurs 1 times
collocate  of  occurs 8 times
node-collocate pair occurs 2 times
3                              the village of #Marlott, in the adjoining #Vale of #Blakemore or #Blackmoor.  The
3                              the village of #Marlott, in the adjoining #Vale of #Blakemore or #Blackmoor.  The


end of output from CLOC mark 2e run on  5 Dec 1983 at 13.53.40
--------------------------------------------------------------
```

Figure 3.15 Collocational analysis produced by CLOC

3.4.2 Examples of CLOC analyses

Some examples of output from CLOC analyses will now be given. They were produced on the DEC 20 computer at the University of Birmingham, and use a version of the text from *Tess of the d'Urbervilles* coded in both upper and lower case, as shown in figure 3.12.

The first run requests a simple alphabetical word-list. References are specified as enclosed in angle brackets. The apostrophe and ♯ are declared as deferred characters. The itemised text is to be saved in a file named HARDYCLOC, so that it may be used in later analyses. The output is shown in figure 3.13.

The second analysis (figure 3.14) uses the already itemised text in the word file HARDYCLOC, and requests a concordance of all words ending in *ing*, *ed* or *ly*. The words are to be sorted alphabetically, the context is to go up to a full stop on either side of the headword where possible, and a line number of up to two figures is to be given as a reference for each entry.

The third analysis (figure 3.15) again uses the itemised text, and produces a condensed list of all pairs of words isolated by the defaults of the COLLOCATIONS command. This means that only pairs occurring together more than once, within a span of four words, will be selected. In the same run, a full set of collocations is requested for words ending in *ing*, the span being five words, and a context width of six words on each side of the keyword being required. Note that the same context is listed twice, because the item *of* occurs twice in one line within a distance of five words from the item *adjoining*.

3.5 The OXEYE package

3.5.1 General features

OXEYE is a package for the syntactic parsing of Modern English texts and was, like OCP, written at the University of Oxford. It was written in SPITBOL (a version of the SNOBOL4 programming language to be discussed in Part II of this book), and is based on the EYEBALL program (see p. 21) originally written in FORTRAN by Ross and Rasche. For full details of OXEYE see Burnard (1976).

3.5.2 The three programs

OXEYE consists of three programs, which can be used separately or in combination. The first, WORDS, splits the text up into words and attempts an initial classification of each word. The results can be fed into the second program, PARSE, which refines the syntactic classification and attempts to define the function of each item in the clause. The third program, STATS, produces a range of statistical analyses based on the parsing carried out in the previous programs. The facilities offered by each program will now be discussed in a little more detail.

The WORDS program allows the user to define the letters of which words may be composed, also a list of word separators, and a list of characters which serve as sentence delimiters. Each of these has a default, so that if the user is satisfied with the default values he need make no specifications. It is also possible to instruct the package to ignore certain characters when sorting, when printing, or both. A word-list in frequency order may be requested.

When the WORDS program has isolated words from the text, it makes an initial attempt to give each of them a syntactic classification. It first looks up each word in a dictionary of grammatical words (articles, demonstratives, pronouns, auxiliaries, prepositions, conjunctions, and the like). If the word is not found, the program invokes a set of simple morphological rules in order to make an informed guess. OXEYE incorporates a facility whereby a user who wishes to analyse a text in some language other than Modern English can specify his own internal dictionary and morphological rules for parsing, and also, if required, his own set of parts of speech.

WORDS produces a word file giving each word in each sentence, with a tentative parsing, and also the number of words in the sentence. Optionally, WORDS can be requested to count the number of syllables in each word, and/or to suppress the in-built facility which expands common contracted forms (for instance *can't* to *can not, he'll* to *he will*).

The PARSE program takes the word file produced by WORDS, and examines the context of each word in order to attempt an analysis of clause structure, in terms of subject (S), predicate (V), complement (C) (including direct and indirect objects), predicate adjunct (A) (that is, adverb-headed phrases), prepositional adjunct (P), and unknown (?) elements. The author of OXEYE explicitly states that no guarantee of the accuracy of this parsing can be made. In practice, users will find that a substantial amount of recoding is necessary, even for fairly simple prose texts (see section 3.5.3). This can be effected by editing the updated word file produced by PARSE. If corrections are not made, the results of any subsequent application of the program STATS will be at best misleading, and at worst meaningless.

The program STATS reads parsings from the word file produced by PARSE, or from another kind of file called a 'parts file'. A parts file contains a summary of the parsing for each sentence, in the form of a series of syntactic codes, one for each word. Such a file can be generated within STATS, and if further analyses are required later, the parts file may then be used by subsequent runs of STATS. The user may at this stage request a word-list (ordered alphabetically or by frequency), an index, a sentence-by-sentence printout of the text with its parsings, or any combination of these. He can also redefine the order of letters for sorting, and instruct the computer to ignore certain letters for sorting, printing, or both.

The statistical output produced by STATS consists mainly of frequency profiles, together with means and standard deviations (for more on these terms see section 3.6; see also Butler, 1985). Tables may be produced for the number of syllables per word, characters per word, and words per sentence, also for words in the whole text, together with measures of vocabulary richness, including the type/token ratio (see section 2.2.1). Similar tables may also be produced for each part of speech, based on the frequency per sentence. The package computes the means and standard deviations for all sentences, also for just those sentences which contain at least one instance of the part of speech concerned. The number of sentences starting with, ending with, and lacking the part of speech under analysis are also printed. A particularly useful feature of OXEYE is an option which allows the user to define syntactic patterns for analysis. The patterns themselves are specified using the conventions of the SNOBOL4 language to be described in Part II of this book. They are, however, quite simple for the user untrained in SNOBOL4 to use.

3.5.3 Examples of OXEYE analyses

In figures 3.16–3.26 are shown a number of analyses of the passage from Hardy's *Tess of the d'Urbervilles* used in earlier examples, run on an ICL 1906A computer.

Figure 3.16 shows the instructions presented to the program WORDS. The package is to take the text from a file called HARDY, and is to produce a word file named HARDYWDS. A word-list is to be given. The symbol # is to be ignored, and the number of syllables in each word is to be counted. Since examples of word-lists have already been given in the sections describing OCP and CLOC, the output from OXEYE is not reproduced here.

```
TEXT HARDY
LETTERS ABCDEFGHIJKLMNOPQRSTUVWXY7#'=
IGNORE #
LIST
FILE HARDYWDS
COUNT SYLLABLES
```

Figure 3.16 Instructions to the program WORDS

Figure 3.17 shows the instruction given to the program PARSE, namely to use the word file HARDYWDS already generated by WORDS, as input to the parsing routines. An extract from the updated word file is shown in figure 3.18. In the columns showing the parsings, the number gives the syllable count for each word. There follows a syntactic coding for the word (or more than one, if the computer cannot decide between alternatives),

```
FILE HARDYWDS
```

Figure 3.17 Instructions to program PARSE

```
HARDYWDS     PARSED ON 02/09/83          16.40.39
LETTERSABCDEFGHIJKLMNOPQRSTUVWXYZ#'-    IGNORE#
PUNCTS0123456789:;<=>? !"£%&()*+, /@[$]↑←    DELIMS.?!:;
NOSORT NOPRINT
100:20:11:0123456789:;<=>? !"#£%&'()*+,
----1:30------------------------------------------------------------
  10003      #ON                       1P   P
  10003      AN                        1D   P
  10003      EVENING                   3N   P
  10003      IN                        1P   P
  10003      THE                       1D   P
  10003      LATTER                    2J   P
  10003      PART                      1N   P
  10003      OF                        1P   P
  10003      #MAY                      1N   P
  10003      A                         1D   ?
  10003      MIDDLE-AGED               3VJ  ?
  20004      MAN                       1N   S
  20004      WAS                       1X   V
  20004      WALKING                   2L   V
  20004      HOMEWARD                  3NJV?
  20004      FROM                      1P   P
  20004      #SHASTON                  2N   P
  20004      TO                        1P   P
  20004      THE                       1D   P
  20004      VILLAGE                   2N   P
  20004      OF                        1P   P
  30005      #MARLOTT                  2N   P
  30005      IN                        1P   P
  30005      THE                       1D   P
  30005      ADJOINING                 3L   P
  30005      #VALE                     1N   P
  30005      OF                        1P   P
  30005      #BLAKEMORE                3N   P
  30005      OR                        1C   ?
  40006      #BLACKMOOR                2N   ?
----2:28------------------------------------------------------------
  40006      #THE                      1D   ?
  40006      PAIR                      1N   ?
  40006      OF                        1P   P
  40006      LEGS                      1N   P
  40006      THAT                      1SDU?
  40006      CARRIED                   1VJ  ?
  40006      HIM                       1U   ?
  40006      WERE                      1V   V
  40006      RICKETY                   3J   C
  50007      AND                       1C   ?
  50007      THERE                     1H   A
  50007      WAS                       1X   V
  50007      A                         1D   C
  50007      BIAS                      2N   C
  50007      IN                        1P   P
  50007      HIS                       1D   P
  50007      GAIT                      1N   P
  50007      WHICH                     1SDU?
  50007      INCLINED                  2VJ  ?
  50007      HIM                       1U   ?
  50007      SOMEWHAT                  2I   ?
  60008      TO                        1P   P
  60008      THE                       1D   P
  60008      LEFT                      1N   P
  60008      OF                        1P   P
  60008      A                         1D   P
  60008      STRAIGHT                  1J   P
  60008      LINE                      1N   P
```

Figure 3.18 Word file after operation of PARSE

and a specification of syntactic function. A considerable number of the parsings are in fact incorrect, and must be corrected manually, with the result shown in figure 3.19.

The instructions for an initial run of the program STATS are shown in figure 3.20. The parsings in the corrected file HARDYWDS are to be used.

```
HARDYWDS     PARSED ON 02/09/83          16.40.39
LETTERSABCDEFGHIJKLMNOPQRSTUVWXYZ#'-    IGNORE#
PUNCTS0123456789:;<=>? !"£%&()*+, /@[$]↑←    DELIMS.?!:;
NOSORT NOPRINT
100:20:11:0123456789:;<=>? !"#£%&'()*+,
----1:30------------------------------------------------------------
   10003     #ON                   1P   P
   10003     AN                    1D   P
   10003     EVENING               2N   P
   10003     IN                    1P   P
   10003     THE                   1D   P
   10003     LATTER                2J   P
   10003     PART                  1N   P
   10003     OF                    1P   P
   10003     #MAY                  1N   P
   10003     A                     1D   S
   10003     MIDDLE-AGED           3L   S
   20004     MAN                   1N   S
   20004     WAS                   1X   V
   20004     WALKING               2L   V
   20004     HOMEWARD              2M   A
   20004     FROM                  1P   P
   20004     #SHASTON              2N   P
   20004     TO                    1P   P
   20004     THE                   1D   P
   20004     VILLAGE               2N   P
   20004     OF                    1P   P
   30005     #MARLOTT              3N   P
   30005     IN                    1P   P
   30005     THE                   1D   P
   30005     ADJOINING             3L   P
   30005     #VALE                 1N   P
   30005     OF                    1P   P
   30005     #BLAKEMORE            2N   P
   30005     OR                    1C   P
   40006     #BLACKMOOR            2N   P
----2:28------------------------------------------------------------
   40006     #THE                  1D   S
   40006     PAIR                  1N   S
   40006     OF                    1P   S
   40006     LEGS                  1N   S
   40006     THAT                  1S   S
   40006     CARRIED               1V   V
   40006     HIM                   1U   C
   40006     WERE                  1V   V
   40006     RICKETY               3J   C
   50007     AND                   1C   ?
   50007     THERE                 1H   S
   50007     WAS                   1V   V
   50007     A                     1D   C
   50007     BIAS                  2N   C
   50007     IN                    1P   P
   50007     HIS                   1D   P
   50007     GAIT                  1N   P
   50007     WHICH                 1S   S
   50007     INCLINED              2V   V
   50007     HIM                   1U   C
   50007     SOMEWHAT              2I   P
   60008     TO                    1P   P
   60008     THE                   1D   P
   60008     LEFT                  1N   P
   60008     OF                    1P   P
   60008     A                     1D   P
   60008     STRAIGHT              1J   P
   60008     LINE                  1N   P
```

Figure 3.19 Corrected word file

```
FILE HARDYWDS
IGNORE #
INDEX
PRINT TEXT
COUNT ALL
WRITEPARTS HARDYPARTS
```

Figure 3.20 Instructions for first run of STATS

```
                                                  ************************************
                                                  * CODING OF GRAMMATICAL CATEGORIES *
                                                  ************************************
                                                  *      ? : UNKNOWN                 *
                                                  *      A : -LY ADVERB              *
                                                  *      B : FUNCTION ADVERB         *
                                                  *      C : CO-ORDINATOR            *
                                                  *      D : DETERMINER              *
                                                  *      F : INFN VERB               *
                                                  *      H : "THERE" SIGNAL          *
                                                  *      I : INTENSIFIER ADVERB      *
                                                  *      J : ADJECTIVE               *
                                                  *      L : PARTICIPLE              *
                                                  *      M : MISCELLANEOUS           *
                                                  *      N : NOUN                    *
                                                  *      O : "NOT"                   *
                                                  *      P : PREPOSITION             *
                                                  *      R : PARTICLE PREP           *
                                                  *      S : SUBORDINATOR            *
                                                  *      T : "TO" INFN               *
                                                  *      U : PRONOUN                 *
                                                  *      V : VERB                    *
                                                  *      X : AUXILIARY VERB          *
                                                  ************************************
                                                  *  CODING OF  SYNTACTIC FUNCTIONS  *
                                                  ************************************
                                                  *      S : SUBJECT                 *
                                                  *      V : PREDICATE               *
                                                  *      A : PREDICATE ADJUNCT       *
                                                  *      P : PREPOSITIONAL ADJUNCT   *
                                                  *      C : COMPLEMENT              *
                                                  *      ? : UNKNOWN                 *
                                                  ************************************
HARDYWDS    PARSED ON 02/09/83        16.40.39
PARAMETERS FOR THIS RUN ...

LETTERS: ABCDEFGHIJKLMNOPQRSTUVWXYZ#'-
NOPRINT:  NOSORT:  IGNORE: #

          1   2  3       4  5   6      7    8  9    1011         12  13  14      15       16   17
  1       #ON AN EVENING IN THE LATTER PART OF #MAY A MIDDLE-AGED MAN WAS WALKING HOMEWARD FROM #SHASTON
          P   D  N       P  D   J      N    P  N    D L          N   X   L       M        P    N
          P   P  P       P  P   P      P    P  P    S S          S   V   V       A        P    P

          18 19  20      21 22        23 24  25        26    27 28         29 30
          TO THE VILLAGE OF #MARLOTT, IN THE ADJOINING #VALE OF #BLAKEMORE OR #BLACKMOOR.
          P  D   N       P  N         P  D   L         N     P  N          C  N
          P  P   P       P  P         P  P   P         P     P  P          P  P
```

```
    1    2    3  4    5    6       7   8    9        10  11    12  1314   15 16  17   18    19
4   #THE PAIR OF LEGS THAT CARRIED HIM WERE RICKETY, AND THERE WAS A BIAS IN HIS GAIT WHICH INCLINED
    D    N    P  N    S    V       U   V    J        C   H     V   D N    P  D   N    S     V
    S    S    S  S    S    W       C   V    C        ?   S     V   C C    P  P   P    S     V

    20  21       22 23  24   25 2627       28
    HIM SOMEWHAT TO THE LEFT OF A STRAIGHT LINE.
    U   I        P  D   N    P  D J        N
    C   P        P  P   P    P  P P        P

    1   2            3    4 5     6    7  8  9  10           11 12   13        14     15 16  17
6   #HE OCCASIONALLY GAVE A SMART NOD, AS IF IN CONFIRMATION OF SOME OPINION, THOUGH HE WAS NOT
    U   A            V    D J     N    S  S  P  N            P  D    N         S      U  X   O
    S   A            V    C C     C    A  A  P  P            P  P    P         A      S  V   V

    18       19 20       21 22
    THINKING OF ANYTHING IN PARTICULAR.
    L        P  U        P  J
    V        P  P        P  P

    1   2     3          4   5     6    7   8    9   10  11 12  13  14  15       1617    18
8   #AN EMPTY EGG-BASKET WAS SLUNG UPON HIS ARM, THE NAP OF HIS HAT WAS RUFFLED, A PATCH BEING
    D   J     N          V   L     P    D   N    D   N   P  D   N   V   L        D N     V
    S   S     S          W   C     P    P   P    S   S   S  S   S   V   C        S S     V

    19    20   21   22 23  24   25    26  27    28   29 30     31 32
    QUITE WORN AWAY AT ITS BRIM WHERE HIS THUMB CAME IN TAKING IT OFF.
    I     L    B    P  D   M    S     D   N     V    R  L      U  R
    C     C    C    P  P   P    A     S   S     V    A  V      C  A

    1          2  3   4   5  6  7       8      9       10 1112   13    14   15 16 17    18
11  #PRESENTLY HE WAS MET BY AN ELDERLY PARSON ASTRIDE ON A GRAY MARE, WHO, AS HE RODE, HUMMED
    A          U  X   L   P  D  J       N      P       P  D J    N     S    S  U  V     V
    A          S  V   V   P  P  P       P      P       P  P P    P     S    A  S  V     V

    1920        21
    A WANDERING TUNE.
    D L         N
    C C         C
```

Figure 3.21 The parsed text

```
   WORD FREQUENCY :       8       7       6       4       3       2       1
      NUMBER SUCH :       1       1       3       2       1       4      81
         %  TYPES :    1.07    2.15    5.37    7.52    8.60   12.90  100.00
         %  TOKENS :    6.01   11.27   24.81   30.82   33.08   39.09  100.00

                  MEAN :      1.43      STANDARD DEVIATION :      1.13

NUMBER OF WORDS (TOKENS)             133
NUMBER OF DISTINCT WORDS (TYPES)     93
TYPE-TOKEN RATIO                     0.699248

YULE'S CHARACTERISTIC K              127.763
YULE'S INDEX OF DIVERSITY            78.2699



-------
TABLE 1
-------

SYLLABLES PER WORD :       1      2      3      4      5
       NUMBER SUCH :     100     20     10      2      1
     % PROBABILITY :   75.18  15.03   7.51   1.50   0.75
 CUM % PROBABILITY :  100.00  24.81   9.77   2.25   0.75

              MEAN :    1.37     STANDARD DEVIATION :    0.78        POPULATION : 133



-------
TABLE 2
-------

WORDS PER SENTENCE :      21     22     28     30     32
       NUMBER SUCH :       1      1      1      1      1
     % PROBABILITY :   20.00  20.00  20.00  20.00  20.00
 CUM % PROBABILITY :  100.00  80.00  60.00  40.00  20.00

              MEAN :   26.06     STANDARD DEVIATION :    4.87        POPULATION : 5
```

Figure 3.22 Extracts from statistical tables produced by STATS

A word index and a printout of the text with parsings are to be produced. Statistics are to be generated for all possible analyses. A parts file called HARDYPARTS is to be produced. The printed text, with parsings, is shown in figure 3.21. Figure 3.22. gives the tables which are printed for word frequency, number of syllables per word, and number of words per sentence. The parts file is reproduced in figure 3.23 and an extract from the word index in figure 3.24.

In a second run of STATS, the package is instructed to read parsings from the parts file, and to count occurrences of two patterns: determiner plus noun (DN) and auxiliary verb plus participle (XL) (see figure 3.25). The results are shown in figure 3.26.

```
PDNPDJNPNDLNXLMPNPDNPNPDLNPNCN
DNPNSVUVJCHVDNPDNSVUIPDNPDJN
UAVDJNSSPNPDNSUXOLPUPJ
DJNVLPDNDNPDNVLDNVILBPDNSDNVRLUR
AUXLPDJNPPDJNSSUVVDLN
```

Figure 3.23 The parts file generated by STATS

```
ADJOINING <L>                   3
AND <C>                         5
AN <D>                  1   8  11
ANYTHING <U>                    8
A <D>           1   5   6       6
                    9  12      12
ARM <N>                         9
AS <S>                      7  12
ASTRIDE <P>                    12
AT <P>                         10
AWAY <B>                       10
BEING <V>                      10
BIAS <N>                        5
BLACKMOOR <N>                   4
BLAKEMORE <N>                   3
BRIM <N>                       10
BY <P>                         11
CAME <V>                       10
CARRIED <V>                     4
CONFIRMATION <N>                7
EGG-BASKET <N>                  8
ELDERLY <J>                    11
EMPTY <J>                       8
EVENING <N>                     1
FROM <P>                        2
GAIT <N>                        5
GAVE <V>                        6
GRAY <J>                       12
HAT <N>                         9
HE <U>            6     7  11  12
HIM <U>                     4   5
HIS <D>           5     9   9  10
HOMEWARD <M>                    2
HUMMED <V>                     12
IF <S>                          7.
INCLINED <V>                    5
```

Figure 3.24 Part of word index generated by STATS

```
READPARTS HARDYPARTS
COUNT 'DN', 'XL'
```

Figure 3.25 Instructions for the second run of STATS

```
----
'DN'
----

FREQUENCY PER SENTENCE :       0       1       2       4       6
           NUMBER SUCH :       1       1       1       1       1
         % PROBABILITY :   20.00   20.00   20.00   20.00   20.00
     CUM % PROBABILITY :  100.00   80.00   60.00   40.00   20.00

                  MEAN :    2.06     STANDARD DEVIATION :    2.40        POPULATION : 5

TOTAL OCCURRENCES : 13


-----
 'XL'
-----

FREQUENCY PER SENTENCE :       0       1
           NUMBER SUCH :       3       2
         % PROBABILITY :   60.00   40.00
     CUM % PROBABILITY :  100.00   40.00

                  MEAN :    0.04     STANDARD DEVIATION :    0.65        POPULATION : 5

TOTAL OCCURRENCES : 2
```

Figure 3.26 Output of second STATS analysis: frequency of patterns DN and XL

3.6 Two statistical packages

3.6.1 A thumbnail sketch of statistical techniques

Two kinds of manipulation of quantitative data are commonly required in linguistic work, as in other fields of study.

We often need to describe the characteristics of one or more sets of data: more specifically, we may be interested in the type of distribution shown by the values, the most typical or 'average' value, and the spread (or 'dispersion') of the values. Thus an important initial stage in analysing a set of data is normally the examination of the *frequency distribution* (the number of observations having each possible value of the variable under consideration), which may be shown in a graphical form as a *bar chart, histogram* or *frequency polygon*. There are several ways of calculating the most central or typical value: the *mean, median* and *mode* are appropriate measures of central tendency for different types of data. The dispersion of a set of data may be crudely measured by the *range* (the difference between the highest and lowest values), but a more common and useful measure is the *standard deviation*, which is the square root of the *variance*.

In many investigations we are concerned not just with the characteristics of a single set of data, but with the comparison of two or more sets. Here, the point at issue is usually whether the characteristics of the data sets are sufficiently different for us to conclude that there is a real effect due to some particular factor we are investigating. It is never possible to be absolutely sure that differences have not arisen 'by chance', due to inherent variability; nevertheless, we can perform tests which allow us to claim 'real' differences with a margin of error (often 5 per cent, 1 per cent or 0.1 per cent) selected by the user.

Two basic types of statistical test are available. *Parametric* tests are suitable only for data which are measured on a scale with arithmetically equal intervals: examples would be scores on a language test, or times taken by different people to utter a particular sentence. *Non-parametric* tests, on the other hand, can be used for data which are not measured on a scale with equal intervals. Some such tests are for use with data which can be ranked: for instance, we might say that one sentence is more acceptable than another in some particular context, though we should presumably not wish to claim that a sentence with a rating of 3 and one with a rating of 4 differed in acceptability exactly as much as sentences rated 4 and 5. Other non-parametric tests are used with data which are classified according to the presence or absence of some characteristic: for example, we could classify each word in a text as either being a noun or not being a noun. Parametric tests often demand quite stringent conditions on the data, in terms of the type of distribution and the similarity of variation in the data sets to be compared; non-parametric tests are much less demanding in their applicability.

Finally, we should mention studies of *correlation*, which attempt to find out whether there is a tendency for high values of one variable to be associated with high values of a second variable (or, indeed, low values of this second variable).

The above provides no more than the barest sketch of statistical techniques. For fuller discussion, readers are referred to Butler (1985).

3.6.2 *The Statistical Package for the Social Sciences (SPSS)*

SPSS is a very flexible and comprehensive package for statistical analysis, available on a wide range of computers. As is implied by the name, it was developed mainly for use by social scientists, and this is reflected in the concept of the 'case', on which SPSS analyses are based. In a sociological investigation, a case could represent a member of the human population being studied, together with values for properties such as age, sex, social class, and so on. This concept is, of course, directly applicable to some types of sociolinguistic study, but it can also be adapted to other kinds of linguistic data.

SPSS will produce frequency distributions, bar charts and a number of descriptive statistics including the mean, median, mode, range and standard deviation. It will allow the production of tables which cross-classify data according to the values of different variables, and will perform tests to assess the degree of association of variables. A variety of parametric and non-parametric tests of significance, measures of correlation, and further more sophisticated types of analysis, are all available. In addition to the normal 'batch' mode, in which output from the analysis goes to a lineprinter or to a named file, there is a conversational or interactive version which sends the results directly to the terminal at which the user is working.

As an example of the application of the SPSS package, let us take the production of a frequency distribution table and descriptive statistics for a hypothetical set of data from a foreign-language test, given in figure 3.27.

```
15 12 11 18 15 15  9 19 14 13 11 12 18 15 16
14 16 17 15 17 13 14 13 15 17 19 17 18 16 14
```

Figure 3.27 Scores of 30 pupils on a language test

A suitable set of SPSS commands for the analysis of these data is shown in figure 3.28. The RUN NAME command gives a title to the analysis, and the package is then informed that only one variable, named SCORE, will be involved. It is also given the information that the data are in free format: they are simply arranged along one or more lines, with blanks separating one value from the next. Since, in this example, a case is just the score for one language learner, there are 30 cases. The VAR LABELS command associates the full title 'SCORE ON LANGUAGE TEST' with the

```
RUN NAME         LANGUAGE TEST SCORES, GROUP A
VARIABLE LIST    SCORE
INPUT FORMAT     FREEFIELD
N OF CASES       30
VAR LABELS       SCORE ON LANGUAGE TEST/
FREQUENCIES      GENERAL = SCORE
STATISTICS       1 3 4 5 9
READ INPUT DATA
15 12 11 18 15 15 9 19 14 13 11 12 18 15 16 14 16 17 15 17 13 14 13 15 17
19 17 18 16 14
END INPUT DATA
FINISH
```

Figure 3.28 SPSS commands and data for analysis of language-test scores

```
SCORE      ON LANGUAGE TEST
                                                    RELATIVE   ADJUSTED     CUM
                                         ABSOLUTE     FREQ       FREQ       FREQ
CATEGORY LABEL                    CODE     FREQ       (PCT)      (PCT)      (PCT)

                                   9.         1        3.3        3.3        3.3

                                  11.         2        6.7        6.7       10.0

                                  12.         2        6.7        6.7       16.7

                                  13.         3       10.0       10.0       26.7

                                  14.         4       13.3       13.3       40.0

                                  15.         6       20.0       20.0       60.0

                                  16.         3       10.0       10.0       70.0

                                  17.         4       13.3       13.3       83.3

                                  18.         3       10.0       10.0       93.3

                                  19.         2        6.7        6.7      100.0
                                          ------     ------     ------
                                 TOTAL       30      100.0      100.0

MEAN          14.933      MEDIAN        15.000       MODE            15.000
STD DEV        2.490      RANGE         10.000

VALID CASES      30       MISSING CASES      0

- - - - - - - - - - - - - - - - - - - - - - - - - - - - - - - - - - - - - - -

LANGUAGE TEST SCORES, GROUP A
```

Figure 3.29 SPSS output for analysis of language-test scores

variable SCORE, and the FREQUENCIES command specifies that it is the variable SCORE which is to be analysed. In the STATISTICS command, five options are selected: numbers 1(mean), 3(median), 4(mode), 5(standard deviation) and 9(range). The package is then told to read the data, which follow thc READ instruction. The end of the data is shown, and the FINISH command signals that the run is to be terminated. The output from this analysis is shown in figure 3.29. Note that the frequency distribution table gives relative frequencies, cumulative frequencies, and also frequencies adjusted for any missing values (of which there are none here), as well as the absolute frequencies.

Examples of the use of SPSS in hypothesis testing on linguistic data can be found in Butler (1985, chapter 12). For an overview of the package itself, see Norušis (1982).

3.6.3 The Minitab package

Minitab was designed as an all-purpose data manipulation package for users with minimal knowledge of computing or statistical techniques. Like SPSS it is available on a wide range of computers. Minitab is based, not on the 'case' principle, but on a 'worksheet' of rows and columns of data, and this probably makes it rather easier to use than SPSS. A second factor making for ease of use is the relative simplicity of its instruction language as compared with that of SPSS. Although not as comprehensive as SPSS, Minitab offers an impressive range of facilities for performing arithmetical operations (such as adding together two columns of data), editing, sorting data into rank order, producing descriptive statistics, and carrying out tests of significance of differences between sets of data.

Figure 3.30 shows a set of Minitab commands for the production of a frequency table and descriptive statistics for the language test data given in figure 3.27. The command SET THE FOLLOWING INTO C1 reads the set of 30 scores, given in free format in a list following the instruction, and sets them into a column which can thereafter be referred to as C1. The other commands request the calculation of the mean, standard deviation and median (the mode and range are not available), and the production of a histogram of the data. The output from the analysis is shown in figure 3.31. Note that Minitab produces a histogram which is sideways-on, and consists of a number of asterisks proportional to the frequency in each class.

Examples of the use of Minitab in significance testing can be found in Butler (1985, chapter 12). For further details of the package itself, see Ryan, Joiner and Ryan (1976).

```
SET THE FOLLOWING INTO C1
15 12 11 18 15 15 9 19 14 13 11 12 18 15 16 14 16 17 15 17 13 14 13 15 17
19 17 18 16 14
AVERAGE OF C1
STANDARD DEVIATION OF C1
MEDIAN OF C1
HISTOGRAM OF C1
STOP
```

Figure 3.30 Minitab commands and data for analysis of language-test scores

3.7 So why learn a programming language?

Packages such as OCP, CLOC or SPSS are powerful, flexible and quite easy to use, and will serve adequately the needs of many types of research. They are, however, designed to perform quite specific kinds of task. If the research worker wishes to carry out analyses involving more than simply

```
-- SET THE FOLLOWING INTO C1
COLUMN        C1
COUNT         30
        15.          12.          11.          18. . . .

-- AVERAGE OF C1
   AVERAGE =       14.933

-- STANDARD DEVIATION OF C1
   ST.DEV. =      2.4904

-- MEDIAN OF C1
   MEDIAN =      15.000

-- HISTOGRAM OF C1

  C1

   MIDDLE OF    NUMBER OF
   INTERVAL     OBSERVATIONS
       9.         1     *
      10.         0
      11.         2     **
      12.         2     **
      13.         3     ***
      14.         4     ****
      15.         6     ******
      16.         3     ***
      17.         4     ****
      18.         3     ***
      19.         2     **


-- STOP
```

Figure 3.31 Minitab analysis output for language-test data

the production of word counts, indexes, concordances and lists of collocations, or if he wishes to perform calculations which are not included in the standard statistical packages, he has two paths open to him: to find someone to write suitable programs for him, or to learn how to write them himself. Helpful as most members of computing departments and services are, rather few of them, at present, are fully conversant either with the kinds of problem a literary or linguistic scholar may wish to investigate, or with a high-level language which is really suitable for the solution of such problems. The arts researcher who has not only a profound knowledge of his own area of interest, but also the means of translating his questions into computer programs, is in a very strong position. He need not be dependent on the expertise and goodwill of others, and is rather more likely to find a satisfactory solution to his problems than his colleague who must enter into a long dialogue with a computer programmer.

A large number of high-level languages can now be implemented on a wide range of computers. Some of these languages, such as FORTRAN and ALGOL, are particularly suitable for scientific applications involving the processing of large quantities of numerical data: text handling is possible in these languages, but somewhat limited, cumbersome and tedious. Other languages, such as COBOL, find their main application in business, where large files of records relating to employees, stock, and the like, must be processed. Yet others, such as BASIC and PASCAL, were developed as tools for teaching the principles of programming, although they are used today for a large range of applications: again, text handling is possible, but the languages are not designed to facilitate it. One language, however, was designed specifically with text manipulation in mind. This is SNOBOL, developed originally at the Bell Telephone Laboratories in 1962. Since then, the language has evolved into what is now known as SNOBOL4.

Scientifically oriented languages such as FORTRAN have built-in facilities which make it easy for users to perform mathematical operations such as finding the squares or square roots of numbers, or calculating trigonometric values such as the sine, cosine or tangent of an angle. SNOBOL4, on the other hand, pays very little attention to such matters: the squares and square roots of numbers, for example, can be calculated by writing appropriate statements or sequences of statements, but there are no built-in 'utilities' which save the user the trouble of doing the necessary programming himself, as there are in, say, FORTRAN or PASCAL. Instead, the computer scientists who developed SNOBOL4 concentrated on making it easy for users to manipulate sequences of letters, punctuation marks and the like (technically known as 'strings'). There are many built-in utilities for finding sequences of particular types of symbol (for example letters), or instances of particular symbols or combinations (for example 'e' or '-ing'). It is, for instance, quite a simple task to isolate from a text all the words which begin with 'e' and end with '-ing', or all the words of more than 7 letters which end in '-able'. Put more generally and more technically, SNOBOL4 allows the programmer to create simple or complex *patterns* of various kinds, and to look for instances of these patterns in the data, by means of the process of *pattern matching*. A further valuable feature of SNOBOL4 is that it allows the representation of data in forms (known as 'data structures') which are appropriate for the kinds of data in which linguists and other arts programmers are interested. For example, we can create a table to keep track of all the different word forms in a text, together with their frequencies, and this table will grow in size automatically as more and more words are found in the text.

Part II of this book gives a thorough grounding in the essentials of SNOBOL4. The reader who works through it conscientiously and does the exercises at the end of each chapter should attain a level of competence which will allow him to write programs for his own purposes, so making him much less dependent on the availability of either suitable package programs or under-employed professional programmers.

Part II

The SNOBOL4 programming language

4 Basic concepts

4.1 Introduction

We saw in section 1.4 that in order to solve any problem whatsoever, the computer must be presented with a set of instructions, called a *program*, showing in detail, step by step, all the stages in the required procedure. We also saw that programs are usually written in a 'high-level language', which is translated into the machine's own 'code' in the process of compilation.

Like other high-level languages, SNOBOL4 requires that the instructions to the computer be presented as a series of *statements*, some of which will have *labels* to enable us to refer to them if we wish to jump from one place to another in a program. Unless we explicitly tell the machine to jump to a particular place in the program, the statements will be obeyed, or 'executed', in the order in which they are presented. We need to tell the computer when it has reached the end of the program, and this is the function of a special statement consisting simply of the label END. We shall deal with the structure and layout of SNOBOL4 programs later.

It cannot be too strongly emphasised that the computer will do only what you tell it: no more, and no less. If you tell it to do something stupid, it will obey you, provided that you have phrased your request in a way it understands. It is thus of vital importance to be absolutely clear about what you are asking the machine to do, and to be totally explicit in your instructions. If the computer does not understand your instructions, it will probably tell you that you have made an error: however, as we have seen, it may well obey foolish but well-formed instructions to the letter.

Such warnings may sound somewhat daunting: in practice, however, errors may result in temporary frustration and even amusement, but rarely have any catastrophic effect on computer installations, as novices sometimes fear! And it is as well to remember that, as in the learning of any language, making mistakes is a very valuable way of making progress.

4.2 Characters and strings

On each computer, a set of *characters*, or symbols, is available. These normally include the letters of the alphabet, numbers, punctuation marks, and some other symbols such as + = / and so on. The blank, or space, is also a character: since it has no visible mark to represent it, this is all too easily forgotten. It is also easy to forget that as far as the computer is concerned, upper case letters such as A, B, C are different characters from the corresponding lower case letters such as a, b, c. In the chapters which follow, we shall normally assume, for simplicity and convenience, that the text to be analysed is in upper case, but an example of a program operating on both upper and lower case characters is given in chapter 14.

A sequence of characters is called a *string*. Thus MEAT is a string consisting of four characters arranged in sequence. Because sequence is a defining characteristic of a string, MEAT, MATE, TEAM and TAME are different strings. In SNOBOL4, strings are often used within programs; they must then be enclosed in quotation marks. Either single or double quotation marks may be used: thus 'MEAT' and "MEAT" are equivalent. The same kind of quote must, however, be used at both ends of the string. Double quotes are useful where the string itself contains an apostrophe, as in "MARY'S DOG"; single quotes are useful where the string contains quoted speech which is itself enclosed in double quotes, as in '"WHAT A LOVELY DAY!" HE SAID.' A quoted string in SNOBOL4 is often called a *literal*. Note that a string can consist of just one character (e.g. A, represented in a program as 'A' or "A"), or even none at all. The so-called 'null string' is a strange but useful one, as we shall see later. Note also that 'A' is different from ' A' (in which a blank precedes the A). The blank, remember, is a character like any other.

4.3 Variables, their names and values

Information is stored in a program in the form of *variables*, each of which can take a range of *values*. A variable can be thought of as a box, which has certain contents (the current value of the variable) and a *name* by which we can refer to it. It is sensible to choose names so that they reflect the contents of the variable. For instance, if we are counting items, then we might use a variable with the name COUNT to hold the current value of the count. Although names can be chosen fairly freely by the programmer, certain rules must be observed:

1 Names can consist of letters, numbers, full stops and underscores (_), but no other characters;
2 they must start with a letter;
3 they can be up to 71 characters long: it is, however, best to choose

names no longer than 10–12 characters, since this minimises typing errors when repeating a name within a program.

The following are examples of valid and invalid names:

Valid	*Invalid*
COUNT	WORD-COUNT (contains a hyphen)
SCORE	5VAR (starts with a number)
VOWEL	
VAR5	
VAR.5	
P183	
WORD_COUNT	

At various points in a program, we may wish to put certain information into one of the 'boxes' which has a name associated with it: that is, more technically, we assign a value to the variable. This is done by using an equals sign, as in the following example:

```
LENGTH  =  5
```

This tells the computer to assign the numerical value 5 to the variable called LENGTH. One particularly important point should be noted here: there must be *at least one blank* each side of the equals sign.

We can also assign strings to variables via their names:

```
WORD = 'PREPOSTEROUS'
```

This statement will assign the string PREPOSTEROUS to the variable called WORD. This use brings out an important difference between the use of the equals sign in SNOBOL4 and that in arithmetic or algebra. In SNOBOL4, = does not mean 'is numerically equal to', but rather 'is assigned the value', where the value can, but need not, be numerical.

We can even assign the contents of one variable to another:

```
SIZE.1  =  LENGTH
```

This means 'assign the contents of the variable named LENGTH to the variable named SIZE.1'. If we have already assigned the value 5 to LENGTH, the value of SIZE.1 now becomes 5 also.

Two further points about the assignment of values to variable names should be noted. Firstly, when execution of a program begins, each variable has the null string as its initial value (i.e., it is empty) until an assignment is made to that variable. Secondly, when an assignment is made, the previous value of the variable is overwritten, and will be lost. The contents of the variable 'box' have been removed, thrown away, and replaced by new contents.

4.4 Operators and expressions

Very often we need to perform operations, such as addition, subtraction, multiplication or division of numbers, or joining strings together. For this, we need special symbols known as *operators*. A simple example of the use of the addition operator, +, is shown below.

```
NEWLENGTH = WORDLENGTH + 1
```

This tells the computer to take the value of the variable called WORDLENGTH (which must, of course, be numerical), and add one to it, then storing the result in a variable called NEWLENGTH. There is nothing to prevent our using the same variable name on both sides of the equals sign. Indeed, such statements are very useful, for example if we want to increment a counter by 1 every time we find an instance of whatever we are counting:

```
COUNT = COUNT + 1
```

This means 'add one to the value of COUNT, and still keep the result in COUNT'. Note that although the above statement is nonsensical in algebra, it is perfectly acceptable in SNOBOL4, because of the special meaning of the equals sign.

Like the equals sign, operators such as + must have at least one blank on either side of them. We shall deal with other arithmetic operators in a later chapter.

One particular operation is so common in SNOBOL4 that no special symbol is used for it. This is *concatenation*, or joining strings together. To do this, we simply use one or more blanks to separate the components to be joined. Consider the following example:

```
DESSERT = 'RICE' ' PUDDING'
```

The result of this statement would be to give the variable DESSERT the string value RICE PUDDING. Note the blank at the beginning of the second concatenated string. The result of

```
DESSERT = 'RICE' 'PUDDING'
```

would be to put the string RICEPUDDING into the variable DESSERT.

We can also concatenate the contents of two or more variables, or the contents of a variable with a literal string:

```
MEAL = SOUP ' ' FISH ' ' MAIN ' ' DESSERT
```

This statement would take the contents of the variables SOUP, FISH, MAIN and DESSERT, concatenate them with blanks between, and assign the resulting string to the variable name MEAL.

```
RESULT  =  'THE NUMBER OF COMMAS IS '  COUNT
```

The above statement will take the current value of the variable COUNT and append it to the string THE NUMBER OF COMMAS IS , (again note the blank after IS), storing the resulting string in RESULT. If the current value of COUNT is 24, the value of RESULT after execution of the above statement will be THE NUMBER OF COMMAS IS 24.

One final piece of nomenclature: the combinations of names and operators, such as COUNT + 1, are called *expressions*. It is the value of an expression which is assigned to the variable name on the left-hand side of the equals sign in the above statements.

Exercises 4

1 Define, and illustrate where appropriate, each of the following terms: 'program', 'label', 'character', 'string', 'variable', 'value', 'name', 'operator', 'expression'.

2 Which of the following are valid names for variables in SNOBOL4? If any are invalid, say why.

```
SEX
NUMBER
CONS2
ALPHA:3
OCCUP.4
3VOWEL
CONS-CLASS
```

3 Each of the following statements contains at least one error. Correct the errors.

```
SIZE-ALPHA   =   10
COUNT   =COUNT   +   1
2SIZE  =  2SIZE+4
```

4 Write statements which will perform the following tasks:

(i) Assign the value 45 to the variable named MAX
(ii) Assign the string value ALL MEN ARE LIARS to the variable named TRUTH
(iii) Add 1 to the value of a variable LCOUNT
(iv) Concatenate the strings SILLY and BILLY with a blank between, and assign the result to a variable named ASS.1
(v) Concatenate the string THE TOTAL COUNT IS with the value of a variable called FINAL, with a blank between, and then assign the concatenated expression to the variable RESULT

5 Pattern matching

5.1 Patterns and pattern matches

Very often, especially in work with texts, it is necessary to search a particular string for the occurrence of a certain character or sequence of characters. We might, for instance, be interested in knowing whether a particular line of text contains the letter E, or the word AND, or a comma, or a more complicated sequence such as T followed by any two vowels followed by N. Examination of strings in this way is called *pattern matching*. As we saw in section 3.7, the main reason for SNOBOL4 being such a useful language for text processing is its extensive and powerful pattern-matching facilities.

Let us now consider how we can test for a simple pattern match. Let us imagine that we have stored a line of text in a variable called LINE (by means of an assignment statement), and that we want to test for the occurrence of the letter E in this line of text. The required pattern matching statement consists of two parts. First we write down what it is we want to look for the pattern in – the so-called 'subject' of the pattern match. In our case, this is the string variable LINE. We then leave one or more blanks, and write the string we wish to test for – in this case 'E'. Note carefully that since this is a string used as data in the program, it must be in quotes.

```
      LINE  'E'
```

Before we go on to look at the results of this pattern matching statement for different values of LINE, one extremely important point must be understood. Two 'modes' of pattern matching are available in SNOBOL4: the so-called 'unanchored' and 'anchored' modes. In the unanchored mode, a pattern match will succeed if the pattern occurs *anywhere at all* in the 'subject' of the match (in our example, if E occurs anywhere at all in the contents of LINE). In the anchored mode, however, the pattern match succeeds only if the pattern occurs *at the very beginning* of the subject (that is, in our example, if E is the very first character in the string stored in LINE). Anchored pattern matching is very useful, since it saves a considerable amount of computer time if the whole subject need not be scanned for a match. Clearly, we need some method of telling the computer whether we want the anchor to be on or off. We can do this by assigning an appropriate value to a special kind of variable, called the anchor *keyword.* Keywords (we shall meet others later) are distinguished from other variables by having special names preceded by the ampersand sign (&). We can establish unanchored mode by assigning a zero value to &ANCHOR:

```
&ANCHOR  =  0
```

Anchored mode is set by assigning any non-zero value (normally 1 is used) to &ANCHOR:

```
&ANCHOR  =  1
```

In practice, any given implementation of the SNOBOL4 language will have a 'default' value of &ANCHOR built into it. That is, the computer will assume a particular value of &ANCHOR unless instructed otherwise. Unfortunately, different implementations of the language may have different default values for &ANCHOR. Until recently, the computer at the University of Nottingham Computing Centre was one of the ICL 1900 series, on which Version 3 of a variant of SNOBOL4 called SPITBOL was run. (SPITBOL, standing for *SP*eedy *I*mplemen*T*ation of SNO*BOL*, is a fast-running variant of the language, incorporating some additional features. We shall discuss differences between SPITBOL and standard SNOBOL at appropriate points in the following chapters.) In this implementation the default value of &ANCHOR was 1 – that is, the computer assumed that the anchor was to be on, unless told otherwise. The university now has a series 2900 machine, on which Version 4 of SPITBOL is run. In the new implementation, the opposite situation obtains: the default is for the anchor to be off, and the programmer needs to specify if he wishes to turn it on. It is therefore desirable for the programmer to find out the default value for &ANCHOR in the particular version of SNOBOL4 supported by the computer installation he uses. For safety's sake, however, it is good practice always to specify the value of &ANCHOR explicitly. We shall adopt this practice here, even in isolated examples of pattern-matching statements. Note that during the execution of a program, the value of &ANCHOR, once declared or set to the default value, remains the same until it is explicitly changed. The value can, if necessary, be changed at will during the course of a program. Usually, however, a program can be written entirely in one mode, so that a single setting of &ANCHOR will suffice, this being placed at or near the beginning of the program. As we have seen, it is best to use the anchored mode whenever possible.

Let us now return to our example of testing for an E in the contents of LINE, and let us assume that we have assigned to LINE the value THE CAT SAT ON THE MAT. If we use the following statements

```
&ANCHOR = 0
LINE 'E'
```

the pattern match will succeed, because the string stored in LINE does contain an E (two, in fact). If, however, we replace the &ANCHOR assignment by

```
&ANCHOR = 1
```

then the pattern match will fail, since the string stored in LINE does not *begin* with an E. On the other hand, the following match would succeed, because the string stored in LINE does begin with TH:

```
&ANCHOR = 1
LINE 'TH'
```

We shall consider in chapter 6 how we can use the results of success or failure in pattern matching. Meanwhile, let us examine a slightly more complex form of pattern match.

Sometimes, we may wish to test whether any of several patterns is present in a string. This could be done in a number of separate statements, one for each pattern, but it is easier and more elegant, and less wasteful of computer resources, to use the *alternation* operator provided in the SNOBOL4 language. In some implementations, this operator is represented by a vertical bar (|) if this is available in the character set of the machine. Some other systems use an exclamation mark (!) for the alternation operator. The user should check which is used in the system to which he has access. In the present account, the vertical bar will be used for alternation. Let us suppose that we wish to know whether a given line of text (stored in LINE) contains one (or more) of the punctuation marks full stop, question mark or exclamation mark. We can write:

```
&ANCHOR = 0
LINE '.' | '?' | '!'
```

Note that the alternation operator, like other operators, must have at least one blank on either side of it.

As a further example of the use of alternation, let us consider how we might test for the presence of F *or* PH *or* V at the beginning of a string stored in a variable called TEXT. The following would achieve the desired result:

```
&ANCHOR  =  1
TEXT  'F'  |  'PH'  |  'V'
```

If TEXT contained any of the strings below, the pattern match would succeed, since each string begins with one of the components of the alternation:

FREDA LIKES HORSES
PHYLLIS HATES DOGS
VERA IS CRAZY ABOUT ALL ANIMALS

If, on the other hand, TEXT contained the string

ALFRED ADORES CAMELS

the pattern match would fail, since, although the string contains one of the components (F), this does not occur at the beginning.

5.2 Assignment of patterns to variable names

Patterns can be assigned to variables, just as strings and numerical values can. Consider, for example, the pattern involving the punctuation marks . ? ! which we wrote earlier. Rather than write the whole pattern out every time we need it in a program, we can assign it to a variable (say PUNCT), and then use the name of this variable in pattern-matching statements. The following statements would thus be equivalent to the single statement written earlier:

```
PUNCT  =  '.'  |  '?'  |  '!'
LINE  PUNCT
```

The last statement here tests for the presence, in the contents of LINE, of whatever is in PUNCT. What is stored in PUNCT must, of course, be a string or an alternation of strings, as indeed it is in our example.

A further example of assignment of a pattern to a variable is given below:

```
&ANCHOR  =  0
SIBILANT  =  'S'  |  'Z'  |  'CI'  |  'CE'
LINE  SIBILANT
```

Here, we have assigned the pattern consisting of S *or* Z *or* CI *or* CE to the variable SIBILANT, and then tested for the occurrence of any of the alternated elements anywhere in the contents of LINE.

The assignment of patterns to variable names is particularly useful where patterns are complicated and are needed several times in a program. Valuable computer time is saved, since the machine needs to compute the pattern only once. Furthermore, the programmer saves a good deal of typing, with a comcomitant increase in accuracy. Note that it is a good idea to choose a name for a pattern-valued variable which reflects what the pattern is about (e.g. SIBILANT in the above example). This helps considerably in making it clear just what particular statements in the program do.

5.3 Concatenation of patterns

Patterns can be concatenated, just as strings can. It does not matter whether the pattern consists of a string, or a variable containing a string – it can still be concatenated with another pattern. Consider the following:

```
&ANCHOR  =  0
LABIODENT  =  'F'  |  'PH'  |  'V'
VOWEL  =  'A'  |  'E'  |  'I'  |  'O'  |  'U'
LINE  LABIODENT  VOWEL
```

This sets up two pattern-valued variables. LABIODENT has as its value the alternation of F, PH and V (note the choice of name to reflect the function of the variable – all the components represent labiodental sounds in English). VOWEL has as its value the alternation of the vowels A, E, I, O and U. The last line then tests the contents of LINE for the occurrence, anywhere in the string, of any of the components F, PH or V, followed immediately by any of A, E, I, O or U. The match would succeed if LINE contained either of the first two strings below, but would fail for the third:

PHILOSOPHY BORES ME	(PH followed immediately by I)
AND FELICITY ADORES ME	(F followed immediately by E)
BUT PHYLLIS ABHORS ME	(PH, but not followed immediately by A, E, I, O or U)

Consider also what will happen if LINE contains the string PHYLLIS IS A PHILISTINE. The first occurrence of PH is not followed by a component of VOWEL, but the computer continues to scan the string (since the anchor is off), and finds a later occurrence of PH which is indeed followed by a component of VOWEL. The pattern match therefore succeeds.

Note that in the above example there are 3 × 5, or 15 substrings which will cause the pattern match to succeed (viz. FA, FE, FI, FO, FU, PHA, PHE, PHI, PHO, PHU, VA, VE, VI, VO and VU). This shows how it is possible to write rather simple patterns which are nevertheless quite powerful.

As a final example of the use of concatenation, and also alternation, let us consider the problem of testing whether a string (stored, let us say, in a variable named TEXTLINE) contains the word HER. At first sight, this seems a rather simple task, not calling for concatenated or alternated patterns. We might be tempted to write simply:

```
&ANCHOR   =   0
TEXTLINE   'HER'
```

This, however, would not achieve our aim, since the pattern match would succeed if, for instance, TEXTLINE contained either of the following strings:

I'D LOVE ANOTHER
I HAVE TWO BROTHERS

What we wish to isolate is not just any successive occurrence of the letters H, E and R, but the word HER. Let us try the following:

```
&ANCHOR   =   0
TEXTLINE   ' HER '
```

The blanks before and after HER in the pattern will ensure that the match fails for strings such as those discussed above, and succeeds for such strings as:

HARRY LOOKED INTO HER EYES.

It will still fail, however, for strings such as the following, in which HER is not followed immediately by a blank:

HE LOVED HER, WITH A PASSION RARE AND INTENSE.
"I LOVE HER", HE SAID.

We can improve matters by allowing any punctuation mark, as well as the blank, to follow HER. We therefore set up a pattern which is an alternation of punctuation marks and the blank:

```
PMARKS   =   ','  |  ';'  |  ':'  |  '.'  |  '?'  |  '!'  |  '"'  |  ' '
```

We can now rewrite our pattern match as:

```
TEXTLINE   ' HER'   PMARKS
```

This will still fail to pick up HER when preceded by quotation marks:

"HER NOSE IS TOO BIG", HE SAID.

We therefore need an alternation of blank and quote as permissible characters before HER. Furthermore, the pattern as written will not match HER at the beginning of a text line, where it will not be preceded by anything, or right at the end, where it will not be followed by anything. To overcome this problem, we insert a blank at the beginning and end of each text line before we test it. The following version builds in these refinements:

```
&ANCHOR  =  0
PMARKS  =  ','  |  ';'  |  ':'  |  '.'  |  '?'  |  '!'  |  '"'  |  ' '
BEFORE  =  ' '  |  '"'
TEXTLINE  =  ' '  TEXTLINE  ' '
TEXTLINE  BEFORE  'HER'  PMARKS
```

5.4 Replacement during pattern matching

Not only can we examine strings during pattern matching but we can also modify them. For instance, let us suppose that we want to replace an occurrence of PH in a line of text, by F. We can write:

```
&ANCHOR  =  0
LINE  'PH'  =  'F'
```

Translated into words, this means 'scan the contents of LINE from left to right until you find an occurrence of PH, and if you find one, replace it by F'. Note that only the first occurrence of PH is replaced. If LINE contains the string

ALL PHILOSOPHERS ARE PHILANDERERS

the result will be

ALL FILOSOPHERS ARE PHILANDERERS

Later, we shall discuss a mechanism by which we can use a replacement statement over and over again until all occurrences of the pattern have been replaced.

Here is a further example of a replacement statement. Imagine that we have split a text into its constituent words, and are storing each word in turn in a variable called WORD (we shall consider later how we can strip off a word at a time from a text). If we wanted to replace the first vowel in the contents of WORD by an asterisk, we could write (with the usual meaning of the pattern VOWEL):

```
&ANCHOR  =  0
WORD  VOWEL  =  '*'
```

One very useful application of replacement statements is in the deletion of material from strings. If we wanted to delete the first occurrence of S from a string stored in WORD, we should write:

```
&ANCHOR  =  0
WORD  'S'  =
```

Since there is nothing on the right-hand side of the equals sign, the first S is replaced by nothing, that is by the 'null string' mentioned earlier. Similarly, given that PUNCT is defined as the alternation of . ? and ! as in an earlier example, the following will delete the first full stop, question mark or exclamation mark from the contents of LINE:

```
&ANCHOR  =  0
LINE PUNCT  =
```

5.5 Value assignment during pattern matching

Earlier, we considered the following statements:

```
PUNCT  =  '.'  |  '?'  |  '!'
LINE  PUNCT
```

This segment of program will search for . or ? or ! and will succeed if *any* of these is found. But we may also want to know *which* of the alternatives has been found. We do this by means of a procedure which attaches a name to a component of a pattern. If the whole pattern is successfully matched, the matched substring is assigned as the value of the attached variable. This is perhaps best understood by example.

```
&ANCHOR  =  0
LINE  PUNCT  .  P
```

This causes the computer to search for . or ? or ! in the contents of LINE. If it finds one of these, it will assign whichever it has found as the value of the variable called P. Note that this is achieved by the use of the full stop as an operator. It is sometimes called the 'conditional value assignment operator', because, as will become clearer below, an assignment is made only if the entire pattern involved in the statement matches. As usual, there must be at least one blank either side of the operator.

As a further example of conditional value assignment during pattern matching, consider the following:

```
&ANCHOR  =  0
LINE  LABIODENT  .  L
```

where LABIODENT is defined as the alternation of F, PH and V as in the earlier example. A search will be made in the contents of LINE for an occurrence of F, PH or V, and if one of these is found it is assigned as the value of L.

Names can be attached to more than one component in a pattern. Consider the following:

```
&ANCHOR  =  0
LABV  =  LABIODENT  .  L   VOWEL  .  V
LINE LABV
```

This will search for one of F, PH or V, followed immediately by one of A, E, I, O or U. If the *whole* pattern matches, then whatever labiodental has been found will be assigned as the value of L, and whatever vowel has been found will be assigned to V. If only one component of the pattern matches successfully, the pattern match as a whole will fail, and no assignment is made to either L or V. Let us suppose that LINE contains the string

ALL PHILOSOPHERS ARE PHILANDERERS

The first character is a vowel, but is not, of course, preceded by any of the components of LABIODENT. The substring PHI, however, matches LABV completely. The whole pattern match succeeds, and the value PH is assigned to L, and the value I to V. Now consider the case where LINE contains the string

PHYLLIS FRIGHTENS ME

LABIODENT is matched by PH, but the following letter, Y, is not a component of VOWEL. The overall pattern match fails, and no assignment is made to either L or V, despite the fact that a partial match has been achieved.

The fact that, when using the conditional value assignment operator, we can cause an assignment to be made only if the *whole* pattern matches is sometimes an undesirable limitation. At times, it is useful to be able to make an *immediate* assignment, as soon as one part of a complex match succeeds, irrespective of whether the rest of the matching succeeds or fails. We can achieve this by means of the 'immediate value assignment operator', written as $. Let us consider an example. Suppose that we wish to test whether a word (stored, let us assume, in a variable named WORD) contains two successive occurrences of the same vowel. We could, of course, write:

```
&ANCHOR  =  0
WORD  'AA'  |  'EE'  |  'II'  |  'OO'  |  'UU'
```

A more elegant way, however, would be to use the $ operator. If VOWEL has been defined in the usual way, we may write:

```
&ANCHOR = 0
WORD VOWEL $ V V
```

Here, the computer will search for an occurrence of any vowel, and as soon as it finds one, the particular vowel found will be assigned as the value of V, irrespective of what follows it in the contents of WORD. Having made the assignment to V, the computer looks for a second occurrence of the vowel which is the value of V, immediately after the first.

In order to show clearly the different effects of the two assignment operators . and $, let us examine the following patterns:

```
VOWELP1 = VOWEL . V 'P'
VOWELP2 = VOWEL $ V 'P'
```

Suppose that the variable TEXT contains the string COMPUTER. If we now write:

```
&ANCHOR = 0
TEXT VOWELP1
```

the VOWEL component of VOWELP1 will match the O of COMPUTER, but as this is not followed directly by P, the overall pattern match fails. The computer now scans the string for a further vowel and finds U, but again this is not followed by P. Further scanning finds the vowel E, but yet again there is no following P. The complete pattern match thus fails each time, and no value is assigned to V. Now consider the following:

```
&ANCHOR = 0
TEXT VOWELP2
```

As before, the VOWEL component of the pattern matches the O of COMPUTER, but this time the value O is immediately assigned to V, even though there is no following P. However, since the complete pattern does not match, the computer scans the string in an attempt to find another vowel. It finds the U, and assigns this as the new value of V. Since there is still no P, further scanning occurs, and the E is found, and assigned as the latest value of V. There is still no complete pattern match, since there is no following P, but E remains as the value of V.

5.6 Precedence of operators in patterns

A familiar problem of elementary mathematics at school is the potential ambiguity of expressions containing more than one arithmetic operator. Consider, for example, the expression $15 - 4 \times 2$. Without further rules or conventions, this could be grouped as either (15 – 4) × 2 or 15 – (4 × 2). The convention adopted in mathematics is that multiplication has a higher 'precedence' than subtraction, so that our expression must actually be evaluated as 15 – (4 × 2). The notion of precedence does not solve all problems of potential ambiguity: for instance, does 15 – 4 – 2 mean (15 – 4) – 2 or 15 – (4 – 2)? Clearly, the subtraction operator has the same precedence wherever it occurs. The convention used here is that this operator 'associates to the left': that is, we first bracket the leftmost pair of numbers connected by the operator.

Precisely analogous problems arise with operators in a programming language such as SNOBOL4. We shall deal with the precedence and association of arithmetic operators such as + and – in a later chapter; meanwhile, we must discuss the application of the concept of precedence to operators used in pattern construction. The assignment operators . and $ have a higher precedence value than the blank used for concatenation, which in turn is of higher precedence than the alternation operator |. As with ordinary arithmetic, we can always used round brackets to make the groupings clear if we wish, and we shall see below that we can also use these to alter the groupings if necessary. Consider the statement:

```
TEXT 'T' VOWEL . V 'S'
```

with VOWEL defined in the usual way. Since the full stop assignment operator has a higher precedence than the concatenation blank, this is equivalent to:

```
TEST 'T' (VOWEL . V) 'S'
```

Again, consider the following:

```
LINE 'Y' | VOWEL . V
```

Since the full stop operator is of higher precedence than the alternation operator, this is equivalent to:

```
LINE 'Y' | (VOWEL . V)
```

Let us now suppose that we wish to find either Y or a vowel, and to assign the result to V. We can alter the grouping of the operators by using brackets as shown below:

```
LINE ('Y' | VOWEL) . V
```

Similarly, if we wanted to find the sequence T + vowel + S in TEXT, and to assign T + vowel to V, we could write:

```
TEXT ('T' VOWEL) . V 'S'
```

Exercises 5

1 Write statements which will test for the presence of each of the following anywhere in the contents of a variable called RECORD (assume that the anchor has already been set to 0):

(i) the letter G
(ii) the word OF followed by a comma (assume here that every occurrence of the word OF will be preceded by a blank)
(iii) *either* A *or* I
(iv) *any* of the following: comma, colon, semicolon
(v) *either* E *or* O, followed by *either* S *or* T

2 For each of the following, construct a suitable pattern and assign it as the value of an appropriately named variable:

(i) any of the vowels A, E, I, O, U
(ii) any of the punctuation marks . ! or ?
(iii) any numerical character
(iv) any letter which can represent a bilabial consonant in English

3 Write statements which will perform each of the following tasks. Assume (i) unanchored pattern matching, (ii) a blank before each word in a text, (iii) the names of any variables you set up in Question 2.

(i) test the contents of a variable LINE for the occurrence of the word HOWEVER followed immediately by a comma
(ii) test the contents of a variable WORD for the occurrence of two successive vowels
(iii) test the contents of a variable TEXT for the presence of a numerical character followed immediately by the letter X
(iv) test the contents of WORD for the presence of a bilabial consonant followed by a vowel

4 Write statements which will perform the following tasks. In each case, specify whether the anchor is to be on or off. You may use names of pattern-valued variables set up in earlier questions.

(i) test WORD to see if it begins with UN
(ii) test LINE to see if it contains the end of a sentence whose last word is IT
(iii) test LINE to see if it has asterisks in positions 1 to 4

5 Write statements which will effect the following changes. Assume any variable names set up in previous questions, and unanchored pattern matching.

(i) replace the first occurrence of the letter F, in the contents of WORD, by the letter V
(ii) replace the first vowel in the contents of LINE by an asterisk

(iii) find, in TEXT, the first occurrence of the word AND which is both preceded and followed by a blank, and replace it by the word BUT
(iv) delete the first occurrence of . ! or ? from the contents of RECORD

6 What will be the results of each of the following sets of statements? Assume unanchored pattern matching.

(i)
```
LINE = "NOBODY LOVES A FAIRY WHEN SHE'S FORTY"
ROUND = 'O' | 'U'
LINE 'F' ROUND . V
```

(ii)
```
TEXT = 'HUMPTY DUMPTY SAT ON A WALL'
VWLS = 'A' | 'O' | 'U'
FINDPAT = VWLS . V 'P'
TEXT FINDPAT
```

(iii)
```
WORD = 'PAN'
PB = 'P' | 'B'
VWLS = 'A' | 'O' | 'U'
STOPV = PB . C VWLS . V
WORD STOPV
```

(iv)
```
WORD = 'ASSUMPTION'
VL = 'O' | 'U'
PAT1 = 'SS' VL $ V 'P'
WORD PAT1
```

7 Write statements which will (assuming unanchored pattern matching):

(i) test for the presence of a vowel in the variable LINE and assign the first vowel to the variable V1
(ii) test for the presence of . , ; or : in TEXT and assign the first occurrence of any of these as the value of P1
(iii) test for the presence in LINE of the letter T followed by any vowel, and assign the vowel in the first successful pattern match to the variable V
(iv) test for the pattern vowel plus P plus vowel in LINE, and assign the first vowel as the value of V, whether or not the rest of the pattern match succeeds

6 Program structure, layout and input/output

6.1 Transfer of control

As we have seen, a SNOBOL4 program consists of a number of statements, which will be executed in the order in which they are presented, unless the computer is told otherwise at a given point. Very often, we need to jump either forwards or backwards in a program, so that some statements are left out for the moment, or some are repeated. This is called *transfer of control*.

In order to tell the machine which statement to transfer to, that statement must have a *label*. Any statement can have a label, though we normally label only those statements to which control is transferred at some point in the program. The rules for the construction of labels are not quite so restrictive as those for names:

1 they can contain any characters other than blanks and semicolons (blanks are used to separate the label from the rest of the statement, and semicolons have a specific function which will be mentioned later);
2 they can be up to 72 characters long, though, as with names, it is best to have a maximum of 10–12 characters in a label;
3 they must begin with either a letter or a number (cf. names, which cannot begin with a number);
4 a label must begin in the first position in the line (otherwise it will be taken as the name of a variable).

The following lists give some valid and invalid labels:

Valid	*Invalid*
Position 1	Position 1
↓	↓
AGAIN	*COUNT (does not begin with letter or number)
MORE	MORE (does not begin in position 1)

COUNT.1 GET WORD (contains a blank)
PRINT
GETWORD
4.COUNT
X%

It is a good idea to choose mnemonic labels, for ease in understanding what the program is doing at any given point. All the labels used in a program must, of course, be different, otherwise an instruction to transfer control would be ambiguous. There must be at least one blank between the label and the rest of the statement, and since anything beginning in the first position in the line will be interpreted as a label, any statement which does not have a label must begin with at least one blank (see comments on program layout below).

6.2 Unconditional and conditional go-to's

An instruction to transfer control to a particular statement with a given label is called a 'go-to'. There are two kinds of go-to: unconditional and conditional.

An unconditional go-to is used when we want to say that *whenever* a particular statement has been executed, the computer is to jump to a statement with a given label. An example of how to do this is given below:

```
     COUNT = COUNT + 1                              :(PRINT)
```

This tells the computer that whenever it has obeyed this statement, and so incremented the value of COUNT by 1, it must go to the statement labelled PRINT. Note that the go-to consists of a colon, followed by the label, in brackets, of the statement to which control is to be transferred. The colon must be separated from the rest of the statement by at least one blank, and there must be no blanks between the colon and the final bracket. The statement to which control is transferred can be anywhere in the program.

Very often, we want to be able to say things such as: 'If such-and-such is so, then jump to the statement labelled X, but if not, then go to the statement labelled Y'. These more complex 'if'-type go-to's are called 'conditional go-to's'. We have already met one kind of condition which can be used in a conditional go-to: the success or failure of a pattern match. We shall meet other kinds of condition later, but for the moment let us concentrate on the pattern matching kind.

Let us suppose that we are counting the number of words beginning with A and the number beginning with E, in a piece of text. We store each word in turn in a variable named WORD (we shall see later how to do this). If WORD contains a string beginning with A we want to increment the value of a variable called ACOUNT; if it begins with E we wish to increment the value of a variable called ECOUNT. The following series of statements will do just this:

```
          &ANCHOR  =  1
          WORD  'A'                              :F(ETEST)
          ACOUNT  =  ACOUNT  +  1                :(NEXT)
ETEST     WORD  'E'                              :F(NEXT)
          ECOUNT  =  ECOUNT  +  1
NEXT
```

This is the most complicated sequence of statements we have met so far, so let us go through it in detail, step by step. First, we set the anchor to 1 so that all the pattern matches will be anchored to the beginning of the string. We then test to see if the contents of WORD begin with A. The go-to at the end of this statement says: 'If the pattern match fails (as shown by the F), go to the statement labelled ETEST.' If the pattern match succeeds, however, the computer will simply go on to execute the next statement, which adds 1 to the value of ACOUNT, as required. Note that if the string in WORD does begin with A, it cannot begin with E, so it would be a waste of time to test for this. Rather, having incremented ACOUNT, we want to proceed with the rest of the program, beginning with the statement labelled NEXT (whose exact nature does not concern us here). We therefore put an unconditional go-to :(NEXT) at the end of the statement incrementing ACOUNT.

If the string in WORD does not begin with A, trasnfer of control occurs, to the statement labelled ETEST, as we have seen. This tests whether the contents of WORD begin with E. If this pattern match fails, the go-to instructs the computer to jump to the statement labelled NEXT. If the match succeeds, the next statement in the series is executed, thereby incrementing ECOUNT as required. After that, the rest of the program proceeds, starting with NEXT.

In the above section of program, we made transfer of control conditional on the failure of a pattern match. We could equally well have wanted to make it conditional on the success of a match, in which case we shoud have written S in the go-to instead of F. Indeed, we can even use both S and F in the same go-to. For example, :S(COUNT.1)F(COUNT.2) means: 'If the pattern match (or other condition) succeeds, go to the statement labelled COUNT.1; if it fails, go to COUNT.2.' Note that only one colon is used in such 'double' go-to's. Below is given a section of program using these facilities, which does exactly the same job as the statements given earlier. One thing which a beginner in programming needs to realise is that there may well be several ways to do a particular job in a program. Sometimes, one way is better than the others, because it uses computer time more efficiently. One example we have already met is the greater efficiency of anchored as compared with unanchored pattern matching.

```
                &ANCHOR  =  1
                WORD  'A'                                    :S(INC.A)
                WORD  'E'                                    :S(INC.E)F(NEXT)
INC.A           ACOUNT  =  ACOUNT  +  1                      :(NEXT)
INC.E           ECOUNT  =  ECOUNT  +  1
NEXT
```

Here, if the word begins with A, we jump to INC.A, and so increment ACOUNT, then pass unconditionally to NEXT. If the pattern match with A fails, the next statement is executed, testing whether the word begins with E. If this pattern match succeeds, we jump to INC.E and increment ECOUNT; if it fails, we jump to NEXT.

6.3 Loops

Conditional go-to's are extremely useful when we want to perform an operation, or a sequence of operations, a number of times. We do this by setting up a 'loop' in the program. Consider the problem of deleting all occurrences of the letter S from a line of text stored in the variable LINE. If we simply write:

```
                &ANCHOR  =  0
                LINE  'S'  =
```

only the first S will be deleted. If we want them all deleted, we must repeat this statement until no more occurrences of S remain. We can do this as follows:

```
                &ANCHOR  =  U
AGAIN           LINE  'S'  =                                 :S(AGAIN)
```

Here, if an S is found in LINE, the conditional go-to causes the computer to loop back to the same statement, repeating it until all the occurrences of S have been deleted. Finally, when the pattern match fails, control passes to the next statement in the program. Note that it is absolutely essential to remember the equals sign in the pattern matching statement. If this is omitted, the same S will be found time and time again, and we shall have created the programmer's nightmare, an infinite loop! Eventually, the computer is likely to give up, telling the programmer that the permissible number of statement executions has been exceeded, but quite a lot of computer time will have been wasted. It is important, however, not to worry too much if this kind of thing happens occasionally at first: it is all part of learning to program; furthermore, as we shall see in a later chapter, there are ways of minimising any wastage of time due to looping which cannot be terminated.

Sometimes, we need to use an unconditional go-to to form a loop, and then a conditional go-to to jump out of the loop. Consider, for example, how we might count the number of commas in a string stored in the variable TEXT, and print out the result. We shall discuss later how to do the printing; for now, let us assume that it is done by means of a statement labelled PRINT. The following statements will do what we require:

```
         &ANCHOR = 0
MORE     TEXT ',' =                     :F(PRINT)
         COMMA = COMMA + 1              :(MORE)
```

The statement labelled MORE searches for a comma, and if one is found, it is deleted (again, note the importance of deletion if the same comma is not to be found over and over again). The value of the counter COMMA is incremented, and the program then loops back unconditionally to search for another comma. When no more commas can be found, control is transferred to the PRINT statement elsewhere in the program.

6.4 The END statement

The computer must be told when it has reached the end of the program, otherwise it will continue to look for instructions. Every SNOBOL4 program must therefore terminate with a statement consisting of just the special label END, starting, as usual, in the first position in the line. Control may 'flow into' the END statement from the previous statement, or we may transfer control to END, unconditionally or conditionally, from a statement earlier in the program.

6.5 Input and output

We have so far said nothing about how we get data for analysis into the computer, or how we print out the results of our programs: that is, about 'input' and 'output' in SNOBOL4.

It is, of course, possible to assign data strings to variables in the course of a program. Usually, however, we shall want to make our programs as general as possible, so that they can be used to operate on different sets of data at different times. We therefore need some way of reading in data (which may be in the form of a linguistic text, a series of numbers, etc.) from outside the program itself. We saw in chapter 1 that data may be typed into a file from a terminal, or punched on cards (though the latter method is now fast becoming obsolete), or transferred on to magnetic tape by an optical character reader. In what follows, we shall assume that a data file has been created. The manner of specifying which data file is to be used on any given occasion of running the program is dependent on the particular operating system for each computer installation, and so will not be discussed here.

In order to read in a line of data for anaysis by a program, we use the special variable name INPUT. Whenever this is used, it causes a line of data from a file to be read in up to 80 character positions, and assigned as the value of a variable specified in the INPUT statement. For instance, if we write:

```
        LINE  =  INPUT
```

this will cause a line of data to be read in and its contents assigned as the value of LINE. We can then go on to perform whatever operations we like on the contents of LINE.

If we keep on reading in data (by means of a loop – see section 6.3) there will come a point where there are no more data in the file. The computer needs to be told what to do when this occurs. For this reason, we must put a failure go-to on the INPUT statement, for instance:

```
READ    LINE  =  INPUT                          :F(NODATA)
```

When the data are exhausted, the program jumps to the statement labelled NODATA.

We must now consider how to make the computer print out the results of an operation, or anything else we may wish to see in the final printout. To do this, we assign whatever we want printed as the value of the special variable called OUTPUT. If, for example, we want to have the string WORDS BEGINNING WITH A VOWEL printed at some point in a program, we write:

```
        OUTPUT  =  'WORDS BEGINNING WITH A VOWEL'
```

We can also assign a variable as the value of OUTPUT, in which case the contents of the variable will be printed. The statement

```
        OUTPUT  =  LINE
```

will cause the current contents of LINE to be printed. We can even use a mixture of quoted strings and variables, or an expression, on the right-hand side of an OUTPUT statement:

```
        OUTPUT  =  'THE NUMBER OF COMMAS IS '  COMMA
```

If the current value of COMMA is 41, the following will be printed out:

```
        THE NUMBER OF COMMAS IS 41
```

As a further example, involving an expression containing an arithmetic operator, consider the statement:

```
          OUTPUT = COUNT + 2
```

This will take the current value of COUNT, add 2 to it, and print the result. Note carefully the difference between the above statement and the following, which will simply print the string COUNT + 2:

```
          OUTPUT = 'COUNT + 2'
```

Note also that if we simply want to read in a data line and print it out, we can use both INPUT and OUTPUT in the same statement:

```
          OUTPUT = INPUT                          :F(NODATA)
```

Finally, it should be noted that since OUTPUT is a variable name, it can be assigned a value during pattern matching. Consider the following, in which VOWEL is defined in the usual way:

```
          &ANCHOR = 0
          LINE 'P' VOWEL . OUTPUT 'S'
```

This will search the contents of LINE for the sequence P + vowel + S, and if the whole match succeeds, the vowel will be assigned as the value of OUTPUT, and therefore printed.

6.6 Program layout

Since we are now almost ready to start writing simple but complete SNOBOL4 programs, it is time to take a closer look at the layout of statements in a program.

We have seen that labels must begin in the first position in the line, and must be separated from the rest of the statement by at least one blank. The clearest way to set out statements is to reserve the first 9 positions for labels, so that the rest of the statement (and any unlabelled statement) starts at position 10, as in the following example:

```
Position 1   Position 10

             &ANCHOR = 1
READ         WORD = INPUT                        :F(END)
             WORD 'A'                            :F(READ)
             OUTPUT = WORD                       :(READ)
END
```

(You should find it very easy to work out exactly what this mini-program does, though this is not the main point at issue here).

No statement may occupy more than the first 72 positions of any given line. If a statement is too long to fit into 72 positions, it may be split between two lines, or even more if necessary. In such cases, the continuation line(s) must begin with a + sign in the first position, this acting as an indication to the computer that it must not interpret what is in this position as being the start of a label. There are strict rules about where a statement may be split. We may divide a statement:

1 at a blank used for concatenation:

```
PRINT     OUTPUT  =  'THE NUMBER OF COMMAS IS '
+ COMMA
```

2 at a blank which is on one side of an operator:

```
          OUTPUT  =  'THE NUMBER OF SYLLABLES IS '  N
+  +  2
```

(Note that the first + here indicates a continuation line since it is in position 1, while the second represents the addition operator)

3 at a blank which separates the components of a statement (e.g. the subject of a pattern match and the pattern itself):

```
VOWELS    FIRSTWORD
+  'A'  |  'E'  |  'I'  |  'O'  |  'U'
```

A statement may *not* be divided in the middle of a variable name: the following statement is thus in error, and would cause program failure:

```
PRINT     OUTPUT  =  'THE FREQUENCY OF "A" IS '  CO
+UNT
```

If we wish to break a statement in the middle of a string, we may *not* simply split it at a blank. Instead, we must divide the string into two parts, closing the quotes at the end of the first part, and reopening them at the beginning of the second:

```
PRINT     OUTPUT  =  'THE NUMBER OF WORDS BEGINNING '
+  'WITH A VOWEL IS '  VCOUNT
```

Note the blank after BEGINNING – if it is not put in, the string printed will contain the 'word' BEGINNINGWITH!

If two or more successive statements are very short, they may be put on the same line. The statements in a multi-statement line must be separated by a semicolon. If the second or subsequent statement in a line has a label, that label must begin in the position immediately after the semicolon. The following are thus equivalent:

```
         &ANCHOR  =  0
READ     LINE  =  INPUT                            :F(END)
         LINE  ','                                 :S(INC)

   &ANCHOR  =  0;READ   LINE  =  INPUT   :F(END);   LINE  ','  :S(INC)
```

The use of multi-statement lines saves space, but makes the program rather more difficult to read. In this book, we shall use such lines only occasionally, where no loss of clarity will result.

One further remark on program layout must be made before we leave this important area. When you are writing a program, it is essential to remember that you, or someone else, will probably need to use the program again some time later, and may have some difficulty in seeing at a glance exactly what each bit of it does unless comments are included to explain the functions of the various parts. Obviously, this is particularly important in the case of long and complex programs, but it is as well to acquire the habit of providing comments even for short ones. Any line of program beginning with an asterisk is taken to be a comment line in SNOBOL4, and is ignored by the computer when compiling the program, but is printed out when the whole program is listed at the beginning of a run. An example involving the use of a comment line is given below:

```
* TEST FOR WORDS CONTAINING A HYPHEN
*
HYPH     WORD  '-'                                 :S(COUNT)
```

Note that lines which are blank except for the initial asterisk can be used to improve the layout visually, as in the second line above.

Exercises 6

1 Which of the following are invalid labels in SNOBOL4, and why?

```
Position 1
↓
GETLINE
DO AGAIN
DO_AGAIN
ERROR.1
3INC
LOOP.2
 LOOP
*FINDP
B$5
```

2 Write statements which will:

(i) add 1 to the value of NUMBER, then transfer control to a statement labelled PRINTOUT
(ii) concatenate the string THE VOWEL COUNT IS plus a blank, with the value of the variable VCOUNT, assign the result to a variable RESULT, and then transfer control to a statement labelled CPRINT
(iii) test for the presence of the letter X in LINE, and transfer control to the statement labelled XCOUNT if the pattern match succeeds
(iv) test for the presence of F followed by a vowel in TEXT, and transfer control to a statement labelled COUNT if the match succeeds, but to MORE if it fails
(v) delete *all* occurrences of the letter E from the contents of a variable called RECORD
(vi) replace *all* occurrences of vowels, in the contents of LINE, by asterisks, and then transfer control to a statement labelled VCOUNT

3 Write a short section of program which will count the number of vowels in the contents of a variable called TEXT, and store the final result in a variable COUNT, then transfer control to a statement labelled PRINTOUT.

4 Divide the following statements into

(i) those which are entirely correct and acceptable
(ii) those which are syntactically correct but would produce unacceptable output
(iii) those which are incorrect and would cause program failure

Give your reasons.

(i)
```
PRINTOUT  OUTPUT  =  'THE TOTAL NUMBER OF WORDS '
   +'I3 ' WCOUNT
```

(ii)
```
PRINT     OUTPUT  =  'THE NUMBER OF VOWELS'
+'IS'  VCOUNT
```

(iii)
```
PRINT.3   OUTPUT  =  'THE NUMBER OF OCCURRENCES OF '
+'THE LETTER X IS ' XCOUNT
```

(iv)
```
          RESULT  =  'THE NUMBER OF FULL STOPS IS '  CO
+UNTFS
```

(v)
```
PRINT     OUTPUT  =  'THE PERCENTAGE OF SATIS
+FIED CUSTOMERS IS ' PERCENT
```

(vi)
```
FINDV     NEXTWD  'A'  |  'E'  |  'I'  |  'O'
+  |  'U'
```

(vii)
```
FINDP     LINE
+ '.'  |  ','
```

7 Three complete programs

7.1 Algorithms, flowcharts and program structure

We are now in a position to tackle the writing of some simple but complete programs, using the facilities discussed so far. In chapter 1, it was pointed out that the writing of a program involves the construction of an algorithm, or series of logically connected steps for solving the problem concerned, and that algorithms are conveniently set out in the form of flowcharts. For the three programs discussed in this chapter, we shall first present an algorithm in the form of a flowchart, which will then be translated into a SNOBOL4 program. As you become more skilled in programming, you will probably find that for most tasks you do not need to write out a flowchart first. Therefore, in succeeding chapters of this book, we shall assume that there is no longer any need to carry out this preliminary step.

The algorithm for a particular task, and the computer program itself, will consist of several phases. The first phase is often termed *initialisation*: in this phase, we set the anchor, set up any patterns which we wish to assign to variable names, and assign initial values to variables. We have seen that if we wish the initial value of a variable to be null (or the numerical equivalent, zero), we do not actually need to state this, since the computer will assume a null value for a variable on the first occasion of its use, unless instructed otherwise. Nevertheless, it is never wrong to assign a zero value to a variable during initialisation; indeed, this is to be encouraged as a safety measure. In later chapters, we shall discuss other types of statement which will form part of the initialisation phase.

The second phase of an algorithm and program is the *processing* phase, in which the calculations, string manipulations, and so on, are carried out. This, then, is the main body of the program.

Many programs, though not all, have a third phase, *termination*, in which headings, results, etc., are printed out. Sometimes, of course, results are printed as part of the processsing phase.

7.2 Program 1: listing the words beginning with a vowel

For our first program, let us consider the problem of reading in words, each word being on a separate data record, and finding and printing all the words which begin with a vowel. A suitable algorithm is shown in flowchart form in figure 7.1. (It may be advisable at this point to revise the conventional symbols used in flowcharts, as set out in chapter 1.)

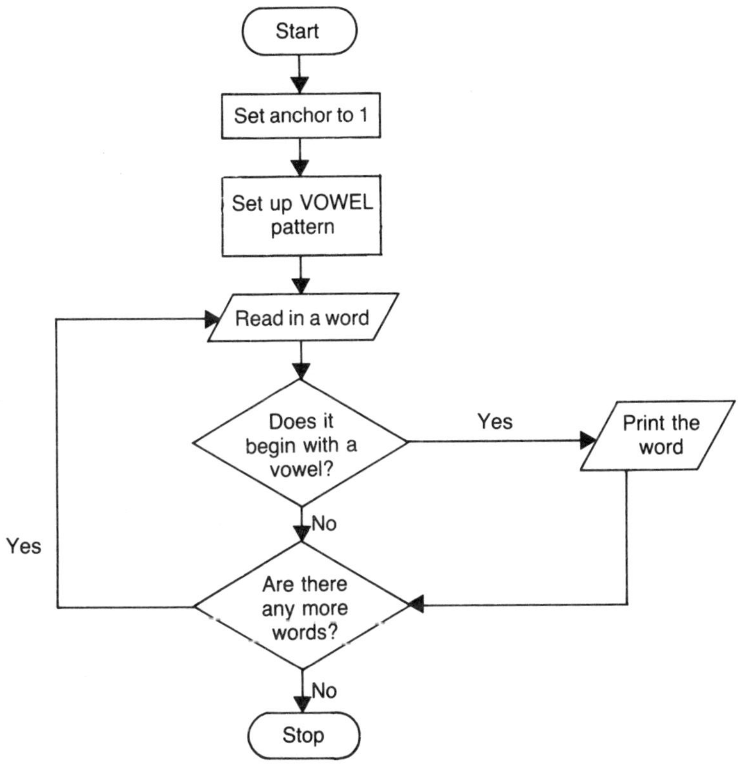

Figure 7.1 Flowchart for reading in words and printing those which begin with a vowel

We may now convert this flowchart into a SNOBOL4 program. We first put in comment lines saying what the program does:

```
* THIS PROGRAM READS IN WORDS, ONE PER DATA RECORD, AND PRINTS
* OUT THOSE WHICH BEGIN WITH A VOWEL.
```

Since we are interested in words which *begin* with a vowel, we shall need to set the anchor to 1 as the first step in our initialisation phase:

```
        &ANCHOR  =  1
```

We now construct a pattern which will match any vowel, and assign the pattern to a suitable variable name:

```
VOWEL  =  'A'  |  'E'  |  'I'  |  'O'  |  'U'
```

Having set up a pattern which can now be used whenever we need it, we may now proceed with the processing phase. The first step is to read a word in. Since we shall need to read in a number of words eventually, we shall have to use a loop which can return to the INPUT statement, as shown in the flowchart. We must therefore give this statement a label: a convenient one is READ. Furthermore, we must provide for the situation where there are no more words to be read in (see the bottom 'diamond' box of figure 7.1). We can use the failure of the INPUT statement to test for this situation; we thus need a failure go-to on this statement, which transfers control to END:

```
READ      WORD  =  INPUT                              :F(END)
```

Having stored our first word in the variable WORD, we must now test to see whether it begins with a vowel. Using the pattern stored in VOWEL, we write:

```
          WORD  VOWEL
```

This is not quite enough, however, since, as shown in the flowchart, we need to consider what we want to happen (i) if the pattern match succeeds, and (ii) if it fails. If it succeeds, we want to print out the contents of WORD: this can be done in the next statement. If it fails, we want to read in another word, if there is one left. We therefore need to add a failure go-to which loops back to READ. We thus replace our original attempt at the vowel-finding statement by the following:

```
          WORD  VOWEL                                 :F(READ)
```

We now write a statement to print the word if it does indeed begin with a vowel. Again, we need to consider what should happen afterwards. Having printed the word, we want to read in another, if there are any more left (see figure 7.1). We therefore need an unconditional go-to transferring control back to READ:

```
          OUTPUT  =  WORD                             :(READ)
```

We have closed the loop, and the cycle repeats until there are no more data records, in which case transfer to END occurs. We must, of course, add END as our last statement. Apart from the END statement, there is no true termination phase in this simple program, since the printing of results occurs as part of the main processing loop.

The complete program is given below, with extra comment lines added to show the beginning of the initialisation and processing phases.

```
* THIS PROGRAM READS IN WORDS, ONE PER DATA RECORD, AND PRINTS
* OUT THOSE WHICH BEGIN WITH A VOWEL.
*
* INITIALISATION
*
          &ANCHOR  =  1
          VOWEL  =  'A'  |  'E'  |  'I'  |  'O'  |  'U'
*
* PROCESSING
*
READ      WORD  =  INPUT                              :F(END)
          WORD  VOWEL                                 :(READ)
          OUTPUT  =  WORD                             :(READ)
END
```

7.3 Program 2: counting commas in a text

As our second problem, let us consider how to count the number of commas in a piece of text, read in line by line. A suitable flowchart is shown in figure 7.2.

We begin our program with comment lines saying exactly what the program does:

```
* THIS PROGRAM COUNTS THE NUMBER OF COMMAS IN A TEXT, READ IN
* LINE BY LINE.
```

The initialisation phase is very simple: we need to set the anchor to zero, since we want to count commas wherever they occur in the lines of text; we also (optionally) set the initial value of a counter variable (let us call it COMMA) to zero:

```
* INITIALISATION
*
          &ANCHOR  =  0
          COMMA  =  0
```

Note that since we shall be looking for a very simple pattern, consisting of just a single character, it is not worth setting up a variable name to hold the pattern, as we did in Program 1.

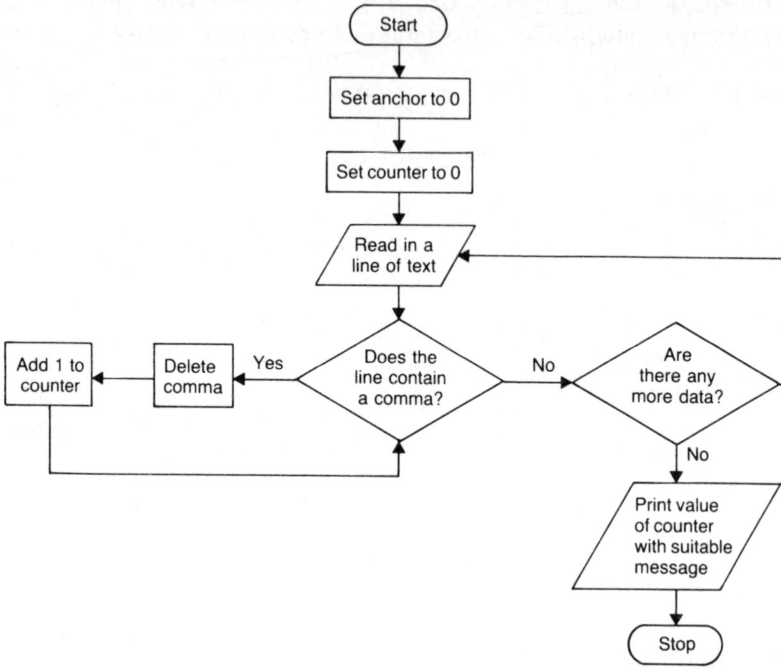

Figure 7.2 Flowchart for counting commas in a text

The processing phase now begins. We read in a line of text, remembering to provide a label so that we can loop back to read more lines, and a failure go-to to cope with the situation where there are no more data, and we want to print out the comma count:

```
* PROCESSING
*
READ      LINE  =  INPUT                                    :F(PRINT)
```

Note the difference between this and the INPUT statement we used in Program 1: in the earlier program, we transferred control directly to END, since we did not want any further action taken when the data ran out; here, on the other hand, we wish to print the final value of COMMA, so we must transfer control to an OUTPUT statement which will constitute the termination phase.

We now test for a comma in the line. There may be more than one of them, so (as shown in figure 7.2) we shall need to loop back to this statement until there are no more commas, in the case where a comma is found at the first attempt. We must also remember to delete each comma as we find it, otherwise the same comma will be found repeatedly. We also need to think about what should happen if no comma is found on the first attempt, or when all the commas in a line have been deleted. We then want to read in another line of text, so that we must loop back to READ. The following statement takes all these requirements into account:

```
MORE      LINE  ','  =                                    :F(READ)
```

If the pattern match is successful, we need to increase the comma count by 1, then loop back to see if there are any more commas in the same line. Our next statement will therefore be:

```
          COMMA  =  COMMA  +  1                            :(MORE)
```

Thus the value of COMMA will be incremented by 1 every time a comma is found. When there are no more commas left in the line, the program loops back to READ (by virtue of the failure go-to on the statement labelled MORE), and another data record is read in. The process continues until there are no more data, and the failure go-to on READ now transfers control to PRINT, in the termination phase of the program. This OUTPUT statement is written so as to print out the final value of COMMA, preceded by a suitable identification:

```
* TERMINATION
*
PRINT     OUTPUT  =  'THE NUMBER OF COMMAS IS '  COMMA
```

Finally, we have the END statement.

The whole program is given below, with extra comment lines to explain what is happening at each stage.

```
* THIS PROGRAM COUNTS THE NUMBER OF COMMAS IN A TEXT, READ IN
* LINE BY LINE.
*
* INITIALISATION
*
          &ANCHOR  =  0
          COMMA  =  0
*
* PROCESSING
*
* READ IN A LINE OF DATA.
*
READ      LINE  =  INPUT                                  :F(PRINT)
```

```
*
* TEST FOR THE PRESENCE OF A COMMA, AND INCREMENT COUNTER IF FOUND.
*
MORE      LINE  ','  =                              :F(READ)
          COMMA  =  COMMA  +  1                     :(MORE)
*
* TERMINATION
*
* PRINT OUT RESULT.
*
PRINT     OUTPUT  =  'THE NUMBER OF COMMAS IS '  COMMA
END
```

7.4 Program 3: counting and printing lines of text containing non-defining relative clauses

As a final example, let us see how we could attempt to count and print out all those lines in an English text which contain a so-called 'non-defining' (or 'non-restrictive') relative clause, that is, a subordinate clause, beginning with a relative pronoun such as *who, which, whom, whose*, not serving to define or identify, but simply to provide more information about the noun to which the clause is linked. Such clauses are normally preceded by a comma, as in the following examples:

MY BROTHER, WHO LIVES IN LONDON, IS A TEACHER.
MRS. SMITH, WHOM WE MET THIS MORNING, IS A VIOLINIST.
THE GIRL, WHOSE NAME WAS MARY POPPINS, SAT DOWN.

We shall not deal here with clauses in which a preposition precedes the relative pronoun, as in the following example:

HIS WIFE, FOR WHOM NOTHING WAS GOOD ENOUGH, LEFT HIM.

We thus define a non-defining relative clause, for our present purposes, as beginning with one of the words *who, which, whom* or *whose*, preceded by a comma and, in normal punctuating practice, a blank. We are now in a position to write a flowchart (see figure 7.3).

It is now a fairly easy task to convert this into a SNOBOL4 program. This time, we shall not go through all the steps verbally – they should be clear from the comment lines in the program – though one or two points will be made at the end.

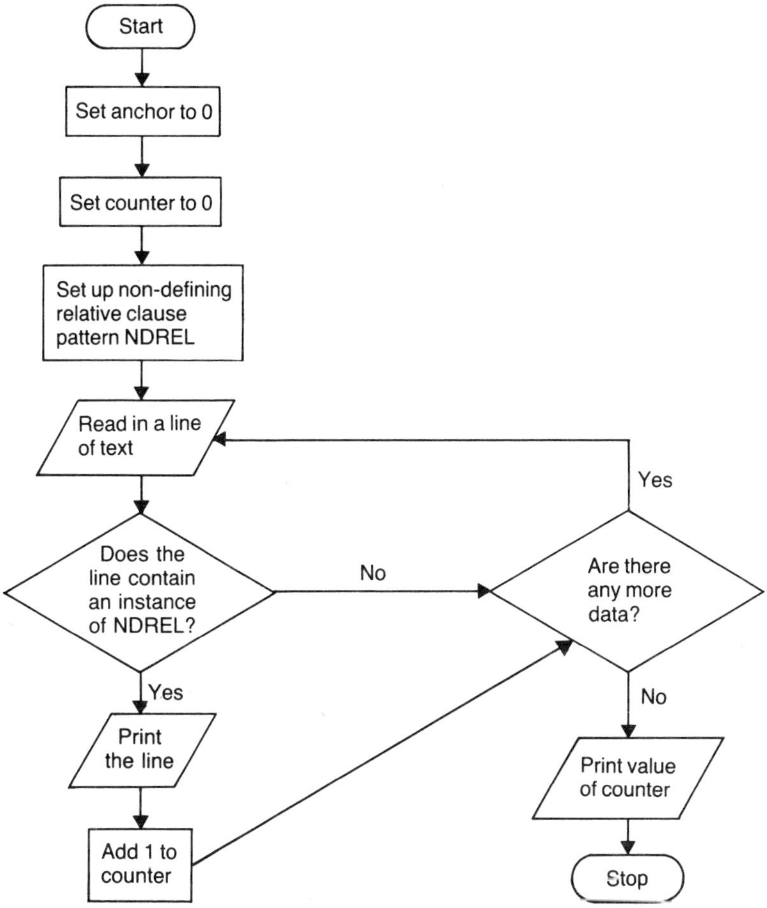

Figure 7.3 Flowchart for isolation of non-defining relative clauses

Note the way in which the pattern NDREL has been defined. It will be remembered from chapter 5 that when isolating particular words from a text we must allow for the case where the word is followed by a punctuation mark rather than by a blank. The only punctuation mark which might possibly be found after a relative pronoun is a comma. We therefore need three components in defining NDREL: the 'comma plus blank' which precedes the relative pronoun, the relative pronoun itself, and the following blank or comma. We could have written this as a single pattern; it is probably clearer, however, to set up the alternations as separate patterns, and then concatenate the three components of NDREL. There is just one further point to note: the use of an OUTPUT statement with nothing on the right-hand side of the equals sign, to produce a blank line in the printout. This is useful for making the output easier to read.

```
* THIS PROGRAM COUNTS AND PRINTS THOSE LINES IN AN ENGLISH TEXT
* WHICH CONTAIN NON-DEFINING RELATIVE CLAUSES IN WHICH THE
* RELATIVE PRONOUN IS NOT PRECEDED BY A PREPOSITION.
*
* INITIALISATION
*
          &ANCHOR  =  0
          REL  =  0
          RELPRON  =  'WHO'  |  'WHICH'  |  'WHOM'  |  'WHOSE'
          PUNCT  =  ' '  |  ','
          NDREL  =  ', '  RELPRON  PUNCT
*
* PROCESSING
*
* READ IN A LINE OF DATA, AND TEST FOR RELATIVE CLAUSE.
*
READ      LINE  =  INPUT                          :F(PRINT)
          LINE  NDREL                             :F(READ)
*
* IF RELATIVE CLAUSE FOUND, PRINT LINE AND ADD 1 TO COUNTER.
* GO BACK TO READ IN ANOTHER LINE.
*
          OUTPUT  =  LINE
          REL  =  REL  +  1                       :(READ)
*
* TERMINATION
*
* PRINT TWO BLANK LINES, THEN RELATIVE CLAUSE COUNT.
*
PRINT     OUTPUT  =
          OUTPUT  =
          OUTPUT  =  'THE NUMBER OF LINES CONTAINING NON-DEFINING '
+  'RELATIVE CLAUSES IS '  REL
END
```

Exercises 7

For each of the following tasks, write a flowchart, and then convert it into a SNOBOL4 program, with appropriate comment lines.

(i) read in data records one at a time and simply print them out

(ii) read in words, one per data record, and print out all those containing the letter M

(iii) read in a text, one line at a time, and print out all the lines containing the word NOW followed by a comma (remember that you need to isolate the *word* NOW, not just the sequence N, O, W)

(iv) read in words, one per data record, and count the number of words beginning with either F or V, then print out the count in a suitable manner

8 Built-in functions

8.1 The concept of a function

In this chapter, we shall begin our discussion of the 'function', a powerful and extremely important mechanism in SNOBOL4 and other programming languages.

In algebra, we say that an expression is a function of x if its value depends in some specifiable way on the value of x. Take, for example, the expression

$$x^3 + 2x^2 + 3x + 4.$$

This is a function of x: its value is 10 when $x = 1$, 26 when $x = 2$, 58 when $x = 3$, and so on. The term 'function' is used in a similar way in computing. A function is something whose value depends on the value of its *argument(s)*. For instance, the length of a string is a function of what the string contains. The string

```
ALL CHILDREN LIKE ICE-CREAM
```

has a length of 27 characters (including blanks), while if we change the string to

```
ICE-CREAM MAKES YOU FAT
```

the length is 23 characters.

When we use a function in SNOBOL4, we are asking the computer to perform an operation or series of operations on a given 'argument' (or sometimes more than one argument), for example 'find the length of the string stored in WORD'. The way in which we should write this is

```
SIZE(WORD)
```

SIZE is the name of a function which computes the length of a string (see section 8.2 below), and WORD is the argument on which we want that function to operate. Note that the argument is in brackets, immediately after the function name.

SIZE takes just one argument. Later on we shall discuss functions which take more than one argument. For example, the function REPLACE takes three arguments, all of which are strings or the names of variables containing strings. If we write

```
REPLACE(TEXT,'A','*')
```

the computer will take the string stored in TEXT, and replace all occurrences of the letter A by asterisks. Note that where there are two or more arguments, these are separated by commas.

The use of a function in a program is usually referred to as a 'function call'. Provided that the arguments with which the function is called are appropriate, a value will be computed, and 'returned' to the program for further use as the programmer wishes. Such values can be of various kinds: the value returned by a call of SIZE is numerical, while that returned by REPLACE is a string. Other functions, to be discussed later, return patterns as values.

Some functions are needed so often that they are built into the SNOBOL4 language itself, and can be brought into operation simply by using the name of the function, with appropriate arguments, as in the examples above. It is also possible for the programmer to define his own functions for special purposes. The way in which this is done will be discussed in chapter 11. In the present chapter we shall look at some useful built-in functions.

8.2 SIZE and LEN

The function SIZE, as we saw above, computes the length of a string, including any internal blanks it may contain. The argument must, of course, be a string or something whose value is a string. The function call

```
SIZE('COMPUTER')
```

would cause the value 8 to be returned, since the string COMPUTER contains 8 characters. If we write

```
WORDLEN  =  SIZE('COMPUTER')
```

the value 8 will be assigned to the variable called WORDLEN.

The argument of SIZE can be a string-valued variable: the following would cause the value 12 to be assigned to LINELENGTH:

```
     LINE  =  'WHAT A PITY!'

     LINELENGTH  =  SIZE(LINE)
```

The argument of SIZE can even be an expression, provided that this evaluates to a string. For instance, the following would assign the value 5 to TOTAL, since the argument of SIZE actually has the value PLANT:

```
     STRING  =  'ANT'

     TOTAL  =  SIZE('PL' STRING)
```

This illustrates a general feature of functions in SNOBOL4: their arguments may consist of expressions of arbitrary complexity, provided that these evaluate to the correct kind of object (e.g. string, number) for the particular function concerned.

Function calls can themselves be used as part of expressions. For instance, a call of SIZE can be used at any point in an expression where a number would be appropriate. The value of the function call will be found, and substituted at that point in the expression. Consider, for example, the situation where we want to measure the length of a word, but if the word contains a hyphen or apostrophe we want to decrease the length by 1, so that we obtain the number of actual *letters* in the word. We could then write:

```
            &ANCHOR  =  0
            WORD  "-"  |  "'"                          :F(OK)
            WORDLEN  =  SIZE(WORD)  -  1               :(REST)
OK          WORDLEN  =  SIZE(WORD)
REST
```

If a hyphen or apostrophe is found in the contents of WORD, the second line of the program segment will compute the length of what is stored in WORD, and subtract 1 from the result (the operator – is used for subtraction, as might be expected). If no hyphen or apostrophe is found, no adjustment is necessary, and the line labelled OK assigns the value of SIZE(WORD) to WORDLEN. It would be easy to amend the above to cover cases where more than one hyphen or apostrophe is present.

While SIZE computes a *number* as a value, the function LEN creates and returns a *pattern* as a value. It has one argument, which can be any positive whole number, or any expression which evaluates to such a number – e.g. LEN(1), LEN(5), LEN(26), LEN(N + 6) are all valid in SNOBOL4 (provided that N is a numerically valued variable). LEN creates a pattern which matches any string of the length given by the argument. Thus LEN(1) matches any single character, LEN(5) matches any sequence of 5 characters, and so on.

LEN is useful in the construction of larger patterns. For example, if we want to write a pattern which will find any string consisting of S, followed by any two characters, followed by T, we put:

```
'S'  LEN(2)  'T'
```

We can now use this pattern in pattern matching statements. For instance:

```
&ANCHOR  =  0
LINE  'S'  LEN(2)  'T'
```

will succeed if LINE contains the string

THERE WAS SOOT ALL OVER THE HEARTH

or the string

THERE WAS SEATING FOR 80 PASSENGERS

or even the string

SQUASH IS SO TIRING

because in all cases the underlined substring matches the pattern. Note that a blank, as usual, counts as a character, as in the last example. The pattern match will, however, fail for the string

ISIDORA SAT IN AN ARMCHAIR

because there is only one character between the S and T of SAT.

We can attach a name to the LEN component of a pattern, and so find out what the characters matched actually are. Say, for example, that we wish to find the first character of a word stored in WORD. We might write:

```
WORD  LEN(1)  .  C
```

The character matched will be assigned as the value of C.

Any statement containing LEN will fail to secure a pattern match if the argument of LEN is bigger than the length of the string to be examined. For instance, since the string COMPUTATION is 11 characters long, any attempt to apply the pattern created by LEN(12) to this string would cause the pattern match to fail.

One word of warning: beginners often confuse LEN and SIZE. Remember that LEN takes a *number* as its argument, and creates a pattern consisting of that number of characters; SIZE takes a *string* as argument, and computes the number of characters in that string. The choice of names for these functions in SNOBOL4 is perhaps rather unfortunate, since it is SIZE which actually returns a length as its value.

8.3 ANY and NOTANY

The two functions ANY and NOTANY, like LEN, return a pattern as their value. The argument of ANY can be any string of characters (except the null string). Its value is a pattern which matches *any one* of the characters in its argument. Consider, for example, the following:

```
PUNCT  =  ANY('.,;:?!')
```

Here, we have created a pattern PUNCT, which matches any of the punctuation marks . , ; : ? ! Note that the above statement does exactly the same job as the following:

```
PUNCT  =  '.'  |  ','  |  ';'  |  ':'  |  '?'  |  '!'
```

The use of ANY is, however, preferable to alternation, since it involves less writing (and therefore potentially less error) and runs faster on the computer. The use of ANY is not, of course, a possible replacement for some examples of alternation: a pattern with ANY is equivalent to an alternation of *single characters only*: if we wish to test an alternation of longer strings, we must use the alternation operator.

The function NOTANY also has a string of characters as its argument, but computes, as a value, a pattern matching any character which is *not* found in its argument. If we wanted to match any character except for the punctuation marks given above, we could write:

```
NOTPUNCT  =  NOTANY('.,;:?!')
```

It should be noted that the argument of ANY and NOTANY, being a string, must be in quotes in examples such as the above. We could, of course, use a string-valued variable name as the argument. The following is equivalent to the definition of PUNCT given above:

```
PMARKS  =  '.,;:?!'
PUNCT  =  ANY(PMARKS)
```

Note also that the order of elements in a string acting as the argument of ANY or NOTANY is immaterial.

8.4 BREAK and SPAN

An extremely useful function is BREAK, which, like ANY and NOTANY, takes a string or string-valued variable as its argument. BREAK creates a pattern which matches everything in a string up to, but not including, the first occurrence of any character in its argument. For example,

```
BREAK('.,;:?!')
```

will match everything up to, but not including, a full stop, comma, semicolon, colon, question mark or exclamation mark. Or, if PMARKS is defined in the same way as in section 8.3, we can write:

```
BREAK(PMARKS)
```

to serve exactly the same purpose.

Let us now consider some examples of the use of BREAK.

```
VOWELS  =  'AEIOU'
WORD  BREAK(VOWELS)
```

This will match everything in the contents of WORD up to, but not including, the first vowel. If WORD contains the string COMPUTERS, the single character C is matched. If WORD contains the string STRIATIONS, the sequence STR is matched.

Now consider the following:

```
LINE  ' A '  BREAK('.')
```

Assuming that the word A is never followed by punctuation, and that we have placed a blank in front of the first word in LINE, this pattern-matching statement will look for the word A, and the pattern BREAK('.') will then match everything between this word and the next full stop. If LINE contains

I'VE BOUGHT A NEW CAR.

BREAK('.') matches the substring NEW CAR, but if LINE contains

IS A WOMAN'S WORK EVER DONE?

the pattern match fails, because there is no full stop.

Note that a pattern created by BREAK can match the null string. If, for instance, we have the word ANGLE stored in WORD, then

```
WORD  BREAK(VOWELS)
```

will succeed, the BREAK pattern matching the null string.

We can, of course, find out exactly what is matched by a BREAK pattern, using the conditional value assignment operator (full stop) or the immediate value assignment operator $. Suppose that we are trying to find all words containing at least two occurrences of S, and we want to know what characters separate the two occurrences. The pattern we need is:

```
BREAK('S')  'S'  BREAK('S')  .  BETWEEN
```

The first BREAK('S') takes us up to the first S, then this S is matched by 'S', then we assign everything up to the next S to the variable name BETWEEN.

One common error in the use of BREAK should be mentioned here. Beginners are often tempted to write patterns such as:

```
BREAK(ANY('AEIOU'))
```

or the equivalent

```
VOWELS  =  ANY('AEIOU')
```

followed by a statement containing BREAK(VOWELS). This is quite incorrect, and will cause program failure. The argument of BREAK must be a *string*; in the above pattern, the argument of BREAK is a *pattern* (in fact, the pattern ANY('AEIOU')). The correct pattern is simply BREAK('AEIOU').

One important feature of BREAK is that since, by definition, it causes the computer to scan a string up to the point where a character within its argument is found, it can often be used, in the anchored mode, to replace unanchored pattern matching, so speeding up the search for a particular substring within a string. Consider, for example, how to find the substring PEACHES in the string STR, where:

```
STR  =  'YOU CAN HAVE PEACHES AND CREAM OR PUMPKIN PIE'
```

If we write:

```
&ANCHOR  =  0
STR  'PEACHES'
```

the match will eventually succeed, though the process will be slow. The use of BREAK and the anchored mode is faster:

```
&ANCHOR  =  1
STR  BREAK('P')  'PEACHES'
```

This expedient can, however, cause problems. Suppose that we wish to find the substring PIE rather than PEACHES. The pattern using BREAK now fails, because BREAK('P') takes us only up to the *first* occurrence of P, and this position is followed, not by PIE, but by PEACHES. A built-in solution to this problem is available in the SPITBOL version of SNOBOL4, though not in the standard language. SPITBOL has an additional built-in function called BREAKX, which differs from BREAK in that if a complete match is not achieved on reaching the first occurrence of a character in the argument of BREAKX, the computer proceeds past this first occurrence to look for others. Thus if, in SPITBOL, we write:

```
STR  BREAKX('P')  'PIE'
```

the pattern match now succeeds, because having failed to find a match at the first P, the computer proceeds to each of the Ps of PUMPKIN and then to the fourth P, where it finally finds a match. BREAKX can be written as a programmer-defined function in standard SNOBOL4.

The function SPAN, like BREAK, takes a string of characters, or a string-valued variable, as its argument. SPAN creates a pattern which matches the longest run of characters all of which are in its argument. For example, if we write:

```
LINE  SPAN('.,;:?!"')
```

then if LINE contains the string

"HAVE YOU PUT THE CAT OUT?" ASKED JANE.

the pattern created by SPAN will match just the first quotation marks. If we delete these and reapply the pattern match, the sequence ?" will be matched, and if we repeated the match once more, the final full stop would be picked up.

As with BREAK, we can find out exactly what has been matched by assigning the value of the SPAN pattern to a variable name. Consider the following:

```
&ANCHOR  =  0
VOWELS  =  'AEIOU'
WORD  SPAN(VOWELS)  .  VRUN
```

If WORD contains the string RAINING, the pattern match will succeed, and the value AI will be assigned to VRUN. If WORD contains PYGMY, the pattern match will fail, since there are no vowels, as defined by the statement assigning a value to VOWELS. If WORD contains CARROTS, the vowel A will be assigned to VRUN.

Using a combination of BREAK and SPAN, we are now in a position to write a pattern which will isolate words, one at a time, from a line of text – clearly a very important operation in many text-handling programs. First we must decide how we are going to define a word. If we define it as 'a sequence of characters bounded by blanks', we let in hyphenated words and words containing apostrophes, which we should indeed normally wish to include. We must, however, define which characters are permissible in a word, so as to exclude, for example, punctuation marks. We also have to decide whether we want numbers to count as word-forming characters. Assuming that we do not, we may define LETTERS as:

```
        LETTERS  =  "ABCDEFGHIJKLMNOPQRSTUVWXYZ'-"
```

or, if we wished to work on a text which also contained lower case letters

```
        LETTERS  =  "ABCDEFGHIJKLMNOPQRSTUVWXYZ"
+                   "abcdefghijklmnopqrstuvwxyz'-"
```

Note that since we need to include the apostrophe in the string, we must use double quotes as string delimiters. We can now define and isolate a word by means of the following pattern:

```
        BREAK(LETTERS)  SPAN(LETTERS)  .  WORD
```

The BREAK part takes us up to the first word-forming character. The SPAN component now matches the sequence of characters up to, but not including, the next non-LETTER character (usually a blank or a punctuation mark). The segment isolated by SPAN is thus a word, and is assigned as the value of the variable WORD, which can then be processed further. Note that this word-isolating pattern can be used in the anchored mode (see earlier comments on BREAK), so speeding up the execution of the program.

8.5 A program using BREAK, SPAN and LEN

We shall now build up a complete program illustrating the use of the functions BREAK, SPAN and LEN. The program isolates words from a text input line by line, and prints out all the words of six or more letters which begin with CON.

In the initialisation phase, we set the anchor to 1 (since we are interested in the beginnings of words), and define the range of characters which can constitute a word:

```
        &ANCHOR  =  1
        LETTERS  =  "ABCDEFGHIJKLMNOPQRSTUVWXYZ'-"
```

We now define a pattern which will isolate words. As we have seen, the following will serve this purpose:

```
        WPAT  =  BREAK(LETTERS)  SPAN(LETTERS)  .  WORD
```

We now begin the processing phase by reading in a line of data:

```
READ     LINE  =  INPUT                         :F(END)
```

By means of WPAT, we can isolate one word at a time from LINE, and assign it to WORD:

```
GETWD    LINE  WPAT  =                          :F(READ)
```

There are three important points to note about this statement. Firstly, it needs a label, since we shall have to loop back to it each time we want to get another word from LINE. Secondly, we must delete each word in turn from the line, once we have found it and stored it in WORD, otherwise we shall keep on finding the same word over and over again. Thirdly, when there are no more words in LINE, we want to read in another line, so we must provide a failure go-to looping back to READ.

We can now test to see if the contents of WORD meet our specifications: at least six letters long, and beginning with CON. This means that the word must have CON, followed by at least three characters. The required statement is:

```
WORD  'CON'  LEN(3)                     :F(GETWD)
```

Two points should be noted here. Firstly, this pattern match will succeed whether the word contains just six characters or more than six: the pattern LEN(3) simply matches three characters, irrespective of whether anything else follows them or not. Secondly, note that if the pattern match fails, we want to retrieve another word from LINE, hence the failure go-to transferring control to GETWD.

If the pattern match succeeds, we want to print out the contents of WORD before fetching another word:

```
OUTPUT  =  WORD                         :(GETWD)
```

All that is now needed to complete the program is the END statement and a number of explanatory comments. The complete program is given below.

```
* THIS PROGRAM PRINTS OUT ALL THE WORDS IN A TEXT WHICH START
* WITH 'CON' AND HAVE AT LEAST 6 LETTERS.
*
* INITIALISATION
*
          &ANCHOR  =  1
          LETTERS  =  "ABCDEFGHIJKLMNOPQRSTUVWXYZ'-"
          WPAT  =  BREAK(LETTERS)  SPAN(LETTERS)  .  WORD
*
```

```
* PROCESSING
*
* READ IN A LINE OF DATA.
*
READ      LINE  =  INPUT                          :F(END)
*
* ISOLATE A WORD FROM THE LINE USING PATTERN 'WPAT'.
*
GETWD     LINE  WPAT  =                           :F(READ)
*
* TEST WORD FOR REQUIRED PATTERN.  IF PATTERN NOT FOUND, GET
* ANOTHER WORD.
*
          WORD  'CON'  LEN(3)                     :F(GETWD)
*
* PRINT WORD IF IT CONFORMS TO PATTERN, AND GET ANOTHER WORD.
*
          OUTPUT  =  WORD                         :(GETWD)
END
```

8.6 TRIM and &TRIM

We end this chapter with a further useful function, TRIM, which takes a string or string-valued variable as its argument, and removes any trailing blanks from the end of the string. It is generally a good idea to remove such trailing blanks from data records as they are input, so that the computer will not scan fruitlessly through these blanks when attempting a pattern match. We might thus write:

```
READ      LINE  =  TRIM(INPUT)                    :F(END)
```

An alternative is to use the keyword &TRIM, which, if set to a non-zero value at the beginning of the program, causes trailing blanks to be removed from all data records as they are read in. The following is thus equivalent to the use of the function TRIM as above:

```
          &TRIM  =  1
READ      LINE  =  INPUT                          :F(END)
```

We shall see in chapter 10 that there are cases where the use of TRIM or &TRIM is essential for the successful application of pattern matching. It is good practice to set &TRIM = 1 in the initialisation phase of all programs, unless there is a special reason for not doing so.

Exercises 8

1 Using built-in functions, write patterns which will

- (i) match a string consisting of the letters P and R separated by any single character
- (ii) match any of the vowels A, E, I, O, U
- (iii) match any string containing at least two commas, and assign everything between the first two commas to the variable INTERCOM
- (iv) match any string consisting of one or more asterisks
- (v) give a successful match with any string which is more than 10 characters long.

2 Write a program to count the number of words in a text which are more than four letters long (including hyphens and apostrophes), and print the result. Assume that the text is to be read in line by line.

3 Imagine that you have a series of data records each containing the name, sex and address of a single individual, the different items of information being separated by asterisks as follows:

```
BLOGGS, F R*M*25 PEABODY CLOSE, AYLESTON
JONES, P*F*60 EGGHEAD CRESCENT, THINGLEY
```

Write a program which will print the names of all the females, and also count the numbers of males and females and print the results.

4 Write a program to print and count those sentences in a text which begin with the word AND. (Note: this question is considerably more difficult than the others. You will find it best to isolate sentences first. Remember that

- (i) a sentence may span more than one line of text
- (ii) the word AND may be followed by a blank or by punctuation
- (iii) sentence-initial AND may be preceded by a quotation mark
- (iv) the A of sentence-initial AND may be the first character in a line of data.

Assume that the text consists of a number of complete sentences, each terminated by . ! or ? and that sentences are separated by at least one blank.)

9 Arithmetic and predicates

9.1 Arithmetic operations

We have already met the addition operator + (section 4.4) and the subtraction operator − (section 8.2). Other arithmetic operations which we may need to perform are:

Operation	*Operator*
Multiplication	*
Division	/
Exponentiation	! or **

Exponentiation is the raising of a number to the power of another number: for example 2^2 ('2 squared') is 4, 2^3 ('2 cubed') is 8, 2^4 ('2 to the fourth') is 16, and so on. In SNOBOL4 only whole numbers can be used as the powers (or 'exponents') to which we raise other numbers: that is, we can square, cube, and so on, but we cannot use the exponentiation operator to raise to fractional powers. This means, unfortunately, that we cannot evaluate square roots (i.e. raise numbers to the power 0.5) in this way. Since there is no square-root function built into SNOBOL4, a special function has to be written by the programmer. We shall discuss such a function in chapter 11. In implementations of the language which use the vertical bar as an alternation operator, rather than the exclamation mark, the exclamation mark can be used to indicate exponentiation, and we shall follow this practice here. In all versions of the language a double asterisk can be used for exponentiation, and this is, of course, the only possibility in cases where the exclamation mark is used for alternation.

As we have seen, the arithmetic operators, like other binary operators, must have at least one blank on either side of them. The result of an arithmetic operation can, as we saw in section 4.4, be assigned as the value of a variable. Some examples follow.

```
P = Q - 4
```

This causes 4 to be subtracted from the current value of Q, and the result is then assigned to P. If Q is 10, P will receive the value 6.

```
Y = X * 3
```

This will multiply the current value of X by 3, and assign the result to Y. If X is 5, the value of Y will become 15.

```
TEMP = TEMP / 2
```

This will halve the current value of TEMP, and assign the result as the new value of the same variable, TEMP.

```
ISQ = I ! 2
```

This will square the current value of I, and assign the result to ISQ.

As we noted briefly in section 5.6, apparent difficulties can arise when two or more operators are present in the same expression. For expressions such as:

```
X + Y + 10
X + Y - Z
```

it does not matter which of the two operations is carried out first: the result is the same whether, for example, X is added to Y and Z then subtracted, or Z is subtracted from Y and the result added to X. In the following cases, however, it does matter which operation is carried out first:

```
2 * 5 + 3
10 - 2 ! 3
```

In the first case, if the multiplication occurs first, the result is $(2 \times 5) + 3 = 13$; but if the addition is carried out first, the result is $2 \times (5 + 3) = 16$. Similarly, the second expression above will have the value $(18 - 2)^3 =$ 4 096 if the subtraction is effected first, but $18 - 2^3 = 10$ if the exponentiation is done first. Because of the possibility of ambiguities of this kind, SNOBOL4 has built into it an order of precedence for arithmetic operators, just as for operators involved in pattern construction: exponentiation is carried out first, then multiplication, then division, and finally addition and subtraction. Thus our first expression above is, in fact, equivalent to (2 * 5) + 3, and the second to 18 − (2 ! 3). Brackets can always be put in to make the programmer's intention absolutely clear, as in the representations just given.

A slightly different kind of problem occurs when an expression contains two or more subtraction operators, with, of course, the same precedence. For instance, is $20 - 8 - 4$ to be read as $(20 - 8) - 4 = 8$, or as 20 – (8 – 4) = 16? If the brackets are not put in, SNOBOL4 adopts the first solution: that is, it starts from the left of the expression, where the expression contains only operators of equal precedence. More technically, the subtraction operator is said to 'associate to the left'.

One point concerning division should be stressed: since the result of dividing any number by zero is infinity, any attempt to divide by zero, or by an expression which evaluates to zero, will cause overflow of the computer's resources, and the program will fail.

In the examples given so far, only numbers or single variables have been connected by operators. We can, however, use complex expressions in arithmetic statements. The following statements are quite valid in SNOBOL4:

```
RATIO = FREQ / (SIZE(WORD) + 1)
W = (12 * S) / ((M ! 2) * ((N ! 3) - N))
```

The first of these would compute the length of the string stored in WORD, add 1 to it, divide the result into the value of FREQ, and assign the final result as the value of RATIO. The second statement would evaluate $M^2 \times (N^3 — N)$, and divide the result into (12 × S). Not all the brackets in this expression are strictly necessary: it is, however, advisable to put them in for clarity of presentation. If an expression contains several sets of brackets, always check that there are equal numbers of right-facing and left-facing brackets.

9.2 Integers and real numbers

It is often important, in numerical computations, to distinguish between 'integers' and 'real' numbers. Integers are whole numbers, which can be positive, negative or zero – e.g. 5, 10, 18 942, +6, −8, −421 041, 0. Note that + and – are being used here as 'unary' operators, since they have only one 'operand', viz. the number which they make positive or negative. The addition and subtraction operators, on the other hand, are 'binary' operators, since they connect two 'operands'. There must be no blank between a unary operator and its operand (e.g. between the – and the number in an integer such as −421 041). Real numbers are those which contain decimal points, and can again be positive, negative or zero, e.g. 1.851, 3.14159, 6.0051, −8.0, 0.00. Note that although −8 and −8.00 have the same numerical value, they are represented differently and are treated differently by the computer.

Quite often, integers are all that is required in a computation. If, for example, we were counting instances of some linguistic item, it would be sensible to use integers for the counter. There are, however, certain problems with the use of integers, especially with regard to their divsiion. Any remainder in the division of one integer by another will be discarded.

For instance, the value of X will be 3 after execution of the following statement, the remainder of 3 being ignored:

```
X = 15 / 4
```

This may be quite acceptable: if, for instance, we had counted the total number of letters in a text in an integer variable TOTAL and the number of words in an integer variable WORDS, then the statement

```
MEANL = TOTAL / WORDS
```

would give the mean word length to the nearest lower integer, and this may be all that is needed. But note that if, for example, the true average is 4.98 words, this will still be reported as 4, the nearest *lower* integer, rather than rounded up to 5, which is really the nearest whole number.

When, as may frequently be the case, greater precision is required, real numbers should be used. For instance, the statement

```
AV = (4.0 + 3.6 + 2.1 + 12.4 + 8.0) / 3.3
```

assigns the value 9.12121 to AV. If an expression contains both integers and real numbers, or variables which have a mixture of integer and real values, then conversion to a real value occurs as soon as a real number is encountered during the evaluation of the expression. Thus the following statement assigns the value 9.5 to MEAN:

```
MEAN = (3 + 4 + 5 + 7) / 2.0
```

It is sometimes useful to be able to convert integers into real numbers, or vice versa. This can be done in SNOBOL4 by means of a built-in function, CONVERT, which we shall meet again in chapter 12. For instance, in calculating the average word length by dividing the value of TOTAL by that of WORDS and assigning the result to MEANL, as discussed above, we can get MEANL more accurately, as a real number, if we convert either TOTAL or WORDS to real form before effecting division. To convert TOTAL to a real, we write:

```
TOTAL = CONVERT(TOTAL,'REAL')
```

This will convert the current value of TOTAL from integer to real form, and assign the result as the new value of TOTAL. Similarly, if we wished to convert a real variable called COEFF to integer form, we could write:

```
COEFF = CONVERT(COEFF,'INTEGER')
```

There is, of course, no reason why the result of the conversion cannot be assigned to a quite different variable name if desired.

9.3 Comparing numbers

SNOBOL4 contains a number of special built-in functions called *predicates*, which differ from other functions in that they succeed or fail depending on the relationship between their arguments. If they succeed, they return the null string as their value, but if they fail, no value is returned: the significance of this seemingly odd fact will become apparent later. The following predicates are available for comparing numbers:

`EQ(X,Y)`	is X equal to Y?
`NE(X,Y)`	is X not equal to Y?
`GT(X,Y)`	is X greater than Y?
`GE(X,Y)`	is X greater than or equal to Y?
`LT(X,Y)`	is X less than Y?
`LE(X,Y)`	is X less than or equal to Y?

Conditional go-to's can be used to transfer control to other parts of the program according to whether the test succeeds or fails. Consider the following example:

```
LT(COUNT,100)                                        :S(NEXT)F(PRINT)
```

This will test whether the current value of COUNT is smaller than 100. If it is, control is transferred to a statement labelled NEXT, but if COUNT is equal to or greater than 100, control passes to the statement labelled PRINT. Complex expressions can be used as arguments for numerical predicates, as in the following example:

```
EQ(P ! 2 + 3 * N,ATOT * 4)                           :S(YES)F(NO)
```

This computes $P^2 + 3N$ and also ATOT $\times$ 4, and tests whether they are equal. If they are, control passes to the statement labelled YES; if not, control is transferred to NO. However complex the expressions, they can be used as the arguments of a numerical predicate, separated by a comma.

Numerical predicates are particularly useful in cases where a loop is to be executed a set number of times. Consider the simple case where just the first 10 records in a data file are to be printed out. The following short program will achieve this:

```
* THIS PROGRAM PRINTS OUT THE FIRST 10 RECORDS FROM  A DATA FILE.
*
* INITIALISATION
*
        I = 0
```

```
* PROCESSING
*
PRINT    OUTPUT  =  INPUT                          :F(NODATA)
         I  =  I  +  1
         LT(I, 10)                                 :S(PRINT)F(END)
*
* THE NEXT LINE PROVIDES FOR THE CASE WHERE THERE ARE FEWER THAN
* 10 RECORDS IN THE DATA FILE.
*
NODATA   OUTPUT  =  'NO MORE DATA'
END
```

Having said what the program does, we initialise the value of a counter to 0. The values of &ANCHOR and &TRIM are unimportant here, as there is no pattern matching to be done. We now read in a data record and print it, using INPUT and OUTPUT in the same statement as shown. Since we shall need to loop back to this statement, we must give it a label, an appropriate one being PRINT. We must also provide for the case where there are fewer than 10 data records in our data file. In this case, control passes to a statement labelled NODATA, and the message NO MORE DATA is printed.

Having output the first line of data, we increment the counter I by 1, then test whether I is less than 10. Obviously, since I has the value 1 at this stage, the test succeeds, and the program loops back to print another record. It goes round this loop until 10 records have been printed (provided, or course, that the data have not been exhausted), at which stage I = 10, and the numerical predicate fails, since I is no longer *less than* 10. Control then passes to the END statement.

There is, in fact, an even more economical way of writing the above program. The two statements which first increment I then test if I is smaller than 10 can be replaced by one statement with the same effect, as follows:

```
I  =  LT(I,9)   I  +  1                            :S(PRINT)F(END)
```

Statements of this type depend on the fact, noted earlier, that if a predicate succeeds, the null string is returned as its value. Thus if, in the above statement, I is indeed less than 9, the effect will be to concatenate the null string (i.e. nothing at all) with the expression I + 1, the end result being that I is incremented by 1, and the program loops back to PRINT. If, however, the predicate fails, no value is returned, I is not incremented, and control passes to END. Note that we now need to ask whether I is less than 9, *not* 10 as before. This is because I is not incremented until after the test, whereas it was incremented before the test in the previous program. Thus after the first record has been printed I is 0 when tested, and after the tenth record has been printed I = 9. Alternatively, we could initialise I to 1 rather than 0, and retain LT(I,10) in the comparison.

Note that it is an easy matter to amend the program to print the first N lines of a data file, where N is any integer, read in from a data record placed right at the beginning of the file. A suitable program (without comment lines) is given below.

```
         I  =  0
         N  =  TRIM(INPUT)
PRINT    OUTPUT  =  INPUT                          :F(NODATA)
         I  =  LT(I,N - 1)  I + 1                  :S(PRINT)F(END)
NODATA   OUTPUT  =  'NO MORE DATA'
END
```

Note the use of TRIM to remove trailing blanks from the data record containing the value of N. SNOBOL4 is able to treat the resulting numeral string as a numerical value. In SPITBOL this step is not strictly necessary, since blanks are ignored when numeral strings are interpreted as numerical values.

9.4 Comparing strings

There are also predicates which compare strings. IDENT tests whether two strings are identical. One or both strings can be the value of a variable. Thus

```
IDENT(STRING,'CRACKER')
```

succeeds if the variable STRING contains the string CRACKER and nothing else. If STRING contained the string CRACKERS, or if CRACKER were preceded by a blank, the predicate would fail. Note that although in most circumstances SNOBOL4 allows numbers and numerical strings to be treated similarly (for instance, in the program written at the end of the last section, the number of data records to be printed was read in as a string, but processed as a number), the following will fail, because IDENT requires its arguments to be of precisely the same type:

```
IDENT(5,'5')
```

DIFFER is the opposite of IDENT, in that it tests whether two strings are different. Consider the following:

```
H2S  =  'ROTTEN EGGS'
DIFFER(H2S,'ROTTEN')
```

This succeeds, because H2S contains ROTTEN EGGS, not just ROTTEN.

Other predicates can be used to compare strings with respect to their alphabetical ordering. In standard SNOBOL4, only one such predicate is available: LGT, which tests whether its first argument is 'lexically greater' (i.e. comes further down an alphabetical listing) than its second argument. Thus

```
LGT('WASP','BEE')
```

succeeds, because WASP is further down an alphabetical listing than BEE. The following, however, fails:

```
LGT('ASP','ASTUTE')
```

Either argument, or indeed both, can be a string-valued variable. Thus the following sequence of statements leads to a successful comparison:

```
WORD 1  =  'DOG'
WORD 2  =  'CAT'
LGT(WORD1,WORD2)
```

The predicate LGT allows us to order *pairs* of words alphabetically. By repeating the comparison of pairs, and swapping the order of items round where necessary, we can alphabetise longer lists of words. The programming required is rather too complex for us to tackle at this stage, but we shall discuss a sorting program in chapter 14.

In the SPITBOL version of SNOBOL4, certain additional predicates, not contained in the standard language, are available:

`LEQ(X,Y)`	is X lexically equal to Y?
`LGE(X,Y)`	is X lexically greater than or equal to Y?
`LLT(X,Y)`	is X lexically less than Y?
`LLE(X,Y)`	is X lexically less than or equal to Y?
`LNE(X,Y)`	is X lexically unequal to Y?

One final point is worth noting: if the second argument of a predicate is omitted, it is assumed to have the null string as its value. Thus if we wish to know whether a variable has the null string as its current value, we may write, for instance:

```
IDENT(STRING)
```

Similarly, if we wished to test whether a variable TEXT had a non-null value, we could write:

```
DIFFER(TEXT)
```

Exercises 9

1 Insert brackets into each of the following expressions to show the ordering of arithmetic operations which will actually be performed by the computer:

(i) N ! 3 + 5 * P − Q / 10
(ii) S + 2 * T − M ! 2
(iii) 0.5 * X ! 2 − Y / 5.0

2 Convert each of the following into a valid SNOBOL4 expression:

(i) add 4 to the value of L and square the result, then divide by the value of N, and finally add 100
(ii) take X per cent of the value of Y, and add a quarter of the value of Z
(iii) the following expression, which is a transformation of a statistical formula:

$$\frac{24(W - (N(N + 1)/4))^2}{N(N + 1)(2N + 1)}$$

3 Which of the following will succeed, and which will fail?

(i) EQ(2 ! 3,11 − 3)
(ii) LE(4 * 3.8 + 2.6,17.8)
(iii) GT(3 / 2,1)
(iv) IDENT('ROCK AND ROLL', 'ROCK')
(v) LGT('RABBIT', 'RABID')
(vi) LLE('COMPUTER', 'CONFUCIUS')

4 Write a program which will read in a text one line at a time, isolate the first 100 words, and calculate an accurate value for the mean length of these 100 words.

5 The statistical 'variance' (see section 3.6.1) of a set of N numbers can be calculated by means of the formula:

$$\text{variance} = \frac{\Sigma(X^2) - ((\Sigma X)^2/N)}{N - 1}$$

where $\sum$ means 'the sum of', so that $(\sum X)^2$ means 'sum all the numbers, then square the result', and $\sum(X^2)$ means 'square each number and then add all the squares together'. Write a program which will calculate the variance of any set of numbers, just one number being present on each data record.

10 More built-in functions, patterns and operators

10.1 The built-in patterns ARB and REM

The built-in pattern ARB matches any string whatsoever. It is useful in determining what lies between two specific substrings. If, for example, we need to find out what separates T and ISH in a string, we may write:

```
BETWEEN  =  'T'  ARB  .  BETW  'ISH'
```

If we have a variable TEXT, whose value is A TICKLISH PROBLEM, then unanchored pattern matching by means of the statement

```
TEXT BETWEEN
```

will assign the substring ICKL to BETW. If TEXT contained A BRITISH CAR, the null string would be assigned to BETW, since there is nothing between T and ISH.

REM is a pattern which matches anything remaining in a string at the point where it is used. Consider the statement

```
TEXT  'B'  REM  .  REST
```

If TEXT contains BRITISH CARS, then after the B is matched the remainder (i.e. RITISH CARS) will be assigned as the value of REST. Note that unless TRIM or &TRIM is used to remove trailing blanks from input data records, such blanks will be included in any assignments made using REM on input data.

10.2 The pattern-valued functions TAB, RTAB, POS and RPOS

In order to understand the use of these functions, it is necessary to think of pattern matching in terms of a cursor moving along a string, stopping at particular positions.

The function TAB takes a single argument, which can be any positive integer, or zero, or any expression evaluating to such a number. The pattern created by TAB takes the cursor along to the position in the string which is given by its argument. For instance, TAB(8) takes the cursor up to the position just after the eighth character in the string. If we have assigned the string COMPUTATION to WORD, and then write

```
WORD  TAB(8)  'I'
```

the pattern match succeeds (irrespective of whether the anchor is on or off), because TAB(8) takes us up to just after the second T:

```
 C O M P U T A T I O N
↑ ↑ ↑ ↑ ↑ ↑ ↑ ↑ ↑
0 1 2 3 4 5 6 7 8
```

TAB can be used to match a substring occurring between some specific substring and a particular position in the string:

```
&ANCHOR  =  0
WORD  'O'  TAB(8)  .  STR
```

If WORD contains the string COMPUTATION, then STR is assigned the value MPUTAT, i.e. everything between the first O and the TAB(8) position. Note that here it is important that the anchor is off, because we have to find some specific substring before the 'tabulator' is applied. If the anchor were on, the pattern match would succeed only if the string began with O.

If it is not possible to move the cursor on to reach the position indicated (because the string is not long enough, or because the cursor has already gone beyond the point specified) the pattern match fails. Thus the above match would fail if WORD contained a string which was less than eight characters long. Consider also the following:

```
&ANCHOR  =  0
TEXT  =  'THIS IS A SHORT SENTENCE'
TEXT  'A'  TAB(30)
```

The attempt to move the cursor to position 30 fails, because there are only 24 characters in the string stored in TEXT. Now consider:

```
&ANCHOR  =  0
TEXT 'E'  TAB(5)
```

The pattern involving TAB will again fail for the value of TEXT given earlier, because by the time the first E has been matched, position 5 has been passed.

The function RTAB is exactly like TAB, except that the cursor starts at the right-hand end of the string instead of the left. Consider the following:

```
&ANCHOR  =  0
LINE  =  'HAVE A GOOD BIRTHDAY'
LINE  'G'  RTAB(4)  .  WISHES
```

First the G of GOOD is matched, then the cursor moves to position 4 as measured from the right-hand end of the string. Thus OOD BIRT is assigned as the value of WISHES.

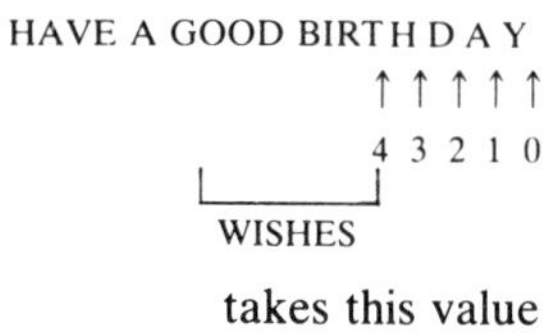

POS and RPOS are similar to TAB and RTAB, except that while TAB and RTAB actually move the cursor to a given position, POS and RPOS merely test whether the cursor is at a particular position. As an example, let us look at the following:

```
&ANCHOR  =  0
LINE  'V'  POS(3)
```

If LINE contains HAVE A GOOD BIRTHDAY, after V is matched, the cursor is indeed in position 3, so the pattern match succeeds. If, however, we write

```
&ANCHOR  -  0
LINE  'D'  POS(8)
```

the match will fail, because the cursor is in position 11, not position 8, when the D of GOOD has been matched:

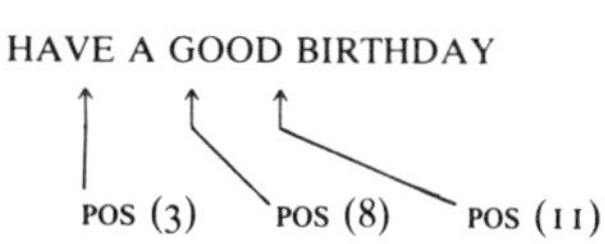

RPOS is similar to POS, but the position is calculated from the right-hand end. RPOS is particularly useful in finding out what comes at the end of a string. Imagine that we have isolated a word from a text, and stored it in WORD, and that we want to know if the word ends in ED. We can write simply:

```
&ANCHOR  =  0
WORD  'ED'  RPOS(0)
```

In the SPITBOL variant of SNOBOL4, we could achieve the same effect more efficiently in anchored mode by writing a pattern with BREAKX:

```
&ANCHOR  =  1
WORD  BREAKX('E')  'ED'  RPOS(0)
```

Note that BREAK would fail to give the correct result here if the word contained another E before the ED ending (see the discussion of BREAKX in section 8.4).

As a second example of the use of RPOS, imagine that we want to isolate the last four letters of a word and assign this substring to the variable LAST4. One way would be:

```
&ANCHOR  =  0
WORD  RPOS(4)  LEN(4)  .  LAST4
```

Alternatively we could use REM instead of LEN:

```
&ANCHOR  =  0
WORD  RPOS(4)  REM  .  LAST4
```

Either of these statements will succeed if there are four or more letters in the word, but fail otherwise. Note carefully what is happening in these pattern matches. Initially, the cursor is *not* at position 4 from the end – it is, in fact, at the beginning. But because the anchor is off, the cursor can move along one position at a time, looking for a match. When the cursor reaches the fourth position from the end of the string, the match is successful. If the anchor were on, the pattern match would fail, because the cursor would be unable to move down the string looking for the pattern required. We could get over this difficulty by using RTAB instead of RPOS, since RTAB, it will be remembered, actually moves the cursor, irrespective of whether the anchor is on or off. The following, therefore, would succeed for a word of four or more letters:

```
&ANCHOR  =  1
WORD  RTAB(4)  LEN(4)  .  LAST4
```

A further warning on the use of RTAB and RPOS is necessary here. These patterns, as we have seen, measure positions from the right of a string. If a string has been read in from a data record, it may well have trailing blanks, and this may cause patterns involving RPOS or RTAB to fail. Consider the following:

```
&ANCHOR  =  0
LINE  =  'THE CAT SAT ON THE MAT
LINE  'MAT'  RPOS(0)
```

This will fail, because when MAT has been matched there are still blanks left before the end of the string – i.e. before the position corresponding to RPOS(0). The solution is to use TRIM or &TRIM to remove trailing blanks from input records (see also the warning on the use of REM in section 10.1).

10.3 The string-valued function DUPL and the related SPITBOL functions RPAD and LPAD

The function DUPL allows a string (which may be a single character or more than one) to be duplicated any required number of times. Suppose that we wish to print a line of 100 asterisks, perhaps as a separating line in a table. We can write:

```
OUTPUT  =  DUPL('*',100)
```

The general form of DUPL is thus:

```
DUPL(STRING,NUMBER)
```

If we wanted to print a sequence of alternating asterisks and dashes, we could write:

```
OUTPUT  =  DUPL('*-',50)
```

As a final cxamplc, imagine that we want to print the value of the variable NAME, but with a margin of 20 blanks on the left. We write:

```
OUTPUT  =  DUPL(' ',20)  NAME
```

In SPITBOL, though not in standard SNOBOL4, the built-in functions LPAD and RPAD are available. Such functions can easily be written by the programmer himself in standard SNOBOL4 (see the exercises for chapter 11). Each of these functions can take three arguments; for instance:

```
OUTPUT  =  LPAD('NAME',20,'*')
```

This will cause the printing of enough asterisks (actually 16) to 'pad out' the string NAME to a total of 20 characters, the string being printed immediately after the asterisks. The general form of LPAD is thus:

```
LPAD(STRING1,NUMBER,STRING2)
```

RPAD is exactly the same as LPAD, except that it pads out on the right. Thus the following statement causes the printing of the string NAME followed by 16 asterisks:

```
OUTPUT  =  RPAD('NAME',20,'*')
```

If the last argument of LPAD or RPAD is omitted, SPITBOL assumes that blanks are to be used for padding. Thus the following causes the printing of 7 blanks, then the string AGE:

```
OUTPUT  =  LPAD('AGE',10)
```

The first argument of LPAD or RPAD can be a string-valued variable. Thus if ADDRESS contains a string, we may write:

```
OUTPUT  =  LPAD(ADDRESS,20)
```

Numerical variables can also be used, since they are automatically converted to strings in this environment.

DUPL, LPAD and RPAD are extremely useful in formatting output, for example in columns.

10.4 The cursor position operator

The cursor position operator @ is a unary operator which takes a variable as its 'operand' (e.g. @X). When encountered in a pattern match, the @ operator causes its operand variable (e.g. X) to be assigned a value which is the current position of the cursor. @ acts like the immediate value assignment operator $ in that the assignment of a value does not wait for a successful match to be achieved. Consider the following:

```
&ANCHOR  =  0
WORD  =  'APPLE'
WORD  @X  'E'
```

The cursor starts in position 0 and moves through positions 1 to 4 before finally finding a match for the E. As it does so, the values 0, 1, 2, 3 and 4 are successively assigned to X. When the pattern match finally succeeds, the value of X is 4.

The following program uses the @ operator to calculate character positions in a line, for the purpose of printing asterisks below the first occurrence of any of the words WILL, WOULD, CAN, COULD, in each line of a text.

```
* THIS PROGRAM PRINTS ASTERISKS UNDER THE FIRST OCCURRENCE OF
* ANY OF THE  WORDS   'WILL', 'WOULD', 'CAN' AND 'COULD'
* IN EACH LINE OF A TEXT.  IF NONE OF THESE WORDS OCCURS, THE
* LINE IS PRINTED WITHOUT ANY MARKING.
*
* INITIALISATION
*
        &ANCHOR  =  0
        &TRIM  =  1
*
* THE PATTERNS WHICH FOLLOW WILL ALLOW THE ISOLATION OF THE
* INDIVIDUAL WORDS REQUIRED, RATHER THAN THE MERE SEQUENCE
* OF LETTERS 'WILL', ETC.
*
        MODALS  =  'WILL'  |  'WOULD'  |  'CAN'  |  'COULD'
        PMARKS  =  ANY(',;:.?!" ')
        BEFORE  =  ANY(' "')
*
* THE PATTERN 'MODPAT' ISOLATES THE REQUIRED ITEMS AND USES THE
* CURSOR POSITION OPERATOR TO CALCULATE THE POSITIONS OF THE
* START AND END OF THE ITEM.
*
        MODPAT  =  BEFORE  @X  MODALS  @Y  PMARKS
*
* PROCESSING
*
* READ IN AND PRINT A DATA LINE, ADDING A BLANK AT START AND
* END TO ENSURE THAT 'MODPAT' WORKS WHERE ONE OF THE REQUIRED
* ITEMS IS AT THE VERY BEGINNING OR END OF A LINE.
*
READ     OUTPUT  =  ' '  INPUT  ' '                  :F(END)
*
* TEST FOR 'MODPAT' IN THIS DATA LINE.  IF FOUND, PRINT ASTERISKS
* UNDER MODAL, THEN A BLANK LINE.  IF NOT FOUND, JUST PRINT BLANK
* LINE.
*
        OUTPUT  MODPAT                               :F(BLANK)
        OUTPUT  =  DUPL(' ',X)  DUPL('*',Y  -  X)
BLANK   OUTPUT  =                                    :(READ)
END
```

The comment lines make this program largely self-explanatory; one or two points, however, deserve mention. Firstly, note that precautions have been taken to ensure that what we isolate is one of the individual words WILL, WOULD, CAN, COULD, and not just the sequences of letters (as in SWILL, CANDLE, TOUCAN, and so on). For discussion of these matters, see section 5.3, where we also dealt with the problem of isolating words occurring at the very beginning or end of a line. Secondly, note that if one of the required modal verbs is found in the pattern match involving MODPAT, the value assigned to X will be the cursor position just before the modal, and the value of Y will be the position just after the modal. This means that when we come to print asterisks under the required word, we need X blanks to take us up to the word to be marked, then (Y – X) asterisks. Thirdly, note that the statement

```
        OUTPUT  MODPAT                              :F(BLANK)
```

does not cause output of another line of text, but uses the line which was assigned to OUTPUT in the previous statement. This is because OUTPUT causes printing only when a value is assigned to it. Finally, note that there is no guarantee that the occurrences of WILL, etc., that we isolate will actually be used as modal verbs. We have given the computer no way of distinguishing between modal and non-modal uses of these words (e.g. 'make your *will*', 'a *can* of peas), and it will therefore print asterisks below each occurrence of these forms, however used.

10.5 The unevaluated expression operator

We saw in section 5.2 that it is in general a good idea to set up at the beginning of a program any patterns which are to be used several times in the program, assigning them to names which can then be used in pattern matching statements. The pattern can then be worked out by the computer just once, and need not be typed out several times. There are times, however, when this practice requires some care.

In section 5.5 we set up the following pattern match for testing whether WORD contained two successive occurrences of the same vowel:

```
        &ANCHOR  =  0
        WORD  VOWEL  $  V  V
```

We might be tempted to set up the pattern at the beginning of the program, assigning it to a name:

```
        DOUBLEV  =  VOWEL  $  V  V
```

Unfortunately, however, this will not give the result we want. The value of

V taken for the final component of the pattern will be its value when the pattern DOUBLEV is worked out at the beginning of the program (presumably the null string), and this will not change when further assignments are made to V during the program run. Thus, as written, the definition of DOUBLEV is equivalent to:

```
DOUBLEV  =  VOWEL  $  V
```

and so will not achieve the desired effect. What we need is some way of deferring the evaluation of V until the pattern DOUBLEV is actually used in a pattern matching statement. We can do this using the 'unevaluated expression operator', unary * (for the distinction between unary and binary operators, see section 9.2). Thus we write:

```
DOUBLEV  =  VOWEL  $  V  *V
```

Now, the value of the second V taken for the match will be its value at the time when the computer reaches that point in the match, i.e. the value just assigned to it by the component VOWEL $ V in the case of a successful match for the first vowel.

The unevaluated expression operator can also be used with an argument of a pattern-valued function, i.e. ANY, NOTANY, LEN, BREAK (and, in SPITBOL, BREAKX), SPAN, POS, RPOS, TAB or RTAB. Let us suppose that at various points in a program we wish to test whether some character occurs at some specified position in a word, but that both the character and the position can vary on different occasions. If we set up the following pattern at the beginning of the program:

```
CHARPOS  =  TAB(N)  CHAR
```

when the pattern is worked out, the values of N and CHAR taken will be those they have at the beginning of the program. i.e. zero or null. We can avoid this by using the unevaluated expression operator as follows:

```
CHARPOS  =  TAB(*N)  *CHAR
```

Now, each time the pattern is used, the values of N and CHAR taken will be those at the time of execution of the pattern-matching statement concerned.

We can also use the unary * operator to apply to whole patterns or to the components of alternation or concatenation. Consider the case where we want to underline various headings at different points in a program, the headings being of different lengths and starting at different positions in the line. If we set up a pattern:

```
UNDER  =  DUPL(' ',N1)  DUPL('-',N2)
```

at the beginning of the program, its value will be worked out using the initial (presumably zero) values of N1 and N2. It would also be incorrect to use the * operator in the following way, because it can be used with the arguments of pattern-valued functions only, and DUPL is a string-valued function:

```
        UNDER  =  DUPL(' ',*N1)   DUPL('-',*N2)
```

We can get round the problem by making * apply to the whole of each DUPL function call, or to the whole pattern, thus:

```
        UNDER  =  *DUPL(' ',N1)   *DUPL('-',N2)
```

or

```
        UNDER  =  *(DUPL(' ',N1)   DUPL('-',N2))
```

10.6 The indirect reference operator

Consider the problem of counting the number of times each possible combination of two vowel letters occurs in a string stored in STRING. We shall presumably need a separate variable to count each combination. We could, of course, write something of the following sort:

```
              &ANCHOR  =  0
AA            STRING   'AA'   =                          :F(AE)
              AA  =  AA  +  1                            :(AA)
AE            STRING   'AE'                              :F(AI)
              AE  =  AE  +  1                            :(AE)
AI
```

and so on through all the possible combinations. This would, however, require some 50 lines of program to do all the tests. Fortunately, there is a much neater way, using the 'indirect reference operator', unary $.

```
              &ANCHOR  =  0
              VPAT  =  (ANY('AEIOU')  ANY('AEIOU'))  .  VLS
TEST          STRING  VPAT  =                            :F(CONT)
              $VLS  =  $VLS  +  1                        :(TEST)
CONT
```

VPAT simply sets up the two-vowel pattern and assigns the two vowels, on matching, to VLS. The statement labelled TEST searches for the pattern and deletes the two vowels if found. The effect of the $ operator is to refer to a variable whose name is the same as the current value of VLS. If VPAT has matched the string AI, which has thus been assigned to VLS, then $VLS refers to a variable called AI, and the statement

```
$VLS = $VLS + 1                         :(TEST)
```

adds 1 to the value of this variable before transferring control back to TEST. If the string EE had been matched, a variable called EE would have been referred to by $VLS, and would have had its value incremented by 1, and so on. The effect of the indirect reference operator, then, is to refer to a name which is the same as the current value of whatever variable is immediately to the right of the operator. As a further example, consider the following:

```
WORD = 'AMPLITUDE'
$WORD = 50
```

This has the effect of assigning the value 50 to a variable called AMPLITUDE.

The indirect reference operator can also be applied to string-valued expressions which are enclosed in parentheses. The following is thus valid in SNOBOL4, and will increment the value of a variable VAR.A by 1:

```
WORD = 'VAR'
$(WORD '.A') = $(WORD '.A') + 1
```

Expressions involving the indirect reference operator can even occur in go-to's, so that labels can be computed as the statement is executed. An example is given below:

```
N = 2 * T + 5                           :($('LOOP.' N)
```

The value of N is computed, then when the go-to is reached, this value, as a string, is concatenated with the string LOOP. and finally the indirect reference operator refers to a name which is the same as this concatenated string. The computer treats this name as a label and transfers control to the statement with that label. If T = 3, N is 11, and 'LOOP.' N is equivalent to LOOP.11. Transfer to the statement labelled LOOP.11 will thus occur. Of course, a statement with such a label must occur in the program, otherwise an error will be signalled.

10.7 A complete program using some of the features discussed in this chapter

To end this chapter, we shall develop a program using RPOS, DUPL and the indirect reference operator.

Let us suppose that we are interested in the vowel qualities of all the monophthongal vowels (i.e. those which do not glide into any other vowel) in a particular poetic text, and have recorded our analysis in terms of two codes for each vowel occurrence, the first giving the height of the highest part of the tongue (H = high, M = mid, L = low), the second indicating which part of the tongue is highest (F = front, C = central, B = back). Let us further suppose that the codings have been typed into a data file, in the following format:

```
*LB*HF*HC*LC*HF*MC*HC etc.
```

with as many pairs of codes per line as convenient, and no asterisk at the end of a line. Our problem is to read in the data, and count and print the frequency of each category (H, M, L, F, C, B) in the data. We can use indirect reference to do this, as in the program set out below.

```
* THIS PROGRAM READS IN DATA ON VOWEL QUALITIES AND COUNTS THE
* NUMBER OF OCCURRENCES OF EACH FEATURE.  FOR EACH VOWEL
* OCCURRENCE THERE ARE TWO CODES:
*           (1)  H = HIGH          (2)  F = FRONT
*                M = MID                C = CENTRAL
*                L = LOW                B = BACK
* THE CODES ARE RECORDED IN THE DATA FILE IN THE FOLLOWING WAY:
* *LB*HF*HC*LC*HF*MC*HC  ETC.
*
* INITIALISATION
*
          &ANCHOR  =  1
          &TRIM  =  1
          H = 0; M = 0; L = 0; F = 0; C = 0; B = 0
          CODES  =  'HMLFCB'
          DATAPAT  =  '*'  ANY(CODES)  .  C1  ANY(CODES)  .  C2
*
* PROCESSING
*
* READ IN A LINE, INCREMENT LINE COUNTER, ISOLATE A PAIR OF CODES.
*
READ      LINE  =  INPUT                          :F(PRINT)
          LINENO  =  LINENO  +  1
GETCODES  LINE  DATAPAT  =                        :S(INC)
*
* IN CASE OF FAILURE, TEST WHETHER DATA IN LINE EXHAUSTED.  IF SO,
```

```
* READ IN ANOTHER LINE.  IF NOT, PRINT MESSAGE INDICATING A DATA
* FORMAT ERROR.
*
          LINE  RPOS(0)                               :S(READ)F(ERR)
*
* IF 'DATAPAT' MATCH SUCCEEDS, INCREMENT APPROPRIATE CODE VARIABLES
* USING INDIRECT REFERENCE.  ISOLATE FURTHER CODES.
*
INC       $C1  =  $C1  +  1
          $C2  =  $C2  +  1                           :(GETCODES)
*
* TERMINATION
*
* PRINT COLUMN HEADINGS.
*
PRINT     OUTPUT  =  'FEATURE'  DUPL(' ',20)  'FREQUENCY'
          OUTPUT  =  DUPL('-',7)  DUPL(' ',20)  DUPL('-',9)
*
* STRIP ONE CODE AT A TIME FROM 'CODES', AND USE INDIRECT
* REFERENCE TO REFER TO EACH CODE VARIABLE IN TURN, PRINTING
* THEIR FINAL VALUES.
*
STRIP     CODES  LEN(1)  .  CH  =                     :F(END)
          OUTPUT  =  DUPL(' ',3)  CH  DUPL(' ',27)  $CH   :(STRIP)
*
* ERROR MESSAGE
*
ERR       OUTPUT  =  'DATA FORMAT INCORRECT IN LINE ' LINENO  :(READ)
END
```

After initial comment lines describing the program and the form of the data input, we set &ANCHOR and &TRIM to 1, and (optionally) initialise to zero the variables for each vowel feature. We also set up a pattern CODES containing a string consisting of the feature codes, and a pattern DATAPAT for breaking out pairs of codes from the data records.

The processing phase begins with the input of a data record. A line counter is then incremented. A pair of codes is isolated, and deleted together with the preceding asterisk. If the code isolation pattern match succeeds, control passes to INC, which uses indirect reference to refer to and increment a variable whose name is the first code letter isolated. A second variable, corresponding to the second code isolated, is also referred to by means of the indirect reference operator, and its value incremented. The program then loops back to attempt the isolation of a further code pair.

If the code isolation statement labelled GETCODES fails, this may be for one of two reasons: there may be no more data codes left in the line; or there may be an error in the data format. We test for the former situation by applying the pattern RPOS(0) to LINE: since we have trimmed all trailing blanks, if we have deleted everything else the cursor will be at the right-hand end of LINE. If this pattern match fails, we know that there must be an error in data format (e.g. only one code, or three codes, or no asterisk). We therefore transfer control to ERR, which prints an error message indicating the line number of the incorrect line. Control is then passed back to READ and processing continues with the next line: in this way, all lines containing data format errors can be picked up in one run of the program.

When all the data have been processed, control is transferred to PRINT. Column headings FEATURE and FREQUENCY are printed, using DUPL (if SPITBOL were being used, it would be easier to use RPAD here). We then strip one code at a time from the string stored in CODES, and use indirect reference to refer to the variable corresponding in name to the current code. The code and the value of the corresponding variable are then printed in suitably formatted columns. When all the codes have been stripped off, control is passed to END.

Note the importance of 'failsafe' devices in programs of this kind. It is quite common for mistakes to be made in the encoding of data, and it is essential to provide a mechanism for spotting such errors. Otherwise, depending on how the program is written, it may simply fail on encountering an error, or, worse still, processing may continue, but give false results.

Exercises 10

1 Describe the result of each of the following if TEXT contains the string THERE'S NO PEACE FOR THE WICKED

```
(i)    TEXT  BREAK('S') 'S' TAB(16) . INTER
(ii)   TEXT  BREAK('F') 'F' TAB(12)
(iii)  TEXT  BREAK('N') 'N' RTAB(0) . LAST
(iv)   &ANCHOR  =  0
       TEXT  POS(3)  'R'
(v)    TEXT  BREAK('E')  'ED'  RPOS(0)
(vi)   &ANCHOR  =  0
       VOWELS  =  'AEIOU'
       TEXT  SPAN(VOWELS)  .  VLS  POS(14)
(vii)  TEXT  BREAK('P')  LEN(5)  .  ITEM
       $ITEM  =  'ON EARTH'
```

2 Write statements which will perform each of the following tasks. Where the distinction between anchored and unanchored pattern matching is important, indicate which is appropriate.

(i) Test whether the fourth character in the string stored in STRING is P
(ii) Test whether the string stored in WORD ends in ISH
(iii) Assign the last two characters of the string stored in WORD, to a variable LAST
(iv) Print the string stored in HEADING, in the centre of a page which is 132 characters wide
(v) Test whether the string stored in CODE ends with a numerical character.

3 Data from an informant test are stored in a file, the data from each informant occupying one record. The informant's name, sex, age, social class (1–5), also the score on the test, are recorded in this order, separated by asterisks, as follows:

```
SMITH, JEAN*F*51*3*38
```

Write a single program which will:

(i) produce a reformatted list of data, with clearly separated columns across the page, and an underlined heading for each column (assume that the page is at least 120 characters wide)
(ii) count and print the numbers of informants in each of the following age groups: up to 20, 21–30, 31–40, 41–50, over 50
(iii) calculate and print the mean score for informants in each of these age groups.

4 Write a program to read in a text line by line, and print out and count all the words which begin and end with the same letter.

11 Programmer-defined functions

11.1 Functions and structured programming

We have seen that there are various built-in functions to perform tasks which are particularly common in programs. SNOBOL4 also allows the programmer to write his own functions to do jobs which, although not provided for by the built-in functions, are nevertheless required several times in a particular program or set of programs.

Most tasks which are suitable for computational solution can be broken down into a series of subtasks. For instance, we might need to isolate a word from a stretch of text, then perform certain tests on the word, and when all the words have been processed we might wish to print out certain results, with appropriate headings. It is good practice, when writing programs, to plan them as a series of 'modules', each corresponding to one subtask. A function can then be written to deal with each module, and the various functions can be brought together as required in the main body of the program. This structured approach to programming encourages us to think problems through with greater clarity; furthermore, it is often the case that functions written for one program may also be useful in others. A further advantage is that functional modules can be tested separately and more thoroughly than if they were woven into the program.

The use of a programmer-defined function requires three things:

1 a definition of the function and its associated arguments;
2 the actual program 'code', or 'procedure', by which the function performs the task it is designed for;
3 a 'call' of the function at some point in the program.

We shall deal with each of these aspects in turn.

11.2 Function definition

To define a function, we must give it a name and say what arguments are associated with it. We do this by means of the built-in function DEFINE.

Let us imagine that on a number of occasions during the execution of a program we wish to count the number of times a character (which may be a different character each time the function is called) occurs in a stretch of text (which may again be different for each function call). We might define a function CHARCT as follows:

```
DEFINE('CHARCT(CHAR,STRING)')
```

This defines the function CHARCT as having two arguments, which we have called CHAR and STRING. These variables are so-called 'dummy' or 'formal' variables, because they are used to stand for whatever values are to be used in an actual call of the function. For instance, if we wanted to know how many times the letter E occurs in the contents of a variable called LINE, CHAR would need to take the value 'E', while STRING would need to take on the value of LINE. On the other hand, if we were interested in the number of commas in a string stored in TEXT, we should need CHAR to have the value ',' and STRING would take the value of TEXT. We shall see shortly how these values are passed to the function during a call of that function.

There are one or two points to notice about the form of the function definition. The name of the function and the names of its arguments are enclosed in a set of quotes, and these in turn are enclosed in brackets. If there is more than one argument (there may be any number, including zero), the individual arguments are separated by commas; the whole set of arguments is enclosed in a set of brackets. In other words, the complex of function name and arguments has the same form as for a built-in function. Note that there are no blanks anywhere in the function definition.

There is one problem which may necessitate the modification of the function definition. When we discuss what happens during a function call, we shall see that the values of a function name and of the arguments are saved before the function procedure is executed again, and restored when the procedure has been completed; we need not, therefore, worry about their values being lost or changed permanently by a function call. We may, however, need to use, within the function procedure itself, variables which are not themselves arguments of the function, and so will not automatically have their values saved and restored at each call of the function. The value of such a variable will thus normally change each time the function is called, and the value it has at the start of one function call will be that with which it was left at the end of the previous call. We can avoid this by making the variable 'local' to the function, so that the computer regards it as being associated with that function, and will treat it like an argument as far as the saving and restoration of values is concerned. As an example of how to include a local variable in the definition of a function, let us consider how to define a function SQRT, which calculates the square root of a number N, and which needs a variable (let us call it TEMP) which is local to the function procedure. We write:

```
DEFINE('SQRT(N)TEMP')
```

The name of the local variable thus follows the bracketed arguments. There may be more than one local variable, with commas between. One final point to note about local variables is that their names can be used elsewhere in the program without fear of confusion between their uses inside and outside the function. That is, the computer would regard TEMP, used outside the function procedure, as a quite different variable from that which is local to the procedure, or, indeed, TEMP used in a different function. Variables which have not been made local may, of course, be used within function procedures, but care is needed since, as we have seen, their values will normally change each time the function is called.

It should be noted that function definitions should come near the beginning of the program, in the initialisation phase, so that they are executed only once.

11.3 Function procedures

The actual body of the function (the 'procedure') which carries out its job may consist of a single statement or more than one; indeed, some functions may be extremely complex, requiring a large number of individual statements. The procedure may come anywhere in the program after the definition statement. It is important, however, not to allow the program to flow into a function from the statement immediately preceding the procedure: the whole point of a function is that it is called up at various points in the program run, and so slotted in as required, rather than simply forming part of an on-going series of sequentially executed statements. One way to avoid flowing into a function is to by-pass it using a go-to on the preceding statement. Probably the safest way, however, is to place all function procedures, with explanatory comments, at the end of the program. This arrangement also has the advantage of making the program easier to follow.

It is, of course, necessary for the computer to know which statement to transfer to each time a particular function is called. The syntax of SNOBOL4 does, in fact, allow for the explicit inclusion of an appropriate label in the function definition statement. Normally, however, a convention is adopted whereby the first statement in a function procedure has a label which is the same as the name of the function itself, and in this case there is no need to specify anything extra in the function definition. The label can be attached to the first actual statement of the procedure, or it can be placed on a line by itself (starting in the first position, of course), with nothing more in the statement. The latter method is often used to make the visual layout clearer. It is also a good idea to mark the end of a function procedure by an appropriate label (e.g. SQRT.END for the function SQRT) on an empty, 'dummy' statement. It may, of course, be necessary to label other statements within the procedure. Since it is perfectly possible to transfer control to any statement with a label, whether inside or outside a procedure, it is good practice to begin each label within a procedure with the name of the function (e.g. SQRT.1, SQRT.2, etc.). In this way, the risk of duplicating labels used elsewhere, and of unintentional transfer into the middle of a function from elsewhere in the program, is minimised.

To exemplify these points, and introduce some further features, let us consider the procedure for the function CHARCT whose definition, repeated below, was discussed earlier:

```
DEFINE('CHARCT(CHAR,STRING)')
```

We shall write this function so that it fails if the string which is the first argument does not occur in the string which is the second argument, but otherwise returns as a value the number of times the first argument occurs in the second. A suitable procedure would be:

```
CHARCT
         STRING  BREAK(CHAR)                    :F(FRETURN)
CHARCT.1 STRING  BREAK(CHAR)  CHAR  =           :F(RETURN)
         CHARCT  =  CHARCT  +  1                :(CHARCT.1)
CHARCT.END
```

Note first that the procedure is written using the dummy arguments given in the function definition. These will automatically be given their real values when the function is called. This particular function computes a value, the number of times CHAR occurs in STRING. We want this value to be returned as the result of the function procedure. To ensure this, we use, as a counter, a variable with the same name as the function itself. Thus the designation CHARCT is being used for three different purposes in the function: (i) as the name of the function itself, (ii) as the label of the first statement in the procedure, (iii) as the variable whose value is to be returned.

A further important point to notice is the way in which we return from the procedure to the main program. The labels RETURN and FRETURN used in the above procedure are not statement labels, as in an ordinary go-to; rather, they indicate that control is to be transferred back to the point where the function was called. If RETURN is used, the function call is taken as having succeeded, and the value returned will be that of the function name variable (in this case, the value of CHARCT). If FRETURN is used, the function call is deemed to have failed, and no value is returned.

Let us now see exactly what the procedure for CHARCT does. First we have a dummy statement with the label CHARCT, so that control can be transferred into the procedure each time the function is called. We could have attached this label to the first statement proper, which tests whether STRING contains any instances of CHAR at all. (Note the use of BREAK here to avoid any assumption of unanchored pattern matching.) If STRING contains no occurrences of CHAR, the function call fails, and control is transferred back using FRETURN. If, however, STRING contains at least one occurrence of CHAR, we delete the first occurrence and then increment the value of CHARCT by one. We then loop back to test whether STRING contains any more instances of CHAR. Note that the statement testing for and deleting CHAR has a label which begins with the function name, in accordance with the practice recommended earlier. When there are no more instances of CHAR in STRING, the use of RETURN transfers control back to the main program, and the function call returns a value which is the current value of CHARCT. The procedure ends with a dummy statement consisting of a label formed from the function name plus .END.

11.4 Function calls

Whenever we wish to call a particular function in a program, we simply write the name of the function followed by the actual value(s) of the argument(s) in brackets. This is exactly the same as for a built-in function: indeed, the only way of telling whether a given function is built-in or programmer-defined is to see if the program contains a definition for the function. Let us consider the situation where we want to use the function CHARCT to count the number of occurrences of the letter E in the contents of a variable called LINE, and that we want to assign the resulting value to the variable ECOUNT. We write:

```
      ECOUNT  =  CHARCT('E',LINE)
```

Note that since E is a string it must be enclosed in quotes as usual.

When such a function call is encountered in the execution of a program, the values of the function name (here, CHARCT) and the arguments (CHAR, STRING) are saved. The computer then assigns the null string as the value of the function name and of any local variables, and assigns to the arguments the values specified in the function call. Thus in the above function call, CHARCT will be given the null string as its value, CHAR will have the value E and STRING will take on the value of LINE. Control is now transferred to the statement labelled CHARCT, and the statements in the procedure are executed. If a return to the main program is made via RETURN, the value of the function call will be that of the variable CHARCT, and will subsequently be assigned to ECOUNT. If a return to the main program is made via FRETURN, no value is returned, and no assignment made to ECOUNT. The values of the arguments CHAR and STRING are restored to what they were before the function was called.

Although there are no local variables in this particular function, if there were any, their initial values would be restored on return via either RETURN or FRETURN.

Note that programmer-defined functions, like built-in functions, can be used as part of a more complex expression. Thus the following statement would be quite valid in SNOBOL4:

```
      TOT   =  EQ(CHARCT(FIRSTCHAR,LINE),5)   TOT   +  1
```

This statement would add 1 to the value of TOT if and only if there were five instances of the character stored in FIRSTCHAR, in the string stored in LINE.

11.5 Some further examples

It will be remembered that SNOBOL arithmetic does not allow the use of 'real' numbers after the exponentiation operator. This means that we cannot compute the square root of a number N simply by writing N ! 0.5. Instead, we may write a function which will perform this calculation, which is very often needed in, for example, statistical calculations.

The argument of the function will clearly be simply the dummy variable N used for the numbers whose square roots we want to find. We shall also need a local variable, which we shall call TEMP, to hold certain values during the calculation. The definition statement, which was in fact discussed earlier, is thus:

```
      DEFINE('SQRT(N)TEMP')
```

The procedure itself is set out below.

```
SQRT
*
*  THE FUNCTION 'SQRT' CALCULATES THE SQUARE ROOT OF A NUMBER N.
*
          TEMP  =  N
SQRT.1    TEMP  =  GT(TEMP,0.000001)  TEMP  /  2.0     :F(RETURN)
SQRT.2    SQRT  =  GT(SQRT  !  2,N)  SQRT  -  TEMP     :S(SQRT.2)
          TEMP  =  GT(TEMP,0.000001)  TEMP  /  2.0     :F(RETURN)
SQRT.3    SQRT  =  LT(SQRT  !  2,N)  SQRT  +  TEMP  :S(SQRT.3)F(SQRT.1)
SQRT.END      .
```

The rationale behind this procedure is basically quite simple. The local variable TEMP is used to store a value by which the value of SQRT may be adjusted up or down, until the square of SQRT is very close indeed to the value of N. Initially, TEMP is set to the value of N; it is then halved successively as finer and finer adjustments are made to SQRT. The easiest way to see how the procedure operates is to follow a specific example through its successive stages. Consider the case where N = 2. Initially, TEMP is assigned the value 2. When SQRT.1 is executed, since the value of TEMP exceeds 0.000001, it is halved, so acquiring the new value 1.0. The statement labelled SQRT.2 is now executed. Since SQRT has the initial value zero, its square is not greater than N, so the predicate fails, and control is passed to the next statement, which halves TEMP again, giving it a value of 0.5. The predicate in statement SQRT.3 succeeds, since SQRT is still zero and hence its square is less than N. Thus SQRT is incremented by the value of TEMP, and so acquires the value 0.5. Statement SQRT.3 is now executed again, and since $(0.5)^2$ is smaller than 2 (the value of N), the value of TEMP (currently 0.5) is again added to SQRT giving 1.0 as the new value of SQRT. Further execution of SQRT.3 achieves success, since $(1.0)^2$ is still less than 2, so 0.5 is again added to SQRT, giving 1.5. The next time SQRT.3 is executed, however, the predicate fails, since $(1.5)^2$ is 2.25, which is greater than N. Therefore SQRT is not incremented, and control passes back to SQRT.1. Since TEMP is still greater than 0.000001, it is halved to give 0.25. In the execution of SQRT.2, since $(\text{SQRT})^2$ is greater than N, SQRT is decremented by the current value of TEMP, to give 1.5 − 0.25, or 1.25. SQRT.2 now operates again, and $(1.25)^2$ is tested to see if it is greater than N. It is not, so SQRT is not decreased, and control passes to the next statement, which halves TEMP to give 0.125. In the execution of SQRT.3, since $(1.25)^2$ is smaller than 2, the value of TEMP (0.125) is added to that of SQRT (1.25) to give 1.375. The square of this is still smaller than 2, so 0.125 is added, giving SQRT a value of 1.5 once again. The next execution of SQRT.3 gives failure of the predicate, so control is passed back to SQRT.1, and TEMP halved again to 0.0625. When SQRT.2 is executed, this new value of TEMP is subtracted from SQRT to give 1.5 − 0.0625, or 1.4375. Thus SQRT is progressively modified until it approaches the true square root of 2, which, to five decimal places, is 1.41421. The approximation process stops, and control is transferred back to the main program, when TEMP falls below 0.000001, this giving the square root to a sufficient degree of accuracy for most purposes.

So far, the functions we have considered have all needed arguments, and have returned values. Neither of these properties is present for all functions. Let us consider the problem of writing a function which will select the next line in a data file which does not begin with an angle bracket, but will skip over any lines which do begin in this way. Such a facility would be useful if, for instance, we wished to incorporate comment lines into a data file. Let us define a function SELECT, which will require no arguments. We must, however, still put in the brackets which would surround the arguments if there were any:

```
DEFINE('SELECT()')
```

The procedure itself could be written as follows:

```
SELECT
          SELECT  =  INPUT                          :F(FRETURN)
          SELECT  POS(0)  '<'                       :S(SELECT)F(RETURN)
SELECT.END
```

A value is returned in this case: that of the variable SELECT, which will be the contents of the next data record not beginning with an angle bracket. A typical call of this function might be:

```
SELECT()  BREAK(',')  ','  BREAK(',')  .  INTER
```

This would call SELECT to return the next non-comment line, and then test its contents for the presence of two commas, assigning everything between them to the variable INTER.

We said above that functions need not return values. As an example of a function which does not return a value, consider the printing and underlining of a string in the centre of a 132-column page, an operation which might be required several times, for different strings, in a program. We may define an appropriate function as below:

```
DEFINE('PRINT(HEADING)N')
```

The procedure itself is very simple:

```
PRINT
          N  =  (132  -  SIZE(HEADING))  /  2
          OUTPUT  =  DUPL(' ',N)  HEADING
          OUTPUT  =  DUPL(' ',N)  DUPL('-',SIZE(HEADING))     :(RETURN)
PRINT.END
```

The procedure simply prints out and underlines the appropriate string in the centre of the page, but returns no value. To print the string stored in the variable HEAD.1, we write:

```
PRINT(HEAD.1)
```

In the above procedure, note the use of a variable N to prevent the computer from having to calculate (132 − SIZE(HEADING)) twice. N is not an argument of PRINT, since it is not specified in a call of the function; it is thus given as a local variable in the function definition.

11.6 Functional composition

A function may be called from anywhere at all in a SNOBOL4 program, even from within another function or indeed the same function. This technique of nesting one function within another, or 'functional composition', allows the building up of quite complex functions from smaller modules, and so facilitates the structured approach to programming recommended earlier.

As an example of functional composition, let us consider the problem of testing whether a given string contains any substrings which are palindromes (i.e. read the same backwards and forwards). We can split this task into three parts. Clearly we need to isolate all the possible substrings of the given string which have two or more characters. For the string REDEEM, for example, there are the following substrings (including the original string): REDEEM, REDEE, EDEEM, REDE, EDEE, DEEM, RED, EDE, DEE, EEM, RE, ED, DE, EE, EM (as well as the individual characters R, E, D, M, which do not concern us), and two of these (EDE, EE) are palindromic. We then need to reverse each substring. Finally, we must test whether the forward and reverse strings are identical. It therefore seems sensible to use three functions, which we shall call SUBSTR, REVERSE and SUBPAL. (Note that REVERSE is a built-in function in SPITBOL and can thus be used without definition by the programmer: indeed, any attempt to redefine it will cause an error. It is not, however, built into standard SNOBOL4, and we shall therefore write our own version below.)

SUBSTR takes three arguments (let us call them STRING, M and N), and returns as a value that substring of STRING which begins after TAB(M) (i.e. at character number M + 1) and is N characters long. For instance, SUBSTR('REDEEM',1,3) would have the value EDE. The definition and procedure for SUBSTR are as follows:

```
           DEFINE('SUBSTR(STRING,M,N)')
           .
           .
           .
SUBSTR
           STRING  TAB(M)  LEN(N)  .  SUBSTR        :S(RETURN)F(FRETURN)
SUBSTR.END
```

REVERSE has one argument (we can call it STRING again, though we need not do so), and one local variable (C) which stores each character stripped from STRING during the procedure. It returns as a value the string which is the reverse of its argument string. For instance, REVERSE('REDEEM') returns MEEDER. The definition and procedure are as shown below:

```
           DEFINE('REVERSE(STRING)C')
           .
           .
           .
REVERSE
           STRING  LEN(1)  .  C  =                    :F(RETURN)
           REVERSE  =  C  REVERSE                     :(REVERSE)
REVERSE.END
```

SUBPAL can now be written so that it calls SUBSTR to isolate the substrings and REVERSE to reverse them, then tests whether the forward and reverse strings are identical and prints strings which are palindromic, together with the number of such strings. SUBPAL has one argument (STRING) and four locals.

```
           DEFINE('SUBPAL(STRING)X,Y,SUB,COUNT')
           .
           .
           .
SUBPAL
           Y  =  SIZE(STRING)
SUBPAL.1   SUB  =  SUBSTR(STRING,X,Y)
           COUNT  =  IDENT(SUB,REVERSE(SUB))  COUNT  +  1     :F(SUBPAL.2)
           OUTPUT  =  SUB
SUBPAL.2   X  =  LT(X,SIZE(STRING)  -  Y)  X  +  1  :S(SUBPAL.1)
           Y  =  GT(Y,2)  Y  -  1                   :F(SUBPAL.3)
           X  =  0                                  :(SUBPAL.1)
SUBPAL.3   OUTPUT  =  'THERE ARE '  COUNT  ' PALINDROMIC '
+                     'SUBSTRINGS IN THE STRING "'  STRING  '"'
+                                                   :(RETURN)
SUBPAL.END
```

The rationale of SUBPAL is as follows. Substrings of the argument are isolated, starting with the whole string, and then decreasing the size of the substrings by one character at a time, until substrings of just two characters are being isolated. For all substring lengths smaller than the length of the original string, there are two or more substrings to be isolated. For a given substring length Y, we isolate all possible substrings, starting at the first character in STRING, and moving along one character at a time. The stages for the string REDEEM are as follows:

Length of substring	Substrings isolated
6	REDEEM
5	REDEE EDEEM

```
            REDE
4            EDEE
              DEEM


            RED
             EDE
              DEE
3              EEM


            RE
             ED
2             DE
               EE
                EM
```

In the procedure, the variable Y is used to store the current length of substrings being isolated. Its value starts at SIZE(STRING) and decreases until it reaches 2, at which point all relevant substrings have been isolated. The variable X is used to store the current position of the beginning of a substring. For any given length of substring (i.e. any given value of Y) the value of X increases from 0 to SIZE(STRING) − Y.

In order to print and count all the palindromic substrings in each of a set of strings read in line by line, we should write a program with an initialisation phase defining the three functions and setting &TRIM (and, for efficiency, &ANCHOR) to 1, followed by the processing phase set out below, and finally the function procedures and the END statement.

```
READ      LINE  =  INPUT                          :F(END)
          SUBPAL(LINE)                            :(READ)
```

Further examples of functional composition will be discussed in chapter 14.

Exercises 11

1 Write (a) the function definition statement, and (b) an appropriate procedure, for each of the following:

   (i) a function LASTC(STRING) whose value is the last character in the string
   (ii) a function DELV(STRING) whose value is the result of deleting all vowels from the string
   (iii) a function STARS(STRING) whose value is the result of replacing all occurrences of non-vowel characters in the string by asterisks
   (iv) a function THREEWD(STRING) whose value is the first three-letter word in the string
   (v) a function FIVEWD(STRING) which will succeed if the string contains just five words, but will fail otherwise.

2 The functions RPAD and LPAD are built into SPITBOL, but not into standard SNOBOL4. Write a definition and procedure for each of these.

3 Write a program which will count the number of words in a text which contain the letter E, and print all such words in five columns spaced across a page of width 132 characters. Write your program in a modular fashion, using functions, so that it can very easily be amended to count and print words containing any other character. Suitable functions would be:

(i) GETWORD(), a function which returns the next word in the text, and fails only when there is no more text (this should be written so that it automatically reads in a new line as required)

(ii) FINDCHAR(STRING,CHAR), which tests for the presence of the character represented by CHAR, in the string represented by STRING

(iii) HEAD(HEADING,LINEWIDTH), which prints a heading centrally on a line of width LINEWIDTH, and underlines it.

12 Arrays, tables and programmer-defined data types

12.1 Referring to collections of values

So far, the only variables we have used have been names and keywords referring to a single value. Often, however, especially in textual work, we need to refer to a collection of values, all of which are related in some way – for instance, the words in a text, or the properties (such as length in words, number and type of constituents) of a sentence. SNOBOL4 provides three kinds of mechanism for handling such collections of values: arrays, tables and programmer-defined data types.

12.2 Arrays

In terms of the 'box and contents' analogy used in section 4.3, an array (of the simplest, one-dimensional type – we shall discuss more complex types later) can be thought of as a set of numbered drawers in a box, in each of which we keep one value in our collection. We can refer to (or 'access') the contents of each drawer by stating its number.

An array can be created, and assigned to a name, by means of a statement such as the following, using the built-in function ARRAY.

```
MONTHS  =  ARRAY(12)
```

In terms of our drawer and box analogy, this creates a box called MONTHS, in which there are 12 drawers. We can refer to any drawer by using its number, or 'index', in angle brackets, after the array name, thus: MONTHS<3>, MONTHS<9>, and so on. We can use these 'array references' in statements just as we have used names so far. For instance, to assign the string APRIL to the fourth element of the array MONTHS (that is, to put APRIL into the fourth 'drawer' of the 'box' called MONTHS) we write:

```
MONTHS<4>  =  'APRIL'
```

We could then go on to use MONTHS<4> in, for example, a pattern match such as:

```
MONTHS<4>  LEN(3)  .  ABBREV
```

which would assign the value APR to ABBREV.

Normally, we create arrays which have the null string as the initial value of each element (that is, each 'drawer' in the 'box' is initially empty). It is, however, possible to create arrays with other initial values for the elements, by providing the value as a second argument of ARRAY. Thus the following statement would create an array of 10 elements, each having the initial value 5:

```
FIVES  =  ARRAY(10,5)
```

and the following creates an array in which each of the 100 elements has the initial string value A:

```
A.ARR  =  ARRAY(100,'A')
```

Note that since A is a string, it must be enclosed in quotes as usual.

If we create an array using a single number as the first or sole argument, as in the examples given so far, the first element will have the index 1, the second the index 2, and so on. This is sufficient for most purposes, but if we wish to start the index somewhere other than at 1, we can do so by specifying the lower and upper bounds of the array, separated by a colon and enclosed overall in quotes, as the first argument of ARRAY, in place of a single number giving the number of elements. Thus to create a 20-element array ARR with the index beginning at 5 and going up to 24, we write:

```
ARR  =  ARRAY('5:24')
```

If we wanted each element to have the initial value X instead of the null string, we should write:

```
ARR  =  ARRAY('5:24','X')
```

It should be noted that numerically valued variables can be used as arguments for ARRAY, and also in array references. Thus if the value 50 has already been assigned to N, the following creates an array of 50 elements:

```
NUMBERS  =  ARRAY(N)
```

and NUMBERS<N> references the 50th element of the array. We can also use numerically valued expressions in array references, so that NUMBERS<N – 20> references the 30th element of the array.

It is interesting to consider what happens if an attempt is made to reference an array using an index which is greater than the number of elements in the array, for instance if we were to write a statement such as:

```
MONTHS<13>  =  'BONUS'
```

The attempt at assignment would fail, because we are trying to access an element which does not exist (in terms of our analogy, we are trying to put something into the 13th drawer of a box which has only 12 drawers).

The failure of an array reference can in fact be turned to good use, provided that we have a failure go-to on the statement. Consider the situation where we want to read 10 numbers from a file in which a collection of more than 10 numbers is stored one per record, and we also wish to assign each of the 10 numbers, in turn, to the 10 elements of an array called NUMDATA. We can write:

```
        &TRIM  =  1
        NUMDATA  =  ARRAY(10)
        I  =  1
READ    NUMDATA<I>  =  INPUT                 :F(DONE)
        I  =  I  +  1                        :(READ)
DONE
```

Note that we have used a loop to read each number into the appropriate array element in turn. This is made possible by using a variable, I, as the index in the array reference, and incrementing I each time a number is read in. Note also that the loop is terminated by failure of the array reference. Up to I = 10, the reference NUMDATA<I> will succeed, but as soon as I reaches 11, there are no more array elements left (that is, the reference is 'out of bounds'), reference fails, and control is transferred to the statement labelled DONE, so that the rest of the program can continue. This device will work for an array of any size; indeed, we do not even need to know the size of the array.

A typical use of an array in text processing would be in a program to count the numbers of words in a text with lengths of 1, 2, 3, 4 letters, and so on (that is, a 'word-length profile' of the text). First we set &ANCHOR and &TRIM to 1, and set up patterns to isolate individual words, as discussed in earlier examples. We shall assume that hyphens and apostrophes are to be counted as letters.

```
        &ANCHOR  =  1
        &TRIM  =  1
        LETTERS  =  "ABCDEFGHIJKLMNOPQRSTUVWXYZ'-"
        WPAT  =  BREAK(LETTERS)  SPAN(LETTERS)  .  WORD
```

We now create an array with 20 elements, assuming that no word (even hyphenated ones) will have more than 20 characters. We shall see below that an error message can be printed if any words of more than 20 characters do occur.

```
WLEN  =  ARRAY(20)
```

We now isolate one word at a time, compute its length, add 1 to the value of the appropriate array element, corresponding to that length, then, provided that assignment to the array element was successful, we go back to get another word. The array reference will fail only if the word is longer than 20 characters: in this case, we go to an error statement which will print the word, with a warning that it is too long for inclusion in the count.

```
READ      LINE  =  INPUT                          :F(PRINT)
GETW      LINE  WPAT  =                           :F(READ)
          N  =  SIZE(WORD)
          WLEN<N>  =  WLEN<N>  +  1               :S(GETW)F(ERR)
```

If the particular word just isolated has a length of 4 letters, then WLEN<4> will be incremented by 1; if the length is 10 letters, WLEN<10> will be incremented, and so on. One additional point should be noticed here. It woud have been possible to combine the last two statements as:

```
WLEN<SIZE(WORD)>  =  WLEN<SIZE(WORD)>  +  1  :S(GETW)F(ERR)
```

If we do, however, the computer has to work out SIZE(WORD) twice (since it appears twice in our statement), while in the version given originally SIZE(WORD) is computed just once and its value assigned to N, thus saving time in the execution of the program.

We now need to print the results in two columns: the first giving the number of letters in the word (corresponding to the indices of successive elements in the array), the second giving the frequency of words with that number of letters (corresponding to the value stored in each successive array element). Let us first give each column a heading:

```
PRINT     OUTPUT  =  'LENGTH'  DUPL(' ',10)  'FREQUENCY'
          OUTPUT  =  DUPL('-',6)  DUPL(' ',10)  DUPL('-',9)
```

This produces the following output:

```
LENGTH          FREQUENCY
------          ---------
```

Our next task is to print the number 1 under LENGTH and the value of WLEN<1> under FREQUENCY, then to print 2 under LENGTH and the value of WLEN<2> under FREQUENCY, and so on until all the array elements have been printed. We can do this using a loop:

```
            I = 1
PRINT.1     OUTPUT = DUPL(' ',3) I DUPL(' ',17) WLEN<I> :F(END)
            I = I + 1                                :(PRINT.1)
```

We thus set a counter I to 1, then print the value of I and the value of WLEN<I> in the appropriate columns, using DUPL to ensure that the values are lined up centrally under the headings. (This is clearly a refinement, but does add considerably to the appearance of the output, and at very little extra cost to the programmer.) We then increment I by 1, and loop round to print the next set of values. The loop continues until the array reference WLEN<I> fails, that is until I exceeds 20.

We now need only the error message discussed earlier, and the END statement:

```
ERR         OUTPUT = 'THE WORD ' WORD ' IS TOO LONG FOR '
+                    'INCLUSION IN THE COUNT'
            OUTPUT =                              :(GETW)
END
```

The complete program for a word-length profile is given below, with appropriate comment lines.

```
* THIS PROGRAM COUNTS THE FREQUENCY OF WORDS OF VARIOUS LENGTHS
* IN A TEXT READ IN LINE BY LINE.  THE HYPHEN AND APOSTROPHE ARE
* COUNTED AS WORD-FORMING CHARACTERS.
*
* INITIALISATION
*
          &ANCHOR = 1
          &TRIM = 1
          LETTERS = "ABCDEFGHIJKLMNOPQRSTUVWXYZ'-"
          WPAT = BREAK(LETTERS) SPAN(LETTERS) . WORD
          WLEN = ARRAY(20)
*
* PROCESSING
*
* READ IN A LINE OF DATA AND ISOLATE A WORD.
*
```

```
READ      LINE  =  INPUT                         :F(PRINT)
GETW      LINE  WPAT  =                          :F(READ)
*
* FIND LENGTH OF WORD AND INCREMENT APPROPRIATE ARRAY ELEMENT,
* THEN ISOLATE NEXT WORD.  FAILURE GO-TO ALLOWS FOR ERROR
* MESSAGE IF WORD IS LONGER THAN 20 CHARACTERS.
*
          N  =  SIZE(WORD)
          WLEN<N>  =  WLEN<N>  +  1              :S(GETW)F(ERR)
*
* TERMINATION
*
* PRINT  HEADINGS.
*
PRINT     OUTPUT  =  'LENGTH'  DUPL(' ',10)  'FREQUENCY'
          OUTPUT  =  DUPL('-',6)  DUPL(' ',10)  DUPL('-',9)
*
* PRINT RESULTS USING A LOOP AND COUNTER.
*
          I  =  1
PRINT.1   OUTPUT  =  DUPL(' ',3)  I  DUPL(' ', 17)  WLEN<I>  :F(END)
          I  =  I  +  1                          :(PRINT.1)
*
* ERROR MESSAGE
*
ERR       OUTPUT  =  'THE WORD '  WORD  ' IS TOO LONG FOR '
+                    'INCLUSION IN THE COUNT'
          OUTPUT  =                              :(GETW)
END
```

So far, we have dealt only with arrays consisting of single, one-dimensional lists of values. We can also set up arrays with more than one dimension. For instance, a two-dimensional array will store a matrix of values, which can be envisaged as occupying the squares of a chess board type of structure (see figure 12.1).

Here, we need two indices to reference the array elements: the first for the rows, the second for the columns. The indices are separated by commas, as in figure 12.1. When we set up an array of this kind, we must enclose the dimensions of the array in quotes. The following statement creates a 3 × 3 array, each element initially having the null string as its value:

```
SQUARE  =  ARRAY('3,3')
```

1,1	1,2	1,3
2,1	2,2	2,3
3,1	3,2	3,3

Figure 12.1 References in a two-dimensional array

Indeed, the dimension of a one-dimensional array can also be enclosed in quotes, though, as we have seen, it is not necessary to do so. Thus instead of our earlier statement

```
        MONTHS  =  ARRAY(12)
```

we could have written

```
        MONTHS  =  ARRAY('12')
```

with the same effect. The reason for having to enclose both dimensions of a two-dimensional array in quotes is that if we omit the quotes, or enclose only the first dimension in them, a *one*-dimensional array will be created, with the number of elements given by the first figure, each element being initialised to the value given by the second figure.

```
        SQUARE  =  ARRAY(3,3)
        SQUARE  =  ARRAY('3',3)
```

Either of these would create a one-dimensional array of 3 elements, each having the initial value 3.

When we wish to reference a two-dimensional array, we pick out the row and column by means of the two indices, separated by commas, within angle brackets. Thus the value in row 2, column 1, of the array SQUARE would be referenced by SQUARE<2,1>.

Two-dimensional arrays are needed less often than simple one-dimensional arrays, but can be useful if we need to cross-classify values.

For instance, if we were interested in the effect of age and sex on some linguistic variable, we might want to create, in the computer, the equivalent of a table giving information on that variable for particular age groupings and for each sex. If we had, say, 5 age groups, then a 5 × 2 array would be an obvious way to store the information. The following program shows how such an array could be used.

```
* THIS PROGRAM READS DATA FROM AN INFORMANT TEST, IN THE
* FOLLOWING FORMAT, BEGINNING AT POSITION 1:
* SEX*AGE GROUP*SCORE
* SEX IS ENCODED AS 1(=MALE) OR 2(=FEMALE), AGE GROUP AS 1 - 5.
* A 2-DIMENSIONAL ARRAY 'MATRIX' HOLDS THE SCORES BY AGE AND
* SEX; ANOTHER 2-DIMENSIONAL ARRAY 'COUNT' HOLDS THE NUMBERS
* OF INFORMANTS IN EACH AGE/SEX CELL.  THE PROGRAM CALCULATES
* THE MEAN SCORE FOR EACH COMBINATION OF SEX AND AGE GROUP.
*
* INITIALISATION
*
          &ANCHOR  =  1
          &TRIM  =  1
          DATAPAT  =  BREAK('*')  .  SEX  '*'  BREAK('*')  .
+         AGE  '*'  REM  .  SCORE
          MATRIX  =  ARRAY('5,2')
          COUNT  =  ARRAY('5,2')
*
* PROCESSING
*
* READ IN A LINE OF DATA; DETERMINE AGE, SEX, SCORE; ADD
* SCORE TO APPROPRIATE ARRAY ELEMENT.
*
READ      LINE  =  INPUT                              :F(HEAD)
          LINE  DATAPAT                               :F(ERR)
          MATRIX<AGE,SEX>  =  MATRIX<AGE,SEX>  +  SCORE
          COUNT<AGE,SEX>  =  COUNT<AGE,SEX>  +  1.0  :(READ)
*
* TERMINATION
*
* PRINT RESULTS.
*
HEAD      J  =  1
```

```
         HEADING1  =  'MALES'
         HEADING2  =  'MEAN SCORES FOR '
         HEADING3  =  ' IN THE 5 AGE GROUPS'
PRINT    HEADING  =  HEADING2  HEADING1  HEADING3
         OUTPUT  =
         OUTPUT  =  HEADING
         OUTPUT  =  DUPL('-',SIZE(HEADING))
         OUTPUT  =
         I  =  1
PRINT.1  OUTPUT  =  'GROUP '  I  DUPL(' ',10)  MATRIX<I,J>
+                   /  COUNT<I,J>
         I  =  LT(I,5)  I  +  1                    :S(PRINT.1)
         J  =  EQ(J,1)  J  +  1                    :F(END)
         HEADING2  =  'FEMALES'
         OUTPUT  =                                 :(PRINT)
*
* ERROR MESSAGE
*
ERR      OUTPUT  =  'DATA FORMAT INCORRECT IN FOLLOWING ENTRY: '
+                   LINE                           :(READ)
END
```

We shall not go through this program line by line. It should nevertheless be studied carefully, not only for the use of arrays, but also with regard to the printing of the headings and results. Note especially the use of one loop (the I-loop) within another (the J-loop) in the printing of results.

12.3 Tables

Arrays are useful when we wish to reference a list of values by means of a numerical index, as in the examples discussed so far. SNOBOL4 also provides a second kind of structure called a *table*, which differs from an array in two important respects. A table can be referenced by any type of object, not just by numbers. We can, for example, set up a table whose values are referenced by strings, a facility which is particularly useful when we want to store information concerned with the words in a text without knowing in advance which words will occur. A second difference between a table and an array is that a table has no fixed size, but grows as required.

If it is known in advance roughly how many variables a table needs to contain, then the table can be created by calling the built-in function TABLE with two arguments, as in the following example:

```
WCOUNT  =  TABLE(100,20)
```

This will set up a table whose initial size is 100, but to which additional capacity is automatically added, 20 at a time, if needed. More usually, we do not know how many variables we may need, and TABLE can then be called with no arguments, but still with the brackets, as follows:

```
WCOUNT  =  TABLE()
```

In this case, the computer assumes a default value of 10 for the initial size, and increases this by 10 each time additional space is required.

References are made to a table in the same way as to an array, except that the index need not be a number. For instance, if we wish to reference the value of a table element labelled by the string 'COMPUTER' and add one to it, we can write:

```
WCOUNT<'COMPUTER'>  =  WCOUNT<'COMPUTER'>  +  1
```

As with arrays, it may be useful to think of tables as boxes containing drawers: in the case of a table, the drawers can be labelled with strings as well as with numbers, and the number of drawers expands as required, while for arrays the drawers can only be identified by number, and there is a fixed number of them.

At the end of a computational sequence involving a table, we may well wish to print the contents of the table. It will be remembered that this can be done for an array by using a loop which outputs the value of each array element in turn, and it is easy to print, alongside this value, the number of the element concerned. With a table, however, we have the probem of not knowing what items have been used to create the table elements (for instance what words have occurred in a text). This problem is solved by converting the table into a two-dimensional array. If there are N different indices for the table (for example, N different word forms in a text being subjected to a word count), the resulting array will be N-by-2. Each row will contain a table index (for instance a word form) in the first column of the array, and the value of that cell of the table in the second column. The conversion procedure is effected by means of the function CONVERT which we met in section 9.2 in relation to the interconversion of integers and real numbers. If we want to convert the table called WCOUNT to an array, we write:

```
WCOUNT  =  CONVERT(WCOUNT,'ARRAY')
```

We could, of course, have used a different variable as the name of the new array.

Let us now see how a table is used in a word-counting program. We shall develop a program for printing all the words in a text ending in ING, together with their frequencies. We first set &TRIM and &ANCHOR, and set up a pattern to isolate words in the normal way:

```
&TRIM   =  1
&ANCHOR  =  1
LETTERS  =  "ABCDEFGHIJKLMNOPQRSTUVWXYZ'-"
WPAT  =  BREAK(LETTERS)  SPAN(LETTERS)  .  WORD
```

We also set up a table, which we shall call INGCOUNT:

```
INGCOUNT  =  TABLE()
```

We now read in a line of text and isolate a word, then delete the word:

```
READ     LINE  =  INPUT                          :F(CONV)
GETW     LINE  WPAT  =                           :F(READ)
```

We now test to see if the word ends in ING. Since, for efficiency, we have set the anchor to be on, we must use RTAB rather than RPOS here (see section 10.2):

```
WORD  RTAB(3)  'ING'                  :F(GETW)
```

If the pattern match fails, we loop back to fetch another word. If it succeeds, we add 1 to the value of the table element INGCOUNT<WORD>. If the first word in the text ending in ING is SLEEPING, the program will now create an element in the table INGCOUNT, with the index SLEEPING, and will add 1 to its initially null value. This element will have its value incremented by 1 every time a further instance of SLEEPING is encountered.

```
INGCOUNT<WORD>  =  INGCOUNT<WORD>  +  1   :(GETW)
```

The program now loops back to search for another word, which will be assigned as the new value of WORD. The next time the reference INGCOUNT<WORD> is encountered, a table element with an index corresponding to the new word is created, if it does not already exist, and so on.

When there are no more data, control is transferred to the label CONV. We now convert the table to an array, so that we can print the contents:

```
CONV     NEWCOUNT  =  CONVERT(INGCOUNT,'ARRAY')     :F(ERR)
```

We put a fail-safe go-to on this statement just in case the conversion goes wrong. This would happen if for some reason the table contained no elements with non-null values (for instance, if there were no words ending in ING in the text).

Printing the array values is now an easy matter. We set up a counter, output the row of the array corresponding to it, and then increment the counter and repeat the process. The loop terminates when the counter exceeds the number of rows in the array (which, as we have seen, we do not need to know).

```
          I = 1
PRINT     OUTPUT = NEWCOUNT<I,1> DUPL(' ',25 - SIZE(NEWCOUNT<I,1>))
+                  NEWCOUNT<I,2>                    :F(END)
          I = I + 1                                 :(PRINT)
```

It now remains only to add the error statement labelled ERR, and the END statement. The writing out of the complete program, with appropriate comment lines, is left as an exercise for the reader.

12.4 Programmer-defined data types

In linguistic and literary applications of computing, we are often interested in entities which all possess a number of attributes relevant to our concerns. For instance, a subject in a language-teaching experiment might be coded for age, sex, social class, IQ and score on a battery of tests; or a word might have its length, part of speech classification and position in sentence recorded. In SNOBOL4 we can refer to such entities and their properties by means of *programmer-defined data types*. These are created by using the built-in function DATA, which sets up the required data type, giving it a name and a number of 'fields' representing the relevant properties. For subjects in a language-teaching experiment we might set up a data type LTSUBJ as follows:

```
DATA('LTSUBJ(AGE,SEX,CLASS,IQ,SCORE)')
```

For words in a text we might set up a data type WORDTYPE:

```
DATA('WORDTYPE(LENGTH,WCLASS,POSN)')
```

Note how the DATA statement is written: the function DATA takes a single argument (in brackets as always), which is written as a string (and therefore enclosed in quotes). The string consists of the name of the data type (here, LTSUBJ or WORDTYPE) followed by the field names, separated by commas and enclosed overall in brackets.

Having set up a data type, we can then create specific objects of that type, and assign them to variables if we wish. Thus if we write:

```
S1  =  LTSUBJ(12,'M',3,105,76)
```

we create an object of the type LTSUBJ, with the values 12 for the AGE field, M for SEX, 3 for CLASS, 105 for IQ and 76 for SCORE, and assign this object as the value of S1. As a further example, consider the following:

```
LONGWD  =  WORDTYPE(24,'NOUN',8)
```

This creates an object of the type WORDTYPE, with a value of 24 for the LENGTH field, NOUN for WCLASS and 8 for POSN, and assigns the object as the value of LONGWD.

The field identifiers act like functions, which can be used to refer to particular fields of a given object. For example:

```
OUTPUT  =  SCORE(S1)
```

prints the value of the SCORE field of the object S1 – that is, 76. If we write:

```
HALFLEN  =  LENGTH(LONGWD)  /  2
```

we halve the value of the LENGTH field of the object LONGWD, and assign the result (which is 12) to the variable HALFLEN.

We can also make assignments to particular fields of given objects by using the field name. For instance, the statement

```
IQ(S1)  = 150
```

changes the value of the IQ field of S1 to 150.

We do not have to specify a value for every field when we create a data object. If, for a data type with, say, five fields, we specify only four values when we create a particular object, these values will be taken as those of the first four fields, and the fifth field will have a null value. Thus:

```
S2  =  LTSUBJ(15,'F',4,125)
```

creates an object of the type LTSUBJ, with 15 as the value of the AGE field, F as the value of SEX, 4 as the value of CLASS, and 125 as the value of IQ, but with a null value for the SCORE field. If we want to leave out a value in the middle of a list of fields rather than at the end, we simply leave nothing between successive commas (equivalent to saying that a given field should have the null string as its value). Thus:

```
WD1  =  WORDTYPE(10,,12)
```

creates an object, assigned to WD1, of the type WORDTYPE, with 10 as the value of the LENGTH field, and 12 as the value of POSN, but with a null value for the WCLASS field.

The following program uses a programmer-defined data type, and calculates the mean length of words in each of the first 10 positions of the sentences of a text.

```
* THIS PROGRAM CALCULATES THE MEAN LENGTH OF WORDS IN EACH OF
* THE FIRST 10 POSITIONS IN THE SENTENCES OF A TEXT.
*
* INITIALISATION
*
          &TRIM = 1
*
* SET UP PATTERNS TO ISOLATE SENTENCES, AND WORDS WITHIN THESE.
*
          LETTERS = "ABCDEFGHIJKLMNOPQRSTUVWXYZ'-"
          WPAT = BREAK(LETTERS) SPAN(LETTERS) . WORD
          SENTEND = '.?!'
          SPAT = (BREAK(SENTEND) ANY(SENTEND)) . SENT
          DEFINE('SENT()')
*
* SET UP A DATA TYPE 'WDFORM' WITH FIELDS CORRESPONDING TO
* LENGTH AND POSITION IN SENTENCE.
*
          DATA('WDFORM(LENGTH,POSN)')
A
* INITIALISE VARIABLES TO 0.
*
          W = 0; L = 0; I = 0; COUNT = 0 ; SUM = 0
*
* INPUT MAXIMUM NUMBER OF WORDS IN THE TEXT, AND CREATE AN
* ARRAY TO STORE INFORMATION ON THESE.
*
      N = TRIM(INPUT)
      WDS = ARRAY(N)
*
* PROCESSING
*
* READ IN THE FIRST LINE OF DATA (THE FUNCTION 'SENT' INPUTS
* THE REST).
```

```
*
         LINE  =  INPUT                              :F(NODATA)
*
* ISOLATE A SENTENCE USING THE FUNCTION 'SENT'.
*
GETSENT  SENTENCE  =  SENT()                         :F(CALC)
*
* P COUNTS THE POSITION OF THE WORD IN A SENTENCE.
*
         P  =  0
*
* ISOLATE A WORD, RECORD POSITION IN SENTENCE, ALSO TOTAL
* WORD COUNT TO DATE.
*
GETWD    SENTENCE  WPAT  =                           :F(GETSENT)
         P  =  P  +  1
         W  =  W  +  1
*
* ASSIGN LENGTH AND POSITION TO APPROPRIATE FIELDS OF 'WDFORM'
* AND ASSIGN THIS DATA OBJECT TO A NEW ELEMENT OF THE ARRAY 'WDS'.
*
         WDS<W>  =  WDFORM(SIZE(WORD),P)             :S(GETWD)F(ERR)
*
* TERMINATION
*
* CALCULATE AND PRINT MEAN LENGTH FOR WORDS IN EACH OF FIRST
* 10 POSITIONS IN SENTENCE.
*
CALC     L  =  LT(L,10)  L  +  1                     :F(END)
INC.I    I  =  LT(I,W)  I  +  1                      :F(MEAN)
         SUM  =  EQ(POSN(WDS<I>),L)  SUM  +  LENGTH(WDS<I>)
+                                                    :F(INC.I)
*
* 'COUNT' COUNTS THE NUMBER OF SENTENCES OF LENGTH L OR GREATER.
*
         COUNT  =  COUNT  +  1                       :(INC.I)
MEAN     OUTPUT  =  'MEAN LENGTH OF WORDS AT POSITION '  L
+        ' = '  SUM  /  COUNT  *  1.0  ' , BASED ON '  COUNT
+        ' SENTENCES'
```

```
          OUTPUT  =
          COUNT  =  0;  I  =  0                       :(CALC)
*
* FUNCTION 'SENT'
*
SENT      LINE  SPAT  =                               :S(RETURN)
          LINE  =  LINE  ' '  INPUT                   :S(SENT)F(FRETURN)
SENT.END
*
* ERROR MESSAGES
*
NODATA    OUTPUT  =  'THERE IS NO TEXT FOR ANALYSIS'     :(END)
ERR       OUTPUT  =  'ARRAY BOUNDS EXCEEDED'
END
```

The logic of the program should be clear from the comments, so we shall simply note here the way in which the data type WDFORM is used. The statement

```
WDS<W>  =  WDFORM(SIZE(WORD),P)                       :S(GETWD)F(ERR)
```

both creates a new object of the type WDFORM, with values for the LENGTH and POSN fields appropriate to the word being processed, and also assigns this object as the value of the next element of the array WDS. In the later statement

```
       SUM  =  EQ(POSN(WDS<I>),L)  SUM  +  LENGTH(WDS<I>)
+                                                     :F(INC.I)
```

we have referred to an object of the type WDFORM by means of a reference to the array element of which it is the value. Field names are applied to the variable WDS<I> in order to refer to the values of particular fields.

A particularly important feature of programmer-defined data types is that they can be used to build up complex networks of structured associations between data objects. A simple but useful kind of data structure is a *linked list*. Each item in the list is linked to the next by having, as the value of one of its fields, the data object which is next in the list. Part of the specification of each item thus 'points' to the next item in the list. The final item in the list has no pointer (that is, it has a null value for the field containing the specification of the next item).

The following program sets up a linked list of all the text lines in a poem which has been typed into a data file with references to stanza numbers in angle brackets on a separate line before each stanza, thus:

```
<1>
(first stanza)
<2>
(second stanza), etc.
```

For each text line, a data object of the type POEMLINE is created, with fields corresponding to the text line itself, the stanza number, the line number within each stanza, and a pointer to the next text line. The final part of the program reads through the linked list representing the poem, and prints out each line which contains a question mark, together with the relevant stanza number and line number. Clearly, any other kind of search could be performed on the linked list, according to the needs of the programmer.

```
* THIS PROGRAM STORES THE TEXT LINES OF A POEM IN A LINKED LIST,
* AND THEN READS THROUGH THE LIST, PRINTING OUT ALL LINES WHICH
* CONTAIN A QUESTION MARK, TOGETHER WITH THE STANZA AND LINE
* NUMBERS.
*
* INITIALISATION
*
          &TRIM   =  1
          &ANCHOR  =  1
          DATA('POEMLINE(LINE,STANZANO,LINENO,NEXT)')
*
* PROCESSING
*
* TEST FOR REFERENCE FOR STANZA 1, THEN ISOLATE FIRST TEXT LINE.
* CREATE A DATA OBJECT OF THE TYPE 'POEMLINE' WITH THE FIRST LINE
* AS THE VALUE OF THE 'LINE' FIELD, 1 AS THE VALUE OF 'STANZANO',
* 1 AS THE VALUE OF 'LINENO', AND AN (AS YET) NULL 'NEXT' FIELD.
*
          INPUT  '<1>'                          :F(ERR)
          L  =  1;  N  =  1
          FIRST  =  POEMLINE(INPUT,N,L)
*
* 'CURRENT' HOLDS THE LINE CURRENTLY BEING PROCESSED, TOGETHER
* WITH ITS PROPERTIES.
*
          CURRENT  =  FIRST
*
* READ IN NEXT LINE AFTER INCREMENTING LINE NUMBER.
```

```
*
INC.L     L  =  L  +  1
          STRING  =  INPUT                          :F(CONT)
*
* TEST TO SEE IF IT IS A REFERENCE LINE.  IF SO, RESET L TO 0
* AND INCREMENT N BY 1.  IF NOT, CREATE AN OBJECT OF THE TYPE
* 'POEMLINE' CORRESPONDING TO THE LINE, AND ASSIGN THIS AS THE
* VALUE OF THE 'NEXT' FIELD OF 'CURRENT', SO CREATING A
* 'POINTER' FROM ONE LINE TO THE NEXT.
*
          STRING  '<'  N  '>'                       :S(RESET.L)
          NEXT(CURRENT)  =  POEMLINE(STRING,N,L)
*
* VALUE OF 'NEXT' FIELD OF CURRENT LINE BECOMES NEW 'CURRENT';
* THAT IS, THE NEW VALUE OF 'CURRENT' IS THE DATA OBJECT WHICH
* CORRESPONDS TO LINE L.  LOOP BACK FOR ANOTHER LINE.
*
          CURRENT  =  NEXT(CURRENT)                 :(INC.L)
RESET.L   L  =  0
          N  =  N  +  1                             :(INC.L)
*
* PROCESS LIST TO ISOLATE LINES CONTAINING '?'.
*
CONT      CURRENT  =  FIRST
TEST      LINE(CURRENT)  BREAK('?')  '?'            :F(NEXTLINE)
          OUTPUT  =  'STANZA '  STANZANO(CURRENT)  ', LINE '
+         LINENO(CURRENT)  ': '  LINE(CURRENT)
*
* USE POINTER TO MOVE TO NEXT LINE.
*
NEXTLINE  CURRENT  =  NEXT(CURRENT)
*
* TEST IF LIST EXHAUSTED:  DATA OBJECT FOR LAST LINE HAS NULL
* 'NEXT' FIELD.
*
          IDENT(CURRENT)                            :S(END)F(TEST)
*
* ERROR MESSAGE
*
ERR       OUTPUT  =  'NO REFERENCE FOR STANZA 1'
END
```

The way in which this program works should be clear from the comment lines. The crucial feature is the use of the NEXT field of the data object as a pointer to the next link in the chain.

12.5 Prototypes

Arrays and programmer-defined data types, also programmer-defined functions, have what is known as a 'prototype'. For a function, the prototype is the string argument of the DEFINE function. Consider the function CHARCT defined as follows in the discussion of programmer-defined functions in section 11.2:

```
DEFINE('CHARCT(CHAR,STRING)')
```

Here, the prototype of CHARCT is the string CHARCT(CHAR,STRING). For a programmer-defined data type, the prototype is the string argument of DATA. For the data type WORDTYPE defined as follows in section 12.4

```
DATA('WORDTYPE(LENGTH,WCLASS,POSN)')
```

the prototype is the string WORDTYPE(LENGTH,WCLASS,POSN). For an array, the prototype is a string corresponding to the first argument of the array, giving the dimensions of the array (usually, as we have seen, this is the only specified argument). Thus for the array MONTHS, defined as

```
MONTHS  =  ARRAY(12)
```

or as

```
MONTHS  =  ARRAY('12')
```

the prototype is the string (not the number!) 12. For the two-dimensional array COUNT, defined as

```
COUNT  =  ARRAY('5,2')
```

the prototype is the string 5,2. It can sometimes be useful to know the prototype of an array, for example if we wish to create a second array with the same number of elements as there are in an original array, but we do not know just how many this is because the original array is the product of conversion from a table. In such cases, the built-in function PROTOTYPE may be used. This function takes an array name as its argument, and returns as its value the string constituting the prototype of the array. Suppose that we have converted a table into a two-dimensional array named NEWARR. We know that there are two 'columns' in this array, but we do not know how many 'rows' there are. The following statement will determine this number and assign it as the value of N:

```
PROTOTYPE(NEWARR)  BREAK(',')  .  N  ',2'  RPOS(0)
```

For further examples of list processing in SNOBOL4 and a discussion of other types of data structure, readers are referred to Griswold (1975).

Exercises 12

1 Write a program which will read in poetry from a file and print a table giving the numbers of lines containing 0, 1, 2, etc. punctuation marks. Assume that the only punctuation marks in the text are the comma, full stop, semicolon, colon, question mark and exclamation mark, and that usually no line will have more than eight punctuation marks.

2 Write a program which will give a list, with frequencies, of all characters, and combinations of characters, in a text which are not upper case letters, numbers or blanks. (Note that combinations such as ," or . . . may occur in some texts, also that other symbols such as % or £ may have been used for special purposes. in encoding the text.)

3 Write a program which will print out all the words which occur only once in a text, in five columns each of width 25 characters, and then print the total number of such words.

4 Write a program which will (i) read each word of a text, together with a following blank or punctuation mark, into a linked list, (ii) search through the list and print out all occurrences of the word AND together with the next word and any associated punctuation, and (iii) finally search the list again,and print all occurrences of the word BUT together with the next word and any associated punctuation.

13 Debugging a SNOBOL4 program

13.1 Types of error

It is quite rare for a program of any complexity to run absolutely correctly first time, and a considerable amount of time may be spent in detecting and correcting errors. In computing jargon, errors are referred to as 'bugs', and the process of detection and correction as 'debugging'. Some bugs are fairly obvious because they are signalled by the system in the form of error reports. Such errors will normally cause the program to fail. Other bugs, however, are much harder to track down and eradicate because, although the program produces unexpected or 'wrong' results, it does not fail, and no error messages are produced. In such cases, the programmer's instrutions were presumably syntactically acceptable to the computer, but their 'semantic' interpretation was not what the programmer intended. Even where the computer does signal an error by means of a report, it may not always be clear exactly where things went wrong, since errors at one point in a program can sometimes be due to operations performed elsewhere in the program. It is often found that a change in the data on which a program operates throws up new bugs: for instance, if a text analysis program has been written to analyse texts typed into a file in a certain format, with certain coding conventions (e.g. signs for capitals, foreign names, and so on), the program may fail or produce nonsensical results (or, even worse, apparently sensible but incorrect results) when used with a differently coded text.

As was mentioned briefly in section 1.3, the way in which the high-level language 'source' program is converted into an 'object' program in machine code varies from one implementation of a language to another. Because of this, the facilities for the detection of errors also differ somewhat as between different implementations. The discussion in the present chapter is based on Version 4 of the SPITBOL variant of SNOBOL4, as run on the ICL 2977 computer at the University of Nottingham.

In this implementation the running of a SPITBOL program can be divided into three phases. In the first phase the SPITBOL program is converted into an intermediate, more compact form. Errors detected at this stage are described by the system as *compilation errors*, though strictly speaking the process of compilation involves the whole of the conversion of source code right through to machine code. The instructions encoded in the intermediate form are then interpreted and carried out during the 'execution' phase, when further errors, known as *execution errors*, may be detected. After the execution phase, there is a *termination* phase, during which the computer outputs certain information about the processes it has carried out.

13.2 Errors signalled by the system

13.2.1 Compilation errors

As each statement is compiled it is printed, together with an identifying number, so that a program listing will precede the results. (It is possible to turn off this listing, but we shall not deal with this here: for details see Griswold, Poage and Polonsky 1971: 173.) Each statement is checked for errors as it is compiled. If none are found, this is indicated in the compilation statistics printed at the end of the listing (in the implementation described here the message is COMP ERRORS 0). If compilation errors are found, the number of such errors is given after the listing. For each line containing an error, a self-explanatory message giving the nature of the error is printed under the program line, together with a marker giving a rough approximation to the position of the error. Only the first error in any line is detected, so it is important, when correcting compilation errors, to check that the statement does not contain more than one error. In the implementation described here, programs containing compilation errors do not proceed to the execution phase. In other implementations, execution is not inhibited provided that the number of compilation errors does not exceed some specified limit, but any attempt to execute a statement containing such an error will cause failure.

An example of a program containing compilation errors, with the messages printed by the system, is given below. Statement 4 should read:

```
VPAT   =  BREAK(VOWELS)  VOWELS  VOWELS
```

In statement 7, the operator + is used without any blank to the left, and in statement 8 the rules for label construction have been flouted, since a label must begin with a letter or number.

```
* THIS PROGRAM COUNTS THE NUMBER OF WORDS IN A TEXT WHICH
* CONTAIN TWO OR MORE SUCCESSIVE VOWELS.
*
* INITIALISATION
*
```

```
1                 &ANCHOR  =  1
2                 &TRIM  =  1
3                 VOWELS  =  ANY('AEIOU')
4                 VPAT  =  BREAK(VOWELS  VOWELS  VOWELS
                                                          !
ERROR 226 -- SYNTAX ERROR. MISSING RIGHT PAREN

        *
        * PROCESSING
        *
5       READ      LINE  =  INPUT                                         :F(PRINT)
6       TEST      LINE  VPAT  =                                          :(READ)
7                 CT  =  CT+  1                                          :(TEST)
                                  !
ERROR 233 -- SYNTAX ERROR. INVALID USE OF OPERATOR


        *
        * TERMINATION
        *
8       %PRINT    OUTPUT  =  'THE NUMBER OF WORDS CONTAINING '

        !
ERROR 214 -- SYNTAX ERROR. BAD LABEL OR MISPLACED CONTINUATION LINE

        +         'TWO SUCCESSIVE VOWELS  IS '  CT
9       END


STORE USED       1511
STORE LEFT       31226
COMP ERRORS      3
REGENERATIONS    0
COMP TIME-MSEC   112
```

13.2.2 Execution errors

Additional errors may be encountered during the execution of a compiled program. Consider a statement such as the following:

```
COUNT  =  COUNT  +  1                              :(NEXT)
```

There is nothing syntactically wrong with this statement, and no error will be signalled during compilation. However, if there is no statement labelled NEXT in the program, any attempt to execute the above statement will fail. Some execution errors are so serious that they always cause program failure; others are less serious, and are said to be 'conditionally fatal'. The number of conditionally fatal errors tolerated before abandoning the job is determined by the value of a keyword, &ERRLIMIT. The default value is zero, so that any execution error causes the program to terminate in failure. &ERRLIMIT can be reset to, say, 10 if the user wishes execution to continue up to a limit of 10 conditionally fatal errors.

On encountering a fatal execution error (or any error, in the default situation), and so terminating the program, the system prints a message, following any output which may already have been generated up to the point where the program failed. The message gives a short description of the error, and indicates which statement was at fault. If no errors are

```
      * THIS PROGRAM COUNTS THE NUMBER OF WORDS IN A TEXT WHICH
      * CONTAIN TWO OR MORE SUCCESSIVE VOWELS.
      *
      * INITIALISATION
      *
1               &ANCHOR  =  1
2               &TRIM  =  1
3               VOWELS  =  ANY('AEIOU')
4               VPAT  =  BREAK(VOWELS)  VOWELS  VOWELS
      *
      * PROCESSING
      *
5     READ      LINE  =  INPUT                               :F(PRINT)
6     TEST      LINE  VPAT  =                                :(READ)
7               CT  =  CT  +  1                              :(TEST)
      *
      * TERMINATION
      *
8     PRINT     OUTPUT  =  'THE NUMBER OF WORDS CONTAINING '
      +         'TWO SUCCESSIVE VOWELS  IS '  CT
9     END


STORE USED      1517
STORE LEFT      31220
COMP ERRORS     0
REGENERATIONS   0
COMP TIME-MSEC  120



ERROR 069 -- BREAK ARGUMENT IS NOT STRING OR EXPRESSION



IN STATEMENT    4
RUN TIME-MSEC   8
STMTS EXECUTED  4
MCSEC / STMT    2000
REGENERATIONS   0
```

found, a message is printed to the effect that normal termination has occurred at a particular statement number (which should be the END statement).

Above is given a version of the program for counting words containing two successive vowels, with the compilation errors corrected. It will be seen that there is still an error, which emerges only during execution. VOWELS has been defined as the *pattern* ANY('AEIOU'), and then used as the argument of BREAK. BREAK, however, requires a *string*, and not a pattern, as its argument. The individual statements are syntactically correct, but the way in which they interact during the execution phase is incorrect.

13.3 Errors during execution which are not signalled by the system

As noted earlier, it is not uncommon for a program to contain no compilation errors, and no execution errors of the type discussed above, and yet to produce no results, or results which are not those intended by the programmer. Because no message is printed as soon as such an error occurs, these bugs are sometimes quite hard to cure. In this section, we shall first consider some frequent sources of this type of error, and then discuss the facilities provided for the tracking down of such errors.

13.3.1 Frequent sources of error

Infinite loops

Consider the following statements:

```
TEST      LINE   ' AND '                          :F(READ)
          ANDCT  =  ANDCT  +  1                   :(TEST)
```

If the pattern match in the first line succeeds, ANDCT will be incremented, and control will pass back to TEST, where the same AND is found again, and the process will continue in an infinite loop. The problem is, of course, caused by the fact that the string being sought is not deleted when it is found. Thus the first line should read:

```
TEST      LINE   ' AND '  =                       :F(READ)
```

In practice, the computer will not go on forever executing a loop, because there is a limit to the total number of statements which can be executed before termination of a program run, and although the system will give no indication of the error itself, it will eventually print a message to the effect that the maximum number of statements has been exceeded. This limit is controlled by the value of the keyword &STLIMIT. The default value is 50 000, so that a considerable amount of valuable computer time may be wasted if a loop is encountered from which there is no exit. For this reason, it is good practice, when testing a program, to reset the value of &STLIMIT to a lower number which will still be adequate for the successful running of the program. For a short program, tested on a small set of data, we might write:

```
&STLIMIT  =  1000
```

For very large programs, or with a large amount of data to be processed, we may, after testing the program, actually need to increase &STLIMIT from the default value, say to 100 000 or even 500 000.

The reason for the infinite loop in the above example is fairly obvious. A subtler case is afforded by the following set of statements:

```
          PAT.1  =  'S'  LEN(2)  'P'
READ      LINE  =  INPUT                          :F(CONT)
```

```
TEST      LINE  PAT1  =                         :F(NEXT)
          CT  =  CT  +  1                       :(TEST)
NEXT ....
CONT ....
```

Because, in the statement labelled TEST, the pattern has been typed in incorrectly (as PAT1 rather than PAT.1), the computer takes PAT1 as a different pattern, with the null string as its value. Since an attempt to match the null string always succeeds, TEST will never fail, and an infinite loop will be set up. This is one of the penalties paid for the great flexibility of SNOBOL4, which, unlike some other languages, allows the programmer to use a new name anywhere in the program without having declared it first, or specifically assigned a value to it.

Statement failure due to more than one possible cause

Consider the case where we wish to read in a line of data and test it for some pattern PAT. We might try to do this economically, in one statement, as follows:

```
READ      INPUT  PAT                            :F(NODATA)
```

Here, the failure go-to is intended to deal with the situation where there are no more lines of data to read in. However, the statement could also fail because the line read in does not contain an instance of PAT. To avoid this, we must use two lines, with separate failure go-to's:

```
READ      LINE  =  INPUT                        :F(NODATA)
          LINE  PAT                             :F(NEXT)
```

Problems involving arrays

Errors can arise due to confusion over the difference between declaring a two-dimensional array with each cell initially null, and declaring a one-dimensional array with each element initially set to some given value. For instance,

```
ARR  =  ARRAY('10,10')
```

creates a 10-by-10 two-dimensional array with each cell initially null, whereas

```
ARR  =  ARRAY(10,'10')
```

or

```
ARR  =  ARRAY('10','10')
```

creates a one-dimensional array of 10 elements, each initially having the value 10.

Problems can also arise when tables are converted to arrays, for the purpose of printing their contents. If for some reason every entry in a table is null, the conversion will fail. If no failure go-to is provided, the non-existence of the required array may not be detected until a reference to the array is made, and this could be considerably further on in the program. All conversion statements should therefore have a failure go-to, as illustrated below:

```
          NEWTABL  =  CONVERT(TABL,'ARRAY')          :F(ERR)
          .
          .
          .
ERR       OUTPUT  =  'CONVERSION TO ARRAY FAILED'
```

Problems due to trailing blanks
Consider the following:

```
          &ANCHOR  =  0
READ      LINE  =  INPUT                             :F(END)
          LINE  '?'  RPOS(0)                         :F(READ)
          OUTPUT  =  LINE                            :(READ)
END
```

The program is intended to print all the text lines in a data file which end with a question mark. Unfortunately, unless there happen to be lines in the file with a question mark in the very last position of the 80 read by the SNOBOL4 program, the pattern match will always fail, because there will normally be trailing blanks at the end of each line, and the computer treats these as characters like any other. The remedy, of course, is to set &TRIM = 1 at the beginning of the program.

13.3.2 Facilities for tracing hidden errors

In tracking down execution errors with non-obvious causes, it is often useful to find out what the values of the program variables were when the program failed, or when it ended 'normally' but gave unexpected results. This can be achieved using the keyword &DUMP. If the value of &DUMP is set to a non-zero value, a 'dump' listing of the program variables and their values is given at the end of the run. In standard SNOBOL4, *any* non-zero value for &DUMP gives a list of the 'natural' variables and keywords, but does not list variables such as individual elements of arrays and tables, which are 'created' when the array or table is declared. In SPITBOL, &DUMP = 1 gives this kind of dump, but &DUMP = 2 gives, in addition, the value of each array and table element and each programmer-defined data object. Variables with null values are not listed. The information given by a dump can be extremely useful in pinpointing where a problem has arisen.

A second useful technique is to keep track of the changes in the values of a variable as the program is executed. To some extent, this can be achieved by inserting OUTPUT statements at appropriate places, to print the values of the variables concerned. An even more useful device, however, is provided by the TRACE facility, which allows the user to obtain a listing, at the end of the output for a run, of all assignments made to any variables he specifies. Let us suppose that we wish to trace assignments to a variable COUNT. We first set the trace mode (usually during initialisation) by assigning some positive integer as the value of the keyword &TRACE. For instance

```
&TRACE  =  1000
```

will allow up to 1 000 individual trace messages to be printed. This statement does not itself cause tracing to occur; to do this, we must use the built-in function TRACE, with the required variable as its argument, in quotes, thus:

```
TRACE('COUNT')
```

This will produce a listing of all assignments made to COUNT, together with the number of the statement in which the assignment was made, and the time (in milliseconds) which has elapsed since the beginning of program execution. An example of a program including both tracing and a dump is given below.

```
          * THIS PROGRAM IS INTENDED TO PRINT THE FIRST LETTER, THEN THE
          * FIRST TWO LETTERS, THEN THE FIRST THREE, ETC., FOR EACH
          * WORD IN A DATA FILE CONTAINING ONE WORD PER LINE.  THE
          * TEST DATA FILE CONTAINS JUST THREE WORDS.
          *
          * INITIALISATION
          *
1                   &STLIMIT = 50
2                   &DUMP = 1
3                   &TRACE = 1000
4                   &TRIM = 1
5                   &ANCHOR = 1
6                   TRACE('FIRSTN')
7                   TRACE('N')
8                   TRACE('WORD')
9                   FIRSTN = LEN(N)  .  OUTPUT
          *
          * PROCESSING
          *
10        READ      WORD = INPUT                           :F(END)
11        INC.N     N = N + 1
12                  WORD FIRSTN                            :S(INC.N)F(READ)
13        END


STORE USED       1260
STORE LEFT       31477
COMP ERRORS      0
REGENERATIONS    0
COMP TIME-MSEC   122

****9*******     FIRSTN = PATTERN
****10******     WORD = 'ONE'
****11******     N = 1
```

```
****11******  N = 2

****11******  N = 3

****11******  N = 4

****11******  N = 5

****11******  N = 6

****11******  N = 7

****11******  N = 8

****11******  N = 9

****11******  N = 10

****11******  N = 11

****11******  N = 12

****11******  N = 13

****11******  N = 14

****11******  N = 15

****11******  N = 16

****11******  N = 17

****11******  N = 18

****11******  N = 19

****11******  N = 20



ERROR 244 -- STATEMENT COUNT EXCEEDS VALUE OF STLIMIT KEYWORD



IN STATEMENT    11
RUN TIME-MSEC   50
STMTS EXECUTED  50
MCSEC / STMT    1000
REGENERATIONS   0


DUMP OF NATURAL VARIABLES

FIRSTN = PATTERN
INPUT = 'ONE'
N = 20
WORD = 'ONE'


DUMP OF KEYWORD VALUES

&ANCHOR = 1
&CODE = 0
&DUMP = 1
&ERRLIMIT = 0
&ERRTEXT = 'STATEMENT COUNT EXCEEDS VALUE OF STLIMIT KEYWORD'
&ERRTYPE = 244
&FNCLEVEL = 0
&FTRACE = 0
&INPUT = 1
&LASTNO = 12
&MAXLNGTH = 5000
&OUTPUT = 1
```

```
&PROFILE = 0
&RTNTYPE = ''
&STCOUNT = 50
&STLIMIT = 50
&STNO = 11
&TRACE = 978
&TRIM = 1
```

The program is intended to print, for each word, one letter, then two letters, then three, and so on. Since the data file contains the words

```
ONE

TWO

THREE
```

the output should be:

```
O

ON

ONE

T

TW

TWO

T

TH

THR

THRE

THREE
```

In fact, no output is produced, except for compilation and execution statistics, the trace and dump information, and an error message to the effect that the permitted number of statements has been exceeded. The trace and dump facilities allow us to track down the source of the error. Since only the string ONE has been assigned to WORD, it is clear that the computer never gets beyond the first data item. The trace of the variable N shows that its value keeps on being incremented, suggesting that we have set up an infinite loop. The dump confirms that only the string ONE has been input, and that the number of statements executed is indeed that set as a maximum in the program. The infinite loop is clearly composed of statements 11 and 12, which in turn means that statement 12 never fails. It will be remembered from p. 191 that such a situation can arise when the null string is being matched. We therefore examine the pattern FIRSTN to see if this could be the case. We note that when this pattern is defined, the value of N is 0, and since LEN(0) is equivalent to the null string, we have located the cause of our problem. We should, of course, have used the unevaluated expression operator, thus:

```
FIRSTN = LEN(*N) . OUTPUT
```

We can also trace labels, or even keywords, if we wish. To trace a label TEST, we set &TRACE to an appropriate value, and also write:

```
TRACE('TEST','LABEL')
```

The nature of the object to be traced is given as a second argument, again in quotes. In fact, the statement

```
TRACE('COUNT')
```

given above is equivalent to:

```
TRACE('COUNT','VALUE')
```

but since VALUE is the default value of the second argument, it can be omitted.

We can also trace individual programmer-defined functions using TRACE (for details, see Griswold, Poage and Polonsky, 1971: 153–7); however, a generally more useful method is to use the special keyword &FTRACE. When this is set to a positive integer, *all* programmer-defined functions are automatically traced, without the need to associate any tracing function with the individual function names. Thus:

```
&FTRACE = 1000
```

will cause tracing of all programmer-defined functions, up to a limit of 1 000 individual trace messages. Each time a function is called, a message is printed, giving the name of the function, the value of its argument(s), and the statement number in which the function call occurs. Each time a function returns, another message is printed, giving the function name and the value, if any, which is returned. In the following program, intended to test a function COMMACT which returns the number of commas in a string, the function does not work properly, and an execution error is signalled, to the effect that a return has been made from 'level zero'. Level zero is, in fact, the level of the main program body, level 1 referring to the level of a function procedure itself. In a function which calls itself recursively (a perfectly legitimate state of affairs in SNOBOL4, as pointed out in section 11.6), there will be additional 'embedded' levels numbered 2, 3, and so on. Our function contains no such recursion, and we should expect it to return from level 1. It seems to have returned from the level of the main program, thus causing an error. The trace information confirms that the function has indeed been called, with the first data line as its argument, and that the correct value for COMMACT has been calculated. It also shows, however, that the function has not even been called to analyse the second line. Examining the program more closely, we see that we have allowed control to flow into the function, after statement 9, because we have failed to provide a go-to which directs control back to READ. Adding this go-to corrects the problem, as seen in the second lot of output reproduced below.

```
        * THIS PROGRAM TESTS THE FUNCTION 'COMMACT', WHICH COUNTS THE
        * NUMBER OF COMMAS IN A STRING.
        *
        * INITIALISATION
        *
1                 &TRIM   =  1
2                 &ANCHOR   =  1
3                 &FTRACE   =  1000
4                 FINDCOM   =  BREAK(',')  ','
5                 DEFINE('COMMACT(STRING)')
6                 N  =  1
        *
        * PROCESSING
        *
7       READ      LINE  =  INPUT                          :F(END)
8                 OUTPUT  =  'THE NUMBER OF COMMAS IN LINE '
        +         N  ' IS '  COMMACT(LINE)
9                 N  =  N  +  1
        *
        * FUNCTION 'COMMACT'
        *
10      COMMACT
11                COMMACT  =  0
12      COMMACT.1 STRING  FINDCOM  =                      :F(RETURN)
13                COMMACT  =  COMMACT  +  1               :(COMMACT.1)
14      COMMACT.END
        *
15      END


STORE USED       1273
STORE LEFT       31464
COMP ERRORS      0
REGENERATIONS    0
COMP TIME-MSEC   127


****8*******   COMMACT('CLEARLY, THIS DATA LINE CONTAINS ONE COMMA.'
****12******   RETURN COMMACT = 1
THE NUMBER OF COMMAS IN LINE 1 IS 1


ERROR 242 -- FUNCTION RETURN FROM LEVEL ZERO


IN STATEMENT     12
RUN TIME-MSEC    14
STMTS EXECUTED   17
MCSEC / STMT     823
REGENERATIONS    0
```

```
       * THIS PROGRAM TESTS THE FUNCTION 'COMMACT', WHICH COUNTS THE
       * NUMBER OF COMMAS IN A STRING.
       *
       * INITIALISATION
       *
1                &TRIM    =  1
2                &ANCHOR  =  1
3                &FTRACE  =  1000
4                FINDCOM  =  BREAK(',')  ','
5                DEFINE('COMMACT(STRING)')
6                N  =  1
       *
       * PROCESSING
       *
7      READ      LINE  =  INPUT                              :F(END)
8                OUTPUT  =  'THE NUMBER OF COMMAS IN LINE '
       +         N  ' IS '  COMMACT(LINE)
9                N  =  N  +  1                               :(READ)
       *
       * FUNCTION 'COMMACT'
       *
10     COMMACT
11               COMMACT  =  0
12     COMMACT.1 STRING  FINDCOM  =                          :F(RETURN)
13               COMMACT  =  COMMACT  +  1                   :(COMMACT.1)
14     COMMACT.END
       *
15     END


STORE USED      1273
STORE LEFT      31464
COMP ERRORS     0
REGENERATIONS   0
COMP TIME-MSEC  141


****8*******  COMMACT('CLEARLY, THIS DATA LINE CONTAINS ONE COMMA.'
****12******  RETURN COMMACT = 1
THE NUMBER OF COMMAS IN LINE 1 IS 1
****8*******  COMMACT('THIS LINE, EVIDENTLY, CONTAINS TWO.')
****12******  RETURN COMMACT = 2
THE NUMBER OF COMMAS IN LINE 2 IS 2
****8*******  COMMACT('BUT THIS ONE CONTAINS NONE AT ALL.')
****12******  RETURN COMMACT = 0
THE NUMBER OF COMMAS IN LINE 3 IS 0


NORMAL END
IN STATEMENT    15
RUN TIME-MSEC   20
STMTS EXECUTED  32
MCSEC / STMT    625
REGENERATIONS   0
```

Exercises 13

1 Correct the following statements, each of which contains at least one error.

(i)
```
                 AV  =  TOTAL/COUNT
```
(ii)
```
       $PRINT    OUTPUT  =  'THE AVERAGE WORD LENGTH IS AV
```
(iii)
```
                 LINE  BREAK(ANY('!.,;:'))  .  UPTOPUNCT
```
(iv)
```
                 OUTPUT  =  'THE NUMBER OF WORDS BEGINNING
       + WITH E IS '  ECOUNT
```

(v)
```
               OUTPUT  =  'THE TOTAL NUMBER OF WORDS IS '  TO
     +TAL                           :(NEXT;3)
```
(vi)
```
               N  =  (SIZE(WORD - 1) / 2) * X
```

2 Each of the following short programs either contains one or more fatal errors or will produce results clearly not intended by the programmer. If you have access to a computer on which SNOBOL4 programs can be run, type in each program and run it with a small amount of suitable data. Then correct any compilation errors and rerun. Finally, correct any execution errors, using the &DUMP and tracing facilities to help you spot them, and then run the programs again, with a number of different data sets. If you have no access to a computer, still try to correct the programs.

(i)

```
* THIS PROGRAM READS IN LINES OF POETRY AND PRINTS OUT THOSE ENDING
* WITH A PUNCTUATION MARK OTHER THAN QUOTATION MARKS.
          &ANCHOR  =  1        TRIM  =  1
          PUNC  =  ANY('.,;:!?')
READ      LINE  =  INPUT
          LINE  BREAK(PUNC)  PUNC  RPOS(0)        :F(READ)
          OUTPUT  =  LINE                         :READ
END
```

(ii)

```
* THIS PROGRAM COUNTS THE NUMBER OF THREE-LETTER WORDS IN
  A TEXT.
          &ANCHOR=1;&TRIM=1
          LETTERS  =  "ABCDEFGHIJKLMNOPQRSTUVWXYZ'-"
          WPAT  =  BREAK(LETTER)  SPAN(LETTER)  .  WORD
READ      LINE  =  INPUT                      :F(PRINTOUT)
*
* ISOLATE WORD, TEST LENGTH, COUNT THREE-LETTER WORDS.
*
GETWD     LINE  WPAT                          :F(READ)
          EQ(SIZE(WORD),3)                    :F(GETWD)
          COUNT=  COUNT + 1                   :(READ)
PRINT     OUTPUT  =  'THE NUMBER OF THREE-LETTER WORDS IS'
  COUNT
END
```

(iii)

```
* THIS PROGRAM PRINTS ALL THE WORDS IN A TEXT WHICH START WITH
* 'A' AND END WITH 'ING'.
          &ANCHOR  =  1;  &TRIM  =  1
          LETTERS  =  "ABCDEFGHIJKLMNOPQRSTUVWXYZ'-"
          PATT1  =  BREAK(LETTERS) SPAN(LETTERS) . WORD
          PATT2  =  'A'  RPOS(3)  'ING'
READ      LINE  =  INPUT                          :F(END)
*
* ISOLATE WORD, TEST FOR REQUIRED PATTERN, PRINT IF PATTERN FOUND.
*
GETWD     LINE  PATT1  =                          :F(GETWD)
          WORD  PATT.2                            :F(GETWD)
          OUTPUT  =  WORD                         :(GETWD)
```

(iv)

```
* THIS PROGRAM USES A FUNCTION 'LENGTH' TO COUNT THE NUMBER OF
* LETTERS, AS OPPOSED TO HYPHENS AND APOSTROPHES, IN A WORD.
* THE PROGRAM PRINTS ALL THE WORDS IN A TEXT WITH MORE THAN
* 8 TRUE LETTERS.
          &ANCHOR  =  1
          &TRIM  =  1
          LETTERS  =  "ABCDEFGHIJKLMNOPQRSTUVWXYZ'-"
          WPAT  =  BREAK(LETTERS)  SPAN(LETTERS)  .  WORD
          PUNCPAT  =  BREAK("'-")  ANY("'-")
          DEFINE('LENGTH(STRING)')
READ      X  =  INPUT                               :F(END)
GETWD     X  WPAT  =                                :F(READ)
*
* USE FUNCTION 'LENGTH' TO CALCULATE NUMBER OF 'TRUE' LETTERS.
* TEST WHETHER THIS IS GREATER THAN 8.  IF SO, PRINT WORD.
*
          GT(LENGTH(WORD),8)                        :F(GETWD)
          OUTPUT  =  WORD
*
* FUNCTION 'LENGTH'
*
LENGTH    X  =  SIZE(WORD)
```

```
LENGTH.1  STRING  PUNCPAT  =                        :F(LENGTH.2)
          X  =  X  -  1                             :(LENGTH.1)
LENGTH.2  LENGTH  =  X                              :(RETURN)
LENGTH.END
*
END
```

14 SNOBOL4 as a research tool: two examples

14.1 Introduction

In this final chapter we shall examine programs written for use in two particular research tasks: an analysis of certain aspects of the style of the American poet Sylvia Plath, and an investigation into the lexical density of English texts.

14.2 SNOBOL4 in the analysis of Plath's poetic style

A detailed account of the research project can be found in Butler (1979): here, after a brief statement of the main issues, attention will be concentrated on some of the programs used.

14.2.1 A summary of the research project

Plath's main poetic oeuvre is contained in four volumes (*The Colossus, Crossing the Water, Ariel* and *Winter Trees*) written over the period 1956–63. Subjectively, it is possible to discern certain trends over this period. The early poems collected in *The Colossus* are characterised by an almost self-conscious attentiveness to technical matters. The resulting collection, though having much of interest to say, is thus especially remarkable for its craftsmanship. As we progress through the three later volumes, the style becomes more direct, though the message becomes ever more complex. This impressionistic observation gave rise to a number of more specific hypotheses concerning particular formal features:

1. The relative frequency of 'end-stopped' lines (that is, lines ending in punctuation) might be expected to be lower in the early work than in the later poems, since one factor making for complication in poetic structure is an exploitation of mis-matching between line divisions and syntactic (clause, phrase) divisions.

2 The total frequency of all punctuation marks might be expected to be higher in the early work.
3 The relative frequency of punctuation associated with formal writing (colon, semicolon) might be expected to be higher in the earlier work, while the frequency of punctuation marks more typical of informal styles (e.g. dash, question mark, exclamation mark) might be expected to show an opposite trend.
4 The word length distribution would be expected to favour longer words in the earlier poems than in the later ones.
5 The sentence length distribution would be expected to favour higher lengths in the earlier poems than in the later ones.
6 'Vocabulary richness', as measured by the ratio of different word 'types' to total word 'tokens', would be expected to be higher in the earlier than in the later poems.

In order to test these hypotheses, a set of programs was written in the SPITBOL variant of SNOBOL4. The word length and sentence length distribution programs will not be discussed here, since a program for producing a word length profile and a function for isolating sentences have been presented elsewhere in this book. In the project itself, hypothesis (6) above was in fact tested by using the COCOA package (see section 3.2) to produce word counts. However, it will be shown that for those who do not have access to such a package, a program to give an alphabetised frequency list of words and a type/token ratio can readily be written in SNOBOL4. The punctuation-counting programs are also presented. For demonstration purposes here, the programs are run on a single Plath poem, 'Apprehensions', the text of which, as entered into the computer, is shown below. The results of the study will not be discussed, except to say that in all but a few minor details each of the hypotheses (1–6) above was strongly supported.

Before we discuss the programs, the conventions used in coding the text should be noted. References to author (A), title of work (W) and stanza number (S) are contained in angle brackets. All upper case letters are preceded by %, and = is used to represent a dash.

```
<A PLATH>
<W APPREHENSIONS>
<S 1>

%THERE IS THIS WHITE HALL, ABOVE WHICH THE SKY CREATES ITSELF=
%INFINITE, GREEN, UTTERLY UNTOUCHABLE.
%ANGELS SWIM IN IT, AND THE STARS, IN INDIFFERENCE ALSO.
%THEY ARE MY MEDIUM.
%THE SUN DISSOLVES ON THIS WALL, BLEEDING ITS LIGHTS.
<S 2>
%A GREY WALL NOW, CLAWED AND BLOODY.
%IS THERE NO WAY OUT OF THE MIND?
%STEPS AT MY BACK SPIRAL INTO A WELL.
%THERE ARE NO TREES OR BIRDS IN THIS WORLD,
%THERE IS ONLY A SOURNESS.
<S 3>
%THIS RED WALL WINCES CONTINUALLY:
%A RED FIST, OPENING AND CLOSING,
```

```
%TWO GREY, PAPERY BAGS=
%THIS IS WHAT %I AM MADE OF, THIS AND A TERROR
%OF BEING WHEELED OFF UNDER CROSSES AND A RAIN OF PIETAS.
<S 4>
%ON A BLACK WALL, UNIDENTIFIABLE BIRDS
%SWIVEL THEIR HEADS AND CRY.
%THERE IS NO TALK OF IMMORTALITY AMONG THESE!
%COLD BLANKS APPROACH US:
%THEY MOVE IN A HURRY.
```

14.2.2 A program to calculate the proportion of end-stopped lines

```
* THIS PROGRAM CALCULATES THE PERCENTAGE OF END-STOPPED
* LINES IN A POETIC TEXT.   = REPRESENTS A DASH.
*
* INITIALISATION
*
          &ANCHOR = 1
          &TRIM = 1
          PUNC = '.?!,;:"=()'
          ENDPUNC = RTAB(1) ANY(PUNC)
          DEFINE('SELECT()')
*
* PROCESSING
*
* USE FUNCTION 'SELECT' TO SELECT A TEXT LINE.
*
READ      LINE = SELECT()                           :F(PRINT)
*
* L COUNTS THE NUMBER OF TEXT LINES.
*
          L = L + 1
*
* TEST FOR END-STOPPING.
*
          LINE ENDPUNC                              :F(READ)
*
* X COUNTS THE NUMBER OF END-STOPPED LINES.
*
          X = X + 1                                 :(READ)
*
* TERMINATION
*
* PRINT RESULTS
*
PRINT     OUTPUT = 'THE NUMBER OF END-STOPPED LINES IS ' X
          OUTPUT  =
          OUTPUT = 'THE NUMBER OF LINES WITHOUT END-STOPPING IS '
+         L - X
          OUTPUT  =
          OUTPUT = 'THE PERCENTAGE OF END-STOPPED LINES IS '
+         X * 100.0 / L                             :(END)
*
* FUNCTION 'SELECT'
*
SELECT
          SELECT = INPUT                            :F(FRETURN)
          SELECT POS(0) '<'                         :S(SELECT)F(RETURN)
SELECT.END
*
END


STORE USED      1303
STORE LEFT      31434
COMP ERRORS     0
REGENERATIONS   0
COMP TIME-MSEC  172


THE NUMBER OF END-STOPPED LINES IS 18
```

```
THE NUMBER OF LINES WITHOUT END-STOPPING IS 2

THE PERCENTAGE OF END-STOPPED LINES IS 90.


NORMAL END
IN STATEMENT    19
RUN TIME-MSEC   98
STMTS EXECUTED  170
MCSEC / STMT    576
REGENERATIONS   0
```

This is a very simple program, only the following features being worthy of note:

1 The function SELECT, discussed in section 11.5, is used to select text lines, skipping over the reference lines in angle brackets.
2 The anchor is set to 'on' for reasons of efficiency. This means, however, that RTAB, rather than RPOS, must be used in defining the pattern ENDPUNC, since otherwise the cursor could not move to the position one character from the right-hand end in order to look for a punctuation mark (see section 10.2).

14.2.4 A program to give a list of all the punctuation marks in a text, with frequencies

```
* THIS PROGRAM SELECTS TEXT LINES FROM A FILE CONTAINING A
* POETIC TEXT, AND PRINTS A LIST OF ALL THE PUNCTUATION MARKS,
* WITH THEIR FREQUENCIES.   = REPRESENTS A DASH.
*
* INITIALISATION
*
          &ANCHOR = 1
          &TRIM = 1
          PUNC = '.?!,;:"=()'
          PUNCPAT = BREAK(PUNC) ANY(PUNC) . P
          PMARKS = TABLE()
          DEFINE('SELECT()')
*
* PROCESSING
*
* SELECT A TEXT LINE.
*
READ      LINE = SELECT()                          :F(CONV)
*
* LOOK FOR PUNCTUATION AND INCREMENT APPROPRIATE ELEMENT OF TABLE.
*
GETPUNC   LINE PUNCPAT =                           :F(READ)
          PMARKS<P> = PMARKS<P> + 1                :(GETPUNC)
*
* TERMINATION
*
* CONVERT TABLE TO ARRAY.
*
CONV      PMARKS = CONVERT(PMARKS,'ARRAY')         :F(ERR)
*
* PRINT RESULTS.
*
          OUTPUT = 'PUNCTUATION MARK' DUPL(' ',10) 'FREQUENCY'
          OUTPUT = DUPL('-',16) DUPL(' ',10) DUPL('-',9)
          I = 1
PRINT     OUTPUT = DUPL(' ',8) PMARKS<I,1> DUPL(' ',21)
+         PMARKS<I,2>                              :F(END)
```

```
                OUTPUT =
                I = I + 1                                :(PRINT)
     *
     * FUNCTION 'SELECT'
     *
     SELECT
                SELECT = INPUT                           :F(FRETURN)
                SELECT POS(0) '<'                        :S(SELECT)F(RETURN)
     SELECT.END
     *
     * ERROR MESSAGE
     *
     ERR        OUTPUT = 'ARRAY CONVERSION FAILED'
     *
     END


STORE USED      1314
STORE LEFT      31423
COMP ERRORS     0
REGENERATIONS   0
COMP TIME-MSEC  191


PUNCTUATION MARK          FREQUENCY
----------------          ---------
        !                     1

        ,                     13

        ?                     1

        :                     2

        =                     2

        .                     10


NORMAL END
IN STATEMENT     23
RUN TIME-MSEC    162
STMTS EXECUTED   210
MCSEC / STMT     771
REGENERATIONS    0
```

There is again little that needs to be said about this program, except that it shows a typical use of the table facility in SNOBOL4.

14.2.4 A program to give an alphabetically ordered word list for a text, with frequencies and a type/token ratio

```
* THIS PROGRAM SELECTS TEXT LINES FROM A TEXT WHICH HAS
* REFERENCE LINES ENCLOSED IN ANGLE BRACKETS, THEN PRODUCES
* AN ALPHABETICAL WORDLIST FOR THE TEXT.
*
* INITIALISATION
*
          &ANCHOR = 1
          &TRIM = 1
          LETTERS = "ABCDEFGHIJKLMNOPQRSTUVWXYZ'-"
          WPAT = BREAK(LETTERS) SPAN(LETTERS) . WORD
          WDS = TABLE()
          DEFINE('PRINT(ARR,COL,HEADING)NCOL,LINE,I,J,K')
          DEFINE('SORTER(A,N)I')
          DEFINE('EXCHANGE(I)TEMP')
          DEFINE('INSERT(J)')
          DEFINE('SELECT()')
```

```
*
* PROCESSING
*
* USE FUNCTION 'SELECT' TO SELECT A TEXT LINE.
*
READ      LINE = SELECT()                         :F(CONV)
*
* ISOLATE A WORD AND INCREMENT THE APPROPRIATE ELEMENT OF TABLE.
*
GETWD     LINE WPAT =                             :F(READ)
          WDS<WORD> = WDS<WORD> + 1
*
* W COUNTS THE NUMBER OF RUNNING WORDS.
*
          W = W + 1                               :(GETWD)
*
* CONVERT TABLE TO ARRAY.
*
CONV      WDS = CONVERT(WDS,'ARRAY')              :F(ERR.1)
*
* FIND PROTOTYPE OF THIS 2-D ARRAY IN ORDER TO COPY EACH WORD
* AND ITS FREQUENCY, AS A SINGLE ITEM, INTO A ONE-DIMENSIONAL
* ARRAY 'NEWWDS' FOR SORTING.
*
          PROTOTYPE(WDS) BREAK(',') . DIM ',2' RPOS(0)   :F(ERR.2)
          NEWWDS = ARRAY(DIM)
*
* COPY THE WORDS AND THEIR FREQUENCIES, SUITABLY FORMATTED,
* INTO THE NEW ARRAY.
*
INC.1     I = I + 1
          NEWWDS<I> = RPAD(WDS<I,1>,19) WDS<I,2>       :S(INC.1)
*
* SORT INTO ALPHABETICAL ORDER USING FUNCTION 'SORTER'.
*
          SORTER(NEWWDS,DIM)
*
* TERMINATION
*
* PRINT HEADING AND CONTENTS OF ARRAY, USING FUNCTION 'PRINT'.
*
          PRINT(NEWWDS,25,'WORDS IN ALPHABETICAL ORDER')
*
* PRINT SUMMARY INFORMATION.
*
          OUTPUT =
          OUTPUT =
          OUTPUT =
          OUTPUT = 'THE TOTAL NUMBER OF WORDS IS ' W
          OUTPUT =
          OUTPUT = 'THE NUMBER OF DIFFERENT WORD FORMS IS ' DIM
          OUTPUT =
          OUTPUT = 'THE TYPE-TOKEN RATIO (BASED ON '
+         'UNLEMMATISED WORD FORMS) IS ' DIM * 1.0 / W   :(END)
*
* FUNCTIONS
*
* FUNCTION 'PRINT'
*
PRINT
          I = SIZE(HEADING)
          OUTPUT = DUPL(' ',(132 - I) / 2) HEADING
          OUTPUT = DUPL(' ',(132 - I) / 2) DUPL('-',I)
          OUTPUT =
          OUTPUT =
          NCOL = 132 / COL
          J = 1
PRINT.1   K = K + 1
*
* COLLECT NCOL ITEMS INTO LINE FOR PRINTING.
*
          LINE = LINE RPAD(ARR<K>,COL)            :F(PRINT.3)
          J = LT(J,NCOL) J + 1                    :S(PRINT.1)
*
* PRINT THE LINE, THEN CLEAR LINE AND RESET J.
*
```

```
PRINT.2   OUTPUT = LINE
          LINE =
          J = 1                                :(PRINT.1)
PRINT.3   OUTPUT = LINE                        :(RETURN)
PRINT.END
*
* FUNCTION 'SELECT'
*
* 'SELECT' SELECTS A TEXT LINE, IGNORING REFERENCE LINES IN
* ANGLE BRACKETS.
*
SELECT
          SELECT = INPUT                       :F(FRETURN)
          SELECT '<'                           :S(SELECT)F(RETURN)
SELECT.END
*
* FUNCTION 'SORTER'
*
* 'SORTER' SORTS AN ARRAY A, OF N ITEMS, INTO ALPHABETICAL
* ORDER.  IT CALLS 'EXCHANGE' AND 'INSERT'.
*
SORTER
          I = LT(I,N - 1) I + 1                :F(RETURN)
          LGT(A<I ,A<I>+ 1>)                   :F(SORTER)
          EXCHANGE(I)
          INSERT(I)                            :(SORTER)
SORTER.END
*
* FUNCTION 'EXCHANGE'
*
* 'EXCHANGE' SWAPS ELEMENTS I AND I + 1 OF AN ARRAY A.
*
EXCHANGE
          TEMP = A<I>
          A<I  = A<I + 1>
          A<I + 1> = TEMP                      :(RETURN)
EXCHANGE.END
*
* FUNCTION 'INSERT'
*
* 'INSERT' INSERTS AN ITEM IN ITS CORRECT POSITION.
*
INSERT
          J = GT(J,1) J - 1                    :F(RETURN)
          LGT(A<J>,A<J + 1>)                   :F(RETURN)
          EXCHANGE(J)                          :(INSERT)
INSERT.END
*
* END OF FUNCTIONS
*
* ERROR MESSAGES
*
ERR.1     OUTPUT = 'ARRAY CONVERSION FAILED'   :(END)
ERR.2     OUTPUT = 'PROTOTYPE OF ARRAY NOT FOUND'
*
END


STORE USED      2402
STORE LEFT      30335
COMP ERRORS     0
REGENERATIONS   1
COMP TIME-MSEC  468
```

1

```
                              WORDS IN ALPHABETICAL ORDER
                              ---------------------------

A              8   ABOVE          1   ALSO           1   AM             1   AMONG            1
AND            6   ANGELS         1   APPROACH       1   ARE            2   AT               1
BACK           1   BAGS           1   BEING          1   BIRDS          2   BLACK            1
BLANKS         1   BLEEDING       1   BLOODY         1   CLAWED         1   CLOSING          1
COLD           1   CONTINUALLY    1   CREATES        1   CROSSES        1   CRY              1
DISSOLVES      1   FIST           1   GREEN          1   GREY           2   HEADS            1
HURRY          1   I              1   IMMORTALITY    1   IN             4   INDIFFERENCE     1
INFINITE       1   INTO           1   IS             5   IT             1   ITS              1
ITSELF         1   LIGHTS         1   MADE           1   MEDIUM         1   MIND             1
MOVE           1   MY             2   NO             3   NOW            1   OF               5
OFF            1   ON             2   ONLY           1   OPENING        1   OR               1
OUT            1   PAPERY         1   PIETAS         1   RAIN           1   RED              2
SKY            1   SOURNESS       1   SPIRAL         1   STARS          1   STEPS            1
SUN            1   SWIM           1   SWIVEL         1   TALK           1   TERROR           1
THE            4   THEIR          1   THERE          5   THESE          1   THEY             2
THIS           6   TREES          1   TWO            1   UNDER          1   UNIDENTIFIABLE   1
UNTOUCHABLE    1   US             1   UTTERLY        1   WALL           5   WAY              1
WELL           1   WHAT           1   WHEELED        1   WHICH          1   WHITE            1
WINCES         1   WORLD          1

THE TOTAL NUMBER OF WORDS IS 140

THE NUMBER OF DIFFERENT WORD FORMS IS 92

THE TYPE-TOKEN RATIO (BASED ON UNLEMMATISED WORD FORMS) IS 0.657142857

NORMAL END
IN STATEMENT   68
RUN TIME-MSEC  2131
STMTS EXECUTED 17139
MCSEC / STMT   124
REGENERATIONS  0
```

This program illustrates one approach to the important task of sorting items into alphabetical or numerical order, and also acts as a further demonstration of the 'structured' approach to programming. It will be remembered that in section 11.1 it was recommended that complex tasks should be broken down into subtasks, and that functions should be written for such subtasks where appropriate. In the production of an alphabetical word list for our poetic text, three subtasks lend themselves very well to treatment as functions. We need to select text lines, rejecting reference lines, and for this we use the function SELECT already familiar from other programs. When words have been isolated, the frequencies of word forms stored in a table, and the table converted to an array, we need to sort the words into alphabetical order (keeping their frequencies with them) before printing out the list: this sorting is carried out by a function SORTER. Finally, we must print the list in an appropriate format, with headings: this is accomplished by means of a function PRINT. SORTER, as we shall see, is a complex function which calls, from within itself, two other functions, which we have called EXCHANGE and INSERT; furthermore, INSERT itself calls EXCHANGE. SORTER thus affords a further example of the 'functional composition' approach discussed in section 11.6.

The first part of the processing phase, from statement 11 to statement 15, contains only familiar material; statements 16–19, however, perhaps require some explanation. As the comment lines in the program indicate, we need to copy the word contained in the first column of a given row of the two-dimensional array WDS, together with its frequency (contained in the second column of that row) as a single string, into a new array (NEWWDS) with a single dimension, so that we can sort these strings into alphabetical order. If we simply sorted the words, and left the frequencies in their original rows in the array, we should get words paired with the wrong frequencies. In order to know how many elements the new array will have, we find the prototype of the original array (for discussion of PROTOTYPE see section 12.5). In statement 19 we have used the SPITBOL function RPAD to format the word and its frequency. If we were using standard SNOBOL4, RPAD would have to be written as a programmer-defined function (see Question 2 of Exercises 11).

We now come to the sorting of the elements of NEWWDS into alphabetical order. Before we proceed, it should be noted that a sorting routine is, in fact, available as a built-in function in SPITBOL, though not in standard SNOBOL. Thus, since the program is written in SPITBOL, we could have omitted the function SORTER, and written statement 20 as:

```
        SORT(NEWWDS)
```

This has not been done because we wished to describe the writing of a sorting function for users of the standard language, and because the function illustrates some important features of good programming. Since, however, SORT is a built-in function in SPITBOL, we cannot use this name for our programmer-defined function, as this would have caused an error through the attempt to redefine a system function. Let us now examine the structure of SORTER.

SORTER takes an array A, with N elements, and sorts these elements into alphabetical order. The technique used is called an 'insertion sort', since each item is inserted at its proper position in the list. Other techniques can be used: for further details the reader should consult Gimpel (1976). The basic logic of the insertion sort is best understood by consideration of a simple example. Consider the sentence

THE CAT SAT ON THE MAT

We start by comparing the first two words. If the first had been alphabetically before the second, we should have left them as they were and passed on to a comparison of the second and third words. In fact, THE and CAT are in the wrong order, and we need to exchange them to give:

    CAT THE SAT ON THE MAT

We now compare words 2 and 3, THE and SAT. Again, they are in the wrong order, so we exchange them, giving:

    CAT SAT THE ON THE MAT

But now we must check to see if SAT is in its correct position with respect to CAT. It is, so we leave things as they are, and go on to compare words 3 and 4, THE and ON. These again need to be exchanged, giving:

    CAT SAT ON THE A MAT

But now, SAT and ON are in the wrong order, so we must exchange these too:

    CAT ON SAT THE A MAT

We must now compare CAT and ON: we find that they are, in fact, in the correct order. Thus we have successfully sent ON back up the list to its correct position by exchanging it for its left-hand neighbour as many times as necessary. The process continues as follows:

    CAT ON SAT THE A MAT

    CAT ON SAT A THE MAT

    CAT ON A SAT THE MAT

    CAT A ON SAT THE MAT

    A CAT ON SAT THE MAT

    A CAT ON SAT MAT THE

    A CAT ON MAT SAT THE

    A CAT MAT ON SAT THE

The logic of the statements constituting SORTER should now be clearer. I is the number of the array element currently being compared with its neighbour. Statement 51 checks that not all the array elements have yet been sorted: if they have, the function returns. Statement 52 then checks if the two items being compared are in the correct alphabetical order. If they are (that is, if the LGT predicate fails), the pair is left as it is, I is incremented and the next pair is compared. If items I and I + 1 are in the wrong order, EXCHANGE is called, in statement 53, to swap them round. Note that the exchange process in statements 57–59 requires the value of one array element to be stored in a temporary variable TEMP (made local to the function) so that it is not lost. If we had written:

```
        A<I>  =  A<I + 1>
        A<I + 1>  =  A<I>                                :(RETURN)
```

then both elements would have had the value of A<I + 1> at the end of the function.

When EXCHANGE has performed the swap, it is necessary to check the new 'earlier' item against those before it in the partially sorted list, and to send the item back to its correct position if necessary. For this purpose, INSERT is called in statement 54, with I as its argument. Statement 62 checks whether we have reached the first item in the list; if we have (that is, if the item being compared is the first, alphabetically, in the list at this point in the sort), the function returns. Otherwise, the value of I (remember that the function has been called with I as argument) is decreased by 1, so that we can now make a comparison between our given item and its left-hand neighbour, as required. Statement 63 tests whether these are in the correct order. If they are (that is, if the LGT predicate fails) there is no more exchanging to be done for that item, and the function returns. If the two items are in the wrong order, EXCHANGE is called to swap them round, and the process is repeated until the item has been inserted in its correct position.

An insertion-sorting function of the type described above can, of course, be adapted to perform other kinds of sorting. For instance, if the items to be sorted were numbers rather than strings, they could be sorted into numerical order by replacing LGT, in our function, by GT. A reverse alphabetical word list (sorted on the ends of words rather than on their beginnings – see p. 13) could be produced by combining SORTER with a function for reversing strings.

Let us now consider briefly the PRINT function used to print the contents of the array in formatted columns with a heading. This is a more sophisticated version of the function written in the suggested answer to Qeustion 3 of Exercises 12. PRINT is defined (in statement 6) with 3 arguments and 5 local variables, used in the course of the function procedure. In a call of PRINT, we specify the name of the array, the width of the columns we wish to have in the printed table, and the heading to be printed centrally on the page and underlined. Thus statement 21 calls PRINT to print the contents of the array NEWWDS in columns of width 25 characters (of which we shall have 5 on a 132-column page), with the heading WORDS IN ALPHABETICAL ORDER. Statements 31–3 print the heading centrally and underline it. Note the use of the local variable I so that SIZE(HEADING) does not have to be computed afresh each time it is needed. The rationale of the rest of the function should be familiar from Question 12.3. Note again the crucial steps (statements 42 and 43) in which LINE is cleared after a line is printed, and J, the counter for the number of elements already concatenated into LINE, reset to 1. Note also that when all the items in the array have been exhausted, if the number of them is not exactly divisible by NCOL, there will be some material left in an incomplete LINE. This must be printed separately at the end (hence statement 44) before the function returns.

Statements 22–9 of the program simply print information on the total number of running words (W), the number of different word forms (equal to the number of elements in the array NEWWDS, that is, DIM), and the type/token ratio (the ratio of different words to total running words) based on unlemmatised word forms (for a discussion of lemmatisation, see p. 14).

14.3 SPITBOL in the calculation of lexical density

An interesting quantitative property of texts, which varies with the context of text production, is the lexical density, defined as the ratio of the number of 'lexical' word tokens to the total number of running words in the text. In this section we shall examine a SPITBOL program, written originally by Michael Stubbs and slightly adapted by the author, which calculates the lexical density of a text. A description of the algorithm underlying the program can be found in Stubbs (forthcoming), which also discusses the concepts of 'lexical word', 'grammatical word' and 'lexical density', and presents some results from data analyses using the program.

The majority of the word forms in a text can be assigned, by means of a series of diagnostic tests, either to the category of lexical words (including nouns, adjectives, adverbs and main verbs) or to the category of grammatical words (including pronouns, determiners, conjunctions, prepositions and auxiliary verbs). Some words, however, can be lexical or grammatical according to context: for instance, *go* can be used as a main (lexical) verb, but also as a grammatical word in the construction *be going to*. The lexical density program uses as part of its input a file containing lists of grammatical and ambiguous words, and also of any items which may occur in the text but are irrelevant to the analysis of lexical density (for example, interjections such as *ah, gosh*, etc.)

In the form given below, the program uses as data for analysis a text from the London–Lund Corpus of Spoken English (see section 2.3.6). Each data record in the corpus begins with 27 columns giving details such as the text category and number, and the identity of the speaker, the text itself occupying columns 28 to 78.

The lexical density program is the largest and most complex discussed in this book. It has been presented in a slightly different format from the other programs in the book, showing the use of lower case letters in comment lines, and of lines of asterisks to separate sections – a useful device in complex programs.

```
*       This program calculates the lexical density and associated
*       statistics for the LUND texts.
*************************************************************************
*
*       Notes on the program:
*
*       Lexical density is defined here according to Jean Ure
*       ('Lexical density and register differentiation', in Perren, G. E.
*       & Trim, J. L. M. (eds.) Applications of Linguistics,  London:
*       Cambridge Univesity Press, 1971), though the program carries
*       out more detailed calculations on the text than she proposes.
*
*       The main limitations on the way the calculation is carried out are
*       (a) it can identify only orthographic words
*       (b) it cannot distinguish between words which are ambiguously
*       grammatical or lexical - such words are however printed out in
*       context for identification.
*       (c) it works only with unlemmatised forms.
*
*       Grammatical words, words which could be either grammatical or
*       lexical, and words which are irrelevant to the calculation (eg
*       interjections, coders' comments), are stored in a separate file.
*       They are read into the program to form three dictionaries
*       in the form of alphabetically arranged arrays.  The program
*       identifies words in the input text, and checks to see
*       whether they occur in any of the dictionaries (by means of
*       a binary search function).  If they do, they are ambiguous or
*       grammatical or irrelevant;  if they don't, they are lexical.
*
*       The program prints lists of grammatical and lexical words, ordered
*       alphabetically and/or by frequency depending on the option set:
*       this is useful for comparing texts even if the overall lexical
*       density calculation is treated with caution.
*
*       The totals in the various categories are used to calculate the
*       lexical density. The ambiguous items are not used in the
*       calculation.
*
*       The program uses programmer-defined functions in order to:
*       read words into three tables, IRRELWORDS, AMBIGWORDS and
*       GRAMWORDS to form dictionaries;
*       perform a binary search of the dictionaries;
*       strip various diacritics etc off the lines of the LUND text so
*       that words can be identified;
*       print out the contents of the tables, in different forms.
*
*************************************************************************
*       INITIALISATION
*
*       Set TEXT to a string giving details of the text to be analysed.
*
                TEXT   =   'LUNDTEXT 10_5: radio commentary, funeral;'
+                          ' sample of first 200 words'
*
*       Set MAXCOUNT to the maximum number of words to be processed.
*
                MAXCOUNT = 200
*
*       Set &STLIMIT to something over 100 times MAXCOUNT
*
                &STLIMIT = 30000
*
*       Set SORTING to 'YES' or 'NO' (upper case and quotes) depending
*       on whether the words are to be sorted and printed or not.
*
```

```
4               SORTING = 'YES'
      *
      *     If SORTING = 'YES', then set CHOICE to 'A' for a normal
      *     alphabetical sort, 'DF' for a sort by descending frequency, or
      *     'BOTH' if both are required.  If SORTING = 'NO', then set
      *     CHOICE to 'NULL'.
      *
5               CHOICE = 'BOTH'
      *
      *     Set PRINTDICT to 'YES' or 'NO' (upper case and quotes) depending
      *     on whether the dictionaries of irrelevant, ambiguous and
      *     grammatical words are to be printed.
      *
6               PRINTDICT = 'YES'
      *
      *     Set ESTLEX and ESTGRAM to reasonable estimates of the number of
      *     lexical and grammatical words likely to be found.  This will speed
      *     up the searches of the tables.
      *
7               ESTLEX = 80
8               ESTGRAM = 40
      *
      ***********************************************************************
9           &ANCHOR = &TRIM = 1
      *
10          LETTER = 'abcdefghijklmnopqrstuvwxyzABCDEFGHIJKLMNOPQRSTUVWXYZ`@-'
11          WORDPAT = BREAK(LETTER) SPAN(LETTER) . WORD
12          STARS = DUPL('*',80)
      *
      ***********************************************************************
      *
      *     Set up tables to store the three dictionaries and the words
      *     found.  Set plausible values for the size of the tables according
      *     to the current contents of the dictionaries.
      *
13              IRRELWORDS = TABLE(40)
14              AMBIGWORDS = TABLE(30)
15              GRAMWORDS  = TABLE(250)
16              IRRELFOUND = TABLE(20)
17              AMBIGFOUND = TABLE(50)
18              GRAMFOUND  = TABLE(ESTGRAM)
19              LEXFOUND   = TABLE(ESTLEX)
      *
      *     Set up programmer defined functions, and patterns they require.
      *
20              DEFINE('DICT(NAMEX,STOP)J,LINE')
21              DEFINE('PRINT1(NAMEX)M,N,TEMP')
22              DEFINE('PRINT2(NAMEX)M,N,TEMP')
23              DEFINE('STRIP(TEXT)REST,S,TEMP')
24              STRING  =  LETTER ' '
25              STRIPPAT = BREAK(STRING) SPAN(STRING) . S
26              DEFINE('FIND(WORDX,LISTX,LENGTH)L,M,U')
27              DEFINE('WORDSPRINT()')
28              DEFINE('PROTOCALC(ARR)')

      *
      ***********************************************************************
      *
      *     PROCESSING
      *
29              OUTPUT = STARS; OUTPUT =  ; OUTPUT =
32              OUTPUT = 'TEXT ANALYSED IS: ' TEXT
33              OUTPUT =  ; OUTPUT =  ; OUTPUT = STARS
      *
      *     Set up the dictionaries.     ***********************************
      *
36              TOTIRREL = DICT(IRRELWORDS,'ENDIRREL')
37              IRRELWORDS = SORT(IRRELWORDS,2)              :F(ERROR1)
38              TOTAMBIG = DICT(AMBIGWORDS,'ENDAMBIG')
39              AMBIGWORDS = SORT(AMBIGWORDS,2)              :F(ERROR1)
40              TOTGRAM = DICT(GRAMWORDS,'ENDGRAM')
41              GRAMWORDS = SORT(GRAMWORDS,2)                :F(ERROR1)
42              IDENT(PRINTDICT,'NO')                        :S(NO.DICT)
      *
      *     Print out the dictionaries if this option is set     *************
      *
43              OUTPUT = ; OUTPUT = 'DICTIONARY OF IRRELEVANT WORDS'
45              OUTPUT = ; PRINT1(IRRELWORDS)
```

```
              OUTPUT = ; OUTPUT = 'DICTIONARY OF AMBIGUOUS WORDS'
              OUTPUT = ; PRINT1(AMBIGWORDS)
              OUTPUT = ; OUTPUT = 'DICTIONARY OF GRAMMATICAL WORDS'
              OUTPUT = ; PRINT1(GRAMWORDS)
              OUTPUT = ; OUTPUT = ; OUTPUT = STARS; OUTPUT = ; OUTPUT =
NO.DICT
*
*       Read in the data, strip off diacritics etc, extract single words,
*       check if they are in the dictionaries, and record them; and print
*       out the ambiguous words in context.
*
              OUTPUT =
              OUTPUT = 'LINES CONTAINING AMBIGUOUS WORDS:'; OUTPUT =
*
*       WORDCOUNT is the count of running orthographic word forms;
*       I, A, G and L are the counts of irrelevant, ambiguous, grammatical
*       and lexical word tokens.
*
              WORDCOUNT = I = A = G = L = 0
              FIRSTLINE = LINE = INPUT              :F(ERROR2)S(COPY)
*
*       The next line can fail for two reasons:  no more data or
*       the value of MAXCOUNT minus irrelevant words is exceeded.
*       In either case go to DATA.END.
*
READ          LINE = LT((WORDCOUNT - I),MAXCOUNT) INPUT    :F(DATA.END)
COPY          COPY = STRLINE = ' ' STRIP(LINE)
NEXT.WORD     STRLINE WORDPAT =                            :F(READ)
              WORDCOUNT = WORDCOUNT + 1
              FIND(WORD,IRRELWORDS,TOTIRREL)               :S(IRREL)
              FIND(WORD,AMBIGWORDS,TOTAMBIG)               :S(AMBIG)
              FIND(WORD,GRAMWORDS,TOTGRAM)                 :S(GRAM)F(LEX)
*
AMBIG         A = A + 1
              AMBIGFOUND<WORD> = AMBIGFOUND<WORD> + 1
*
*       The next two lines print out ambiguous words, plus a question
*       mark, in context.
*
              COPY BREAKX(' ') . AX ' ' (WORD REM) . BX
              OUTPUT = '  ' AX ' ?' BX                     :(NEXT.WORD)
*
IRREL         I = I + 1
              IRRELFOUND<WORD> = IRRELFOUND<WORD> + 1      :(NEXT.WORD)
GRAM          G = G + 1
              GRAMFOUND<WORD> = GRAMFOUND<WORD> + 1        :(NEXT.WORD)
LEX           L = L + 1
              LEXFOUND<WORD> = LEXFOUND<WORD> + 1          :(NEXT.WORD)
*
*************************************************************************
*
*       Sort the output if this option has been set.
*
DATA.END      IDENT(SORTING,'YES')                         :F(NO.SORT)
              IDENT(CHOICE,'DF')                           :S(DF.SORT)
*
A.SORT        OUTPUT = ; OUTPUT = ; OUTPUT = STARS; OUTPUT =
              OUTPUT = 'WORDS SORTED ALPHABETICALLY'
              OUTPUT =
              IRRELFOUND = SORT(IRRELFOUND,1)              :F(ERROR3)
              AMBIGFOUND = SORT(AMBIGFOUND,1)              :F(ERROR3)
              GRAMFOUND  = SORT(GRAMFOUND,1)               :F(ERROR3)
              LEXFOUND   = SORT(LEXFOUND,1)                :F(ERROR3)
              WORDSPRINT()
*
              IDENT(CHOICE,'BOTH')                         :F(PROTO)
*
DF.SORT       OUTPUT = ; OUTPUT = ; OUTPUT = STARS; OUTPUT =
              OUTPUT = 'WORDS SORTED BY DESCENDING FREQUENCY'
              OUTPUT =
              IRRELFOUND = RSORT(IRRELFOUND,2)             :F(ERROR3)
              AMBIGFOUND = RSORT(AMBIGFOUND,2)             :F(ERROR3)
              GRAMFOUND  = RSORT(GRAMFOUND,2)              :F(ERROR3)
              LEXFOUND   = RSORT(LEXFOUND,2)               :F(ERROR3)
              WORDSPRINT()                                 :(PROTO)
*
*************************************************************************
*
```

```
NO.SORT    IRRELFOUND = CONVERT(IRRELFOUND,'ARRAY')     :F(ERROR4)
           AMBIGFOUND = CONVERT(AMBIGFOUND,'ARRAY')     :F(ERROR4)
           GRAMFOUND  = CONVERT(GRAMFOUND,'ARRAY')      :F(ERROR4)
           LEXFOUND   = CONVERT(LEXFOUND,'ARRAY')       :F(ERROR4)
*
************************************************************************
*
*     Calculate the size of the arrays, ie the no of word types.
*
PROTO      ITP = PROTOCALC(IRRELFOUND)                  :F(ERROR5)
           ATP = PROTOCALC(AMBIGFOUND)                  :F(ERROR5)
           GTP = PROTOCALC(GRAMFOUND)                   :F(ERROR5)
           LTP = PROTOCALC(LEXFOUND)                    :F(ERROR5)
*
*     Calculate totals of word tokens and types ignoring irrelevant
*     words.
*
           TTP = ATP + GTP + LTP
           T   = A + G + L
************************************************************************
*
*     Print out the text statistics.
*
*
           OUTPUT = STARS; OUTPUT = ; OUTPUT =
*
           OUTPUT = 'TEXT STATISTICS - based on unlemmatised word forms'
           OUTPUT =
           OUTPUT = '                 '
+                   'No of types   No of tokens  Type-token ratio'
           OUTPUT = '                 '
+                   'ie different  ie running'
           OUTPUT = '                 '
+                   'words         text words'
           OUTPUT = '                 '
+                   '------------  -----------   ----------------'
           OUTPUT =
           OUTPUT = 'Whole text:      '
+          LPAD(TTP,8) LPAD(T,13) DUPL(' ',8) '1 : ' ((T * 1.0) / TTP)
           OUTPUT =
           OUTPUT = 'Grammatical:     '
+          LPAD(GTP,8) LPAD(G,13) DUPL(' ',8) '1 : ' ((G * 1.0) / GTP)
           OUTPUT = 'Lexical:         '
+          LPAD(LTP,8) LPAD(L,13) DUPL(' ',8) '1 : ' ((L * 1.0) / LTP)
           OUTPUT = 'Ambiguous:       '
+          LPAD(ATP,8) LPAD(A,13) DUPL(' ',8) '1 : ' ((A * 1.0) / ATP)
           OUTPUT = 'Irrelevant:      '
+          LPAD(ITP,8) LPAD(I,13) DUPL(' ',8) '1 : ' ((I * 1.0) / ITP)
*
           OUTPUT =
           OUTPUT = 'Provisional lexical density (ignoring ambiguous '
+                   'words): '   (L * 100.0) / (G + L) ' %'
           OUTPUT =  ;  OUTPUT  =

************************************************************************
*
*     Print out a check of the first and last lines processed.
*
           OUTPUT = ; OUTPUT = ; OUTPUT = STARS; OUTPUT =  ; OUTPUT =
           OUTPUT = 'FIRST LINE OF DATA PROCESSED:'
           OUTPUT = FIRSTLINE
           OUTPUT = 'LAST LINE OF DATA PROCESSED:'
           OUTPUT = LINE
           OUTPUT =  ; OUTPUT =  ; OUTPUT = STARS          :(END)
*
************************************************************************
*     Function bodies
*
FIND
*     This function performs a binary search to find a given
*     word WORDX in a list LISTX of any length stored in an array.
*     L and U are the lower and upper bounds of a segment of the
*     list being searched at any one time, and M is the middle item.
*
           L = 1
           U = LENGTH
FIND.M     M = (L + U) / 2
```

```
                LEQ(WORDX,LISTX<M,2>)          :S(RETURN)
                LGT(WORDX,LISTX<M,2>)          :S(FIND.MOVE)
                U = M - 1                      :(FIND.CHK)
FIND.MOVE L = M + 1
FIND.CHK  LE(L,U)                              :S(FIND.M)F(FRETURN)
FIND.END
*
*************************************************************************
*
DICT
*      This function forms dictionaries by reading words into a
*      table (which will later be converted into a 2-dimensional
*      array by the built-in function SORT).
*
DICT.RD  LINE = INPUT                          :F(ERROR6)
*
*      Ignore if a comment line.
              LINE '*'                         :S(DICT.RD)
*
*      Stop when termination marker reached.
*
              LINE STOP                        :S(RETURN)
DICT.WD       LINE WORDPAT =                   :F(DICT.RD)
              DICT = DICT + 1
              NAMEX<DICT> = WORD               :(DICT.WD)
DICT.END
*
*************************************************************************
*
PRINT1
*     This function prints out the contents of a 2-dimensional
*     array with about 70 to 80 chars per line.
*
            M = M + 1
            TEMP = TEMP '   ' NAMEX<M,2>       :F(PRINT1.OUT)
            LT(SIZE(TEMP),70)                  :S(PRINT1)
            OUTPUT = TEMP; TEMP =              :(PRINT1)
PRINT1.OUT  OUTPUT = TEMP                      :(RETURN)
PRINT1.END
*
*************************************************************************
*
PRINT2
*           This function prints out the contents of a 2-dimensional
*           array with 3 word + frequency pairs per line, right
*           justified to cols 21 and 26, 47 and 52, 73 and 78.
*
             N = 1
PRINT2.INCM  M = M + 1
             TEMP = TEMP LPAD(NAMEX<M,1>,21) LPAD(NAMEX<M,2>,5)
+                                              :F(PRINT2.OUT)
             N = LT(N,3) N + 1                 :S(PRINT2.INCM)
             OUTPUT = TEMP; TEMP =             :(PRINT2)
PRINT2.OUT   OUTPUT = TEMP; TEMP =
             OUTPUT =                          :(RETURN)
PRINT2.END
*
*************************************************************************
*
STRIP
*           This function strips diacritics off the lines of transcrip-
*           tion, and also removes the first 27  columns, where there is
*           no text.
*
            TEXT TAB(27) REM . REST
STRIP.LOOP  REST STRIPPAT =                    :F(STRIP.SET)
            TEMP = TEMP S                      :(STRIP.LOOP)
STRIP.SET   STRIP = TEMP                       :(RETURN)
STRIP.END
*
*************************************************************************
*
WORDSPRINT
*
           OUTPUT =
           OUTPUT = 'WORD TYPES FOUND (UNLEMMATISED), '
+                   'WITH FREQUENCY'
```

```
                OUTPUT =
                OUTPUT = 'IRRELEVANT WORDS'
                PRINT2(IRRELFOUND)
                OUTPUT = 'AMBIGUOUS WORDS'
                PRINT2(AMBIGFOUND)
                OUTPUT = 'GRAMMATICAL WORDS'
                PRINT2(GRAMFOUND)
                OUTPUT = 'LEXICAL WORDS'
                PRINT2(LEXFOUND)                    :(RETURN)
      *
      WORDSPRINT.END
      *
      ************************************************************************
      *
      PROTOCALC
      *
               PROTOTYPE(ARR) BREAK(',') . PROTOCALC ',2' :S(RETURN)F(FRETURN)
      *
      PROTOCALC.END
      ************************************************************************
      *
      * ERROR MESSAGES
      *
      ERROR1    OUTPUT = 'DICTIONARY SORT FAILS'           :(END)
      ERROR2    OUTPUT = 'NO TEXT TO READ IN'              :(END)
      ERROR3    OUTPUT = 'SORT OF WORDS FOUND FAILS'       :(END)
      ERROR4    OUTPUT = 'TABLE CONVERSION FAILS'          :(END)
      ERROR5    OUTPUT = 'PROTOTYPE CALCULATION FAILS'     :(END)
      ERROR6    OUTPUT = 'NO DICTIONARY TO READ IN'
      *
      END


  STORE USED      4346
  STORE LEFT      28391
  COMP ERRORS     0
  REGENERATIONS   2
  COMP TIME-MSEC  1063
```

```
*****************************************************************************

TEXT ANALYSED IS: LUNDTEXT 10_5: radio commentary, funeral; sample of first 200 words

*****************************************************************************

DICTIONARY OF IRRELEVANT WORDS

  -  @  @h  @m  ah  aha  alas  b  c  d  e  ch  f  f@  g  gosh  h  hey  hm
  i  j  k  l  m  n  o  oh  oho  ooh  ouch  ow  p  q  r  s  syll  sylls
  t  tut  tut-tut  u  v  w  wow  x  y  yippee  z

DICTIONARY OF AMBIGUOUS WORDS

  am  are  aren`t  be  been  being  did  do  does  doing  go  going  had
  hadn`t  has  hasn`t  have  haven`t  having  is  isn`t  one  past  was
  wasn`t  well  were

DICTIONARY OF GRAMMATICAL WORDS

  a  about  above  across  after  against  all  along  alongside  although
  amid  amidst  among  amongst  an  and  any  anybody  anyone  anything
  anywhere  apropos  as  at  atop  because  before  behind  below  beneath
  beside  besides  between  beyond  both  but  by  can  can`t  cos  could
  couldn`t  dare  daren`t  despite  dhi  didn`t  doesn`t  don`t  during
  each  ei  either  else  every  everybody  everyone  everything  everywhere
  except  few  for  from  he  he`d  he`ll  he`s  her  here  hers  herself
  him  himself  his  how  however  if  in  inside  into  it  it`d  it`ll
  it`s  its  itself  less  many  may  mayn`t  me  mhm  might  mine  minus
  more  most  much  must  mustn`t  my  myself  needn`t  neither  never
  nevertheless  no  no-one  nobody  none  nonetheless  noone  nor  not
  nothing  notwithstanding  of  off  on  or  other  ought  oughtn`t  our
  ours  ourselves  out  outside  over  per  plus  shall  shan`t  she  she`d
  she`ll  she`s  should  shouldest  shouldn`t  since  so  some  somebody
  someone  someplace  something  somewhere  than  that  that`d  that`ll
```

```
  that's  the  thee  their  theirs  them  themself  themselves  then  there
  there'd  there'll  there's  there've  therefore  therewith  these  they
  they'd  they'll  they're  they've  thine  this  those  thou  though
  through  throughout  thus  thy  till  to  too  toward  towards  uhuh
  under  underneath  until  up  upon  us  very  via  we  we'd  we'll  we're
  we've  what  what'd  what'll  what's  what've  whatever  when  whenever
  where  wherever  whether  which  whichever  while  whilst  who  whom
  whose  why  will  with  within  without  won't  would  wouldn't  ye  yeah
  yes  yet  you  you'd  you'll  you're  you've  your  yours  yourself  yourselves
  I  I'd  I'll  I'm  I've  OK


*****************************************************************************


LINES CONTAINING AMBIGUOUS WORDS:

  he ?is safe - -
  ?was he in steadier hands - - -
  for this ?is a long


*****************************************************************************


WORDS SORTED ALPHABETICALLY


WORD TYPES FOUND (UNLEMMATISED), WITH FREQUENCY

IRRELEVANT WORDS
                     -    27

AMBIGUOUS WORDS
                    is     2                  was     1

GRAMMATICAL WORDS
                     a     4                after     1                  all     1
                    an     1                  and    13                   as     1
                    at     1               behind     1                   by     1
                   for     2                   he     2                  her     1
                   him     2                  his     1                   in     3
                    it     3                 it's     1                  its     1
                 never     1                   of     7                   on     2
                  that     2                  the    18                their     2
                  then     1                 this     2                   to     1
                 we've     1                 with     1

LEXICAL WORDS
               abreast     1             accident     1          adventurous     1
               bearing     1               become     1              breasts     1
                 broad     1             carriage     3            carriages     1
                coffin     1                 crew     1            daughters     1
            displaying     1               draped     1                draws     1
                 eight     1               enamel     1               escort     1
                family     2               father     1                first     1
               flanked     1            formation     1            forty-two     1
               gallant     1                 gold     1                  got     1
                   gun     2                hands     1           impression     1
              insignia     1                   la     1                 lead     1
                  life     1                 limp     1                 long     2
                  mass     1             measured     1                  men     1
              mourners     2               moving     1                naval     1
            ninety-two     1         overwhelming     1                 pace     1
              presents     1              private     1                 rear     1
              recently     1                right     1                 rise     1
                 ropes     1                 safe     1              sailors     1
                   say     1             se@ri@n     1            secretary     1
                 seems     1                short     1           silk-hatted     1
                slight     2           solidarity     1                 sons     1
                square     1             steadier     1            steadying     1
              strength     1                  two     1                 walk     1
                   Air     1                Brown     1          Christopher     1
         Christopher's     1            Churchill     5                Dixon     1
                 Force     1               Garter     1                 Jack     1
                Jeremy     1                 John     1               Julian     1
                  Lady     1                Major     1                 Mary     1
```

```
      Montague    1              Mr    9           Nicholas    1
     Peregrine    1           Piers    1          Randolph    1
         Royal    1          Sandys    1             Sarah    1
           Sir    1          Soames    3             Union    1
       Winston    1       Winston's    1

**********************************************************************************

WORDS SORTED BY DESCENDING FREQUENCY


WORD TYPES FOUND (UNLEMMATISED), WITH FREQUENCY

IRRELEVANT WORDS
             -   27

AMBIGUOUS WORDS
            is    2             was    1

GRAMMATICAL WORDS
           the   18             and   13                 of    7
             a    4              in    3                 it    3
           for    2              he    2                him    2
            on    2            that    2              their    2
          this    2           after    1                all    1
            an    1              as    1                 at    1
        behind    1              by    1                her    1
           his    1            it's    1                its    1
         never    1            then    1                 to    1
         we've    1            with    1

LEXICAL WORDS
            Mr    9       Churchill    5           carriage    3
        Soames    3          family    2                gun    2
          long    2        mourners    2             slight    2
       abreast    1        accident    1        adventurous    1
       bearing    1          become    1            breasts    1
         broad    1       carriages    1             coffin    1
          crew    1       daughters    1         displaying    1
        draped    1           draws    1              eight    1
        enamel    1          escort    1             father    1
         first    1         flanked    1          formation    1
     forty-two    1         gallant    1               gold    1
           got    1           hands    1         impression    1
      insignia    1              la    1               lead    1
          life    1            limp    1               mass    1
      measured    1             men    1             moving    1
         naval    1      ninety-two    1       overwhelming    1
          pace    1        presents    1            private    1
          rear    1        recently    1              right    1
          rise    1           ropes    1               safe    1
       sailors    1             say    1             se@ri@n    1
     secretary    1           seems    1              short    1
    silk-hatted   1      solidarity    1               sons    1
        square    1        steadier    1          steadying    1
      strength    1             two    1               walk    1
           Air    1           Brown    1        Christopher    1
 Christopher's    1           Dixon    1              Force    1
        Garter    1            Jack    1             Jeremy    1
          John    1          Julian    1               Lady    1
         Major    1            Mary    1           Montague    1
      Nicholas    1       Peregrine    1              Piers    1
      Randolph    1           Royal    1             Sandys    1
         Sarah    1             Sir    1              Union    1
       Winston    1       Winston's    1
```

```
*******************************************************************************

TEXT STATISTICS - based on unlemmatised word forms

                     No of types    No of tokens   Type-token ratio
                     ie different   ie running
                     words          text words
                     ------------   ------------   ----------------

Whole text:               129            200         1 : 1.5503876

Grammatical:               29             78         1 : 2.68965517
Lexical:                   98            119         1 : 1.21428571
Ambiguous:                  2              3         1 : 1.5
Irrelevant:                 1             27         1 : 27.

Provisional lexical density (ignoring ambiguous words): 60.4060914 %


*******************************************************************************

FIRST LINE OF DATA PROCESSED:
10 5   1   10 1 1 a     11   ^fl/anked£                                        /
LAST LINE OF DATA PROCESSED:
10 5   3  620 1 1 a     12   ^[se@ri@n] . ^{S\arah} and M\ary£ -               /

*******************************************************************************

NORMAL END
IN STATEMENT    216
RUN TIME-MSEC   4475
STMTS EXECUTED 26974
MCSEC / STMT    165
REGENERATIONS   2
```

One noteworthy feature of the initialisation phase is the assignment, to certain variables, of values some or all of which will normally need to be changed from one run of the program to the next. TEXT is a string variable containing details of the text to be analysed, and will be used as a heading for the results. The value of MAXCOUNT sets a limit to the number of words to be processed, so that the user can, for example, analyse just the first 200 words of the text, or 1 000 words, or whatever. For safety, &STLIMIT is set to a value which will be sufficient for the processing of MAXCOUNT words of text. SORTING is set to 'YES' or 'NO' according to whether the lists of words found by the program are to be sorted and printed or simply counted. If sorting is to be carried out, this can be alphabetical (CHOICE = 'A'), by descending frequency (CHOICE = 'DF') or both (CHOICE = 'BOTH'). CHOICE is set to 'NULL' if no sorting is to be done. A further choice afforded to the user is whether to request a printout of the dictionaries of irrelevant, ambiguous and grammatical words (PRINTDICT = 'YES' or 'NO'). The assignment of suitable values of ESTLEX and ESTGRAM simply ensures that the tables which will contain the lexical and grammatical words start with roughly the right number of elements: they will, of course, be expanded automatically if necessary.

Statement 9 of the program introduces a feature which can be used for compression: the assignment of a value to more than one variable in a single statement. In this case, the value 1 is given to both &ANCHOR and

&TRIM. Further examples of multiple assignment can be found in statements 64, 65 and 67. Statement 10 declares the set of word-forming characters: note that it includes lower as well as upper case letters, since the text contains both. The symbol ` is used in the text for apostrophes, and @ is used for the 'schwa' vowel [ə] in certain items for which a phonetic transcription is given. The tables set up in statements 13–15 will contain the dictionaries of irrelevant, ambiguous and grammatical words, and the tables created in statements 16–19 will store the four types of word found in the text.

The program makes use of 7 programmer-defined functions, each written to perform some specific subtask.

DICT reads words from the file containing lists of irrelevant, ambiguous and grammatical words, and stores them in a table which is the first argument of the function. The file to be read contains comment lines starting with an asterisk, which are ignored by DICT. The list of words in any particular category ends with a marker which is given as the second argument of the function.

PRINT1 and PRINT2 both print information stored in two-dimensional arrays (which may, of course, have been derived by conversion of a table). PRINT1 prints the contents of the second column of such an array in lines of 70–80 characters, and is used to print the dictionaries if this option has been set (that is, if PRINTDICT = 'YES'). PRINT2 prints the contents of both columns, with three pairs of columns across a page. It is used to print the lists of the various types of words found, with their frequencies.

STRIP is necessary in this program because of the format of the text used as data for analysis. As mentioned earlier, each data record in the London–Lund corpus has non-textual information in positions 1–27, and this must be removed before the main processing of each line can begin. The text also contains certain diacritic marks indicating such things as stress and intonation, and these too must be removed. STRIP does this by isolating sequences of word-forming characters and blanks, and concatenating them into a new line, skipping over any other characters.

FIND searches for any given word in a list of words stored in an array. It is used to find out, for each word in the text, whether it occurs in one of the lists of irrelevant, ambiguous and grammatical words. FIND uses a technique known as a 'binary search', which is best understood by means of an example.

Imagine that we have a list of just 9 words in alphabetical order: APPLE, BANANA, CHERRY, DAMSON, FIG, GREENGAGE, LEMON, PEAR, PLUM. The middle item in a list of 9 is the fifth. We can express this more generally if we consider that our list has a lower bound which is item number 1, and an upper bound which is the last item on the list, here number 9. That is:

```
M = (L + U) / 2
```

Statement 154 of the program

where M is the number of the middle item, L is the lower bound and U is the upper bound. It may be that the word we are looking for happens to be this middle item, and we can test this by means of the predicate LEQ in SPITBOL as in statement 155 (or we could use IDENT which, unlike LEQ, is available in standard SNOBOL4 too). If we are searching for the word FIG, this middle item is indeed the one we are looking for, and the function can return a successful result.

But suppose that we are looking for some word other than FIG, so that the LEQ predicate fails. We now determine whether the required word would occur in the upper or the lower part of the alphabetical list. This is done by testing whether the word we want is 'lexically greater than' the middle item in the list (statement 156). If it is (as it will be if, for instance, we are searching for PEAR), we can ignore the upper half of the list. We therefore reset the lower boundary of our search segment to the item below the middle one (statement 158). We shall see below that the search process is cyclic, and also that the upper bound, U, may need to be decreased. It is obvious, then, that eventually we might create the situation where L becomes greater than U. If this situation arises there is clearly no point in continuing the search, and we have failed to find the required item. Statement 159 checks for this eventuality, and if it fails, so does the function. If, however, the predicate in statement 159 succeeds, we go back to statement 154 to calculate the mid-point of the new, reduced list, and the cycle repeats. Eventually, we shall either find the required word at the mid-point of the search segment, or we shall fail to find it at all, in which case we can say that the word does not occur in the list.

So far, we have considered only the situation where statement 156 succeeds. If it fails, as it would if we were searching for APPLE, we can ignore the *lower* half of the list. In this case we reset the *upper* bound of the search segment to be the item which is one above the middle of the current segment (statement 157). We again check that lower and upper bounds have not met and crossed (statement 159). If they have not, we go back to statement 154 to calculate the mid-point of a new search segment.

Let us now follow through the steps in a search for the item PEAR in our list of 9 items. Since at first L = 1 and U = 9, M acquires the value 5 in statement 154. The fifth word in the list is not PEAR but FIG, so that the LEQ predicate in statement 155 fails. The LGT predicate in statement 156, however, succeeds. Control therefore passes to statement 158, and the lower bound is reset to 5 + 1, or 6. The comparison in statement 159 succeeds, since L is 6 and U is 9. We therefore go back to statement 154 and calculate a new value of (6 + 9)/2, or 7, for M. Note that because L and U are integers the remainder is ignored. This deals with the situation where, as here, there is an even number of items in the segment being searched (here, the 4 items from 6 to 9 inclusive), so that there is no item which is precisely in the middle. In this case, the lower item (here, number 7) is taken as the one for further comparisons. Statement 155 now tests whether item 7 is the one we want. It is not (the seventh item is LEMON), so statement 156 checks whether the required word, PEAR, is lexically greater than the word at position 7, LEMON. This succeeds, control passes to statement 158, and the lower bound is reset to 7 + 1, or 8. Since U is still

9, the comparison in statement 159 succeeds and we go back once again to statement 154. M is given a new value of (8 + 9)/2, or 8 in integer arithmetic. Finally, the predicate in statement 155 succeeds, since the item at position 8 is PEAR, the word we are searching for. The function therefore returns successfully.

It is left as an exercise for the reader to work out the steps involved in searching for (i) a word which is in the upper half of the list (such as APPLE), and (ii) a word which is not on the list at all (such as STRAWBERRY).

The function WORDSPRINT is used to print the lists of irrelevant, ambiguous, grammatical and lexical words found by the program, together with a heading. It calls PRINT2 to format and output the individual lists.

The function PROTOCALC returns the number of elements in a two-dimensional array. As we shall see later, it is used to determine the number of words of each type which have been found in the text.

Once the programmer-defined functions are understood, the operation of the main body of the program is fairly straightforward. The first part of the processing phase reads in the three dictionaries and then uses the function SORT (which is built into SPITBOL though not into standard SNOBOL4 – see section 14.2.4) to sort the words into alphabetical order.

SORT takes as its first argument the name of a one- or two-dimensional array or table. If the function is to operate on a one-dimensional array, no second argument is necessary. If the contents of a table are to be sorted, the function automatically converts the table to a two-dimensional array in just the same way as the function CONVERT. When operating on a two-dimensional array (either specified as the first argument or derived from a table acting as first argument), SORT requires a second argument giving the column of the array containing the values which are to act as the 'key' for sorting. Consider statements 36 and 37. Statement 36 calls DICT to form a table which is indexed by the number of each word in sequence in the dictionary, and whose elements contain the word itself. When SORT is called in statement 37, it converts the table to an array with the numbers in column 1 and the words in column 2. Since we have specified 2 as the value of the second argument, the words are taken as the sorting key, and are rearranged into alphabetical order, though each word remains associated with its own frequency.

Note that in statement 36, TOTIRREL will contain the total number of words in the IRRELWORDS dictionary, since the function DICT is written in such a way that it returns as its value the number of items read in. This value is needed later for the binary search procedure carried out by FIND.

If a printout of the dictionaries has been requested, PRINT1 is used to achieve this; otherwise, this part of the program is skipped by means of the go-to in statement 42.

The next part of the program reads in the textual data line by line, strips off the first 27 columns and the diacritics using the function STRIP, isolates words using the pattern WORDPAT, keeps a count of the number of words so far isolated, and attempts to find each word in one of the three dictionaries. If the word is found in a dictionary, a counter for that category of words is incremented. If an ambiguous word is found, the line containing that word is printed out with a question mark in front of the ambiguous word. If the word being processed is not in any of the dictionaries, it is counted as a lexical word.

In the next section of the program, the tables of words found are sorted and printed in whatever way has been selected by the user, if SORTING has been set to 'YES'. Note that since the tables are referenced by the words themselves, each element containing the frequency of the relevant word, the words will be in column 1 of the two-dimensional array generated by SORT, and the frequencies in column 2. For an alphabetical sort, therefore, with the words themselves as key, we must specify 1 as the first argument of SORT, as in statements 91–4. Statements 103–6 introduce a further SPITBOL function, RSORT, which is identical to SORT except that it produces a list in *reverse* alphabetical order or, if sorting on numbers, a list in *descending* numerical order. Since 2 is given as the second argument of the function, statements 103–6 request sorting of the word/frequency pairs in descending numerical order of the frequency. WORDSPRINT is used to print the lists of sorted words.

If no sorting has been carried out, we still need to convert the tables to arrays in order to use the function PROTOCALC to find the number of elements in each. This number is, of course, the number of words found in each category, so that we now have all the information we require in order to calculate the lexical density.

The final phase of the program prints out the statistics for the text. For each category of word, the program prints the number of word types (different words), the number of word tokens (running text words) and the type/token ratio. The value of the lexical density, based on the ratio of lexical words to the sum of lexical and grammatical words, is also printed. This is a provisional value, in that it does not take into account the ambiguous words found by the program. Since these are printed out in context for the user to examine, an adjusted value for the lexical density can easily be calculated manually from the text statistics after the potentially ambiguous items have been assigned to either the grammatical or the lexical category. The program finally prints the first and last lines of data processed.

14.7 Conclusion

It is hoped that the discussion in part II of this book, and especially the programs presented in this final chapter, will have convinced the reader of the rewards to be gained from the considerable effort involved in learning a high-level computer language, and of the power and usefulness of SNOBOL4, in particular, as a language for use in linguistic and literary research. There is much important and exciting work yet to be done in the area of computational text analysis, and it is the author's hope that this book will help provide the tools for the job.

Appendix: model answers to exercises

Exercises 4

2 All are valid except:

`ALPHA:3`	(colon not permitted in a name).
`3VOWEL`	(name must begin with a letter).
`CONS-CLASS`	(hyphen not permitted in a name).

3

`SIZE_ALPHA   =   10`	(hyphen not permitted in a name).
`COUNT   =   COUNT   +   1`	(= operator must have at least one blank on either side).
`SIZE2   =   SIZE2   +   4`	(name may not begin with a number; + operator must have at least one blank on either side).

4

(i) `MAX   =   45`

(ii) `TRUTH   =   'ALL MEN ARE LIARS'`

(iii) `LCOUNT   = LCOUNT   +   1`

(iv) `ASS.1   =   'SILLY '   'BILLY'` <u>or</u>
`ASS.1   =   'SILLY'   ' BILLY'`

(v) `RESULT   =   'THE TOTAL COUNT IS '   FINAL`

Exercises 5

1

(i) `RECORD   'G'`

(ii) `RECORD   ' OF,'`

(iii) `RECORD   'A'   |   'I'`

(iv) `RECORD   ','   |   ':'   |   ';'`

(v) `RECORD   ('F'   |   'O')   ('S'   |   'T')`

2

(i) `VOWEL   =   'A'   |   'E'   |   'I'   |   'O'   |   'U'`

(ii) `PUNCT   =   '.'   |   '!'   |   '?'`

(iii) `NUMBER   =   '0' | '1' | '2' | '3' | '4' | '5' | '6' | '7' | '8' | '9'`

(iv) `BILAB   =   'P'   |   'B'   |   'M'`

3 (i) `LINE ' HOWEVER,'`
(ii) `WORD VOWEL VOWEL`
(iii) `TEXT NUMBER 'X'`
(iv) `WORD BILAB VOWEL`

4 (i)
```
&ANCHOR = 1
WORD 'UN'
```
(ii)
```
&ANCHOR = 0
LINE ' IT' PUNCT
```
(iii)
```
&ANCHOR = 1
LINE '****'
```

5 (i) `WORD 'F' = 'V'`
(ii) `LINE VOWEL = '*'`
(iii) `TEXT ' AND ' = ' BUT '`
(iv) `RECORD PUNCT =`

6 (i) The value O is assigned to V.
(ii) The pattern match fails: there is no occurrence of AP, OP or UP.
(iii) The value P is assigned to C, and A to V.
(iv) The value U is assigned to V (even though there is no following P) because the immediate value assignment operator has been used.

7 (i) `LINE VOWEL . V1`
(ii) `TEXT ('.' | ',' | ';' | ':') . P1`
(iii) `LINE 'T' VOWEL . V`
(iv) `LINE VOWEL $ V 'P' VOWEL`

Exercises 6

1 The invalid labels are:

`DO AGAIN`	(contains a blank)
` LOOP`	(does not begin in position 1)
`*FINDP`	(does not begin with a letter or number)

2 (i)
```
         NUMBER = NUMBER + 1                            :(PRINTOUT)
```
(ii)
```
         RESULT = 'THE VOWEL COUNT IS ' VCOUNT          :(CPRINT)
```
(iii)
```
         &ANCHOR = 0
         LINE 'X'                                       :S(XCOUNT)
```
(iv)
```
         &ANCHOR = 0
         TEXT 'F' VOWEL                                 :S(COUNT)F(MORE)
```

(assuming that VOWEL has been defined as in Exercises 5)

(v)
```
         &ANCHOR = 0
AGAIN    RECORD 'E' =                                   :S(AGAIN)
```
(vi)
```
         &ANCHOR = 0
MORE     LINE VOWEL = '*'                               :S(MORE)F(VCOUNT)
```

3
```
         &ANCHOR = 0
AGAIN    TEXT VOWEL =                                   :F(PRINTOUT)
         COUNT = COUNT + 1                              :(AGAIN)
```

4 (i) Incorrect: the + sign for continuation must be in position 1.
(ii) Syntactically correct, but would lead to the output of VOWELSIS.
(iii) Correct and acceptable.
(iv) Incorrect: a statement must not be split in the middle of a variable name.
(v) Incorrect: the string quotes must be closed on the first line and reopened on the second.
(vi) Correct and acceptable.
(vii) Correct and acceptable, if rather odd!

Exercises 7

(i)

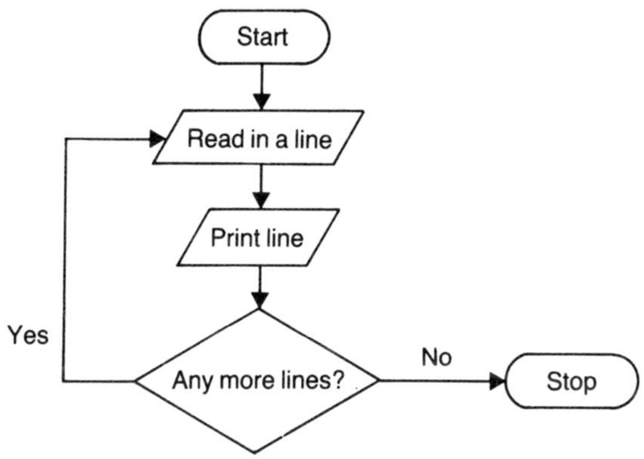

Figure E7.1 Flowchart for printing all records from a data file

```
* THIS PROGRAM READS DATA RECORDS FROM A FILE AND PRINTS THEM.
*
READ     OUTPUT = INPUT                          :S(READ)
END
```

(ii)

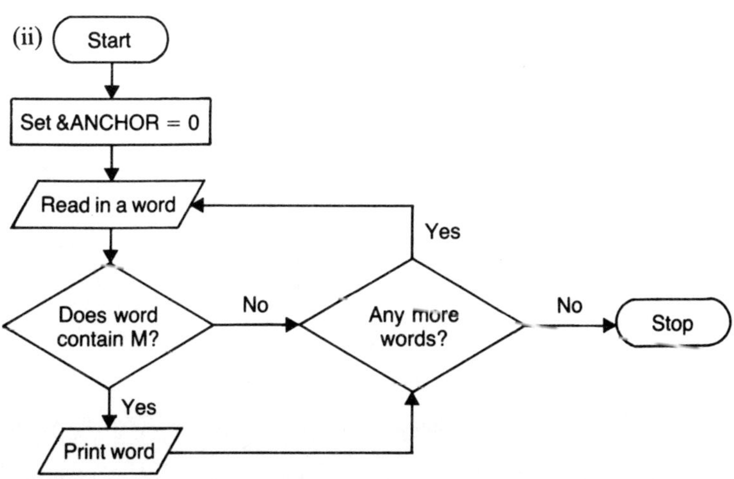

Figure E7.2 Flowchart for printing all words containing M

```
* THIS PROGRAM READS IN WORDS, ONE PER DATA RECORD, AND PRINTS
* ALL THOSE CONTAINING THE LETTER 'M'.
*
* INITIALISATION
*
         &ANCHOR  =  0
*
* PROCESSING
*
* READ A WORD IN.
*
READ     WORD  =  INPUT                              :F(END)
*
* TEST FOR 'M'.
*
         WORD  'M'                                   :F(READ)
*
* IF WORD CONTAINS 'M', PRINT IT.
*
         OUTPUT  =  WORD                             :(READ)
END
```

(iii)

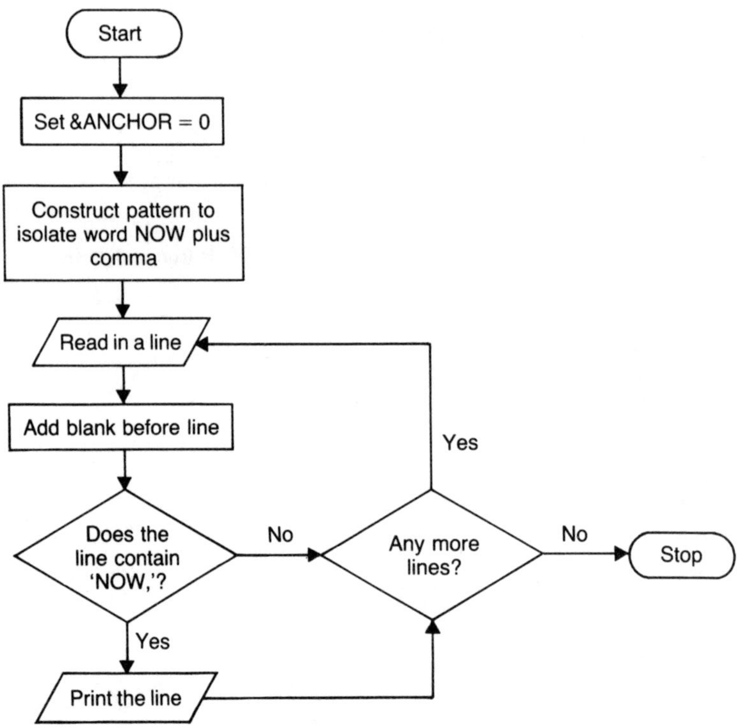

Figure E7.3 Flowchart for printing all text lines containing NOW plus a comma

(Note that the way the pattern will be constructed means that a blank must be added before each line which is read in.)

```
* THIS PROGRAM READS IN A TEXT, ONE LINE AT A TIME, AND PRINTS
* ALL LINES CONTAINING THE WORD 'NOW' FOLLOWED BY A COMMA.
*
* INITIALISATION
*
        &ANCHOR  =  0
*
* SET UP PATTERNS TO FIND 'NOW,'
*
        BEFORE   =  ' '  |  '"'
        NOWPAT   =  BEFORE  'NOW,'
*
* PROCESSING
*
* READ IN A LINE AND ADD INITIAL BLANK IN CASE 'NOW' IS THE FIRST WORD.
*
READ    LINE  =  ' '  INPUT                         :F(END)
*
* TEST FOR NOWPAT AND PRINT LINE IF SUCCESSFUL.
*
        LINE  NOWPAT                                :F(READ)
        OUTPUT  =  LINE                             :(READ)
END
```

(iv)

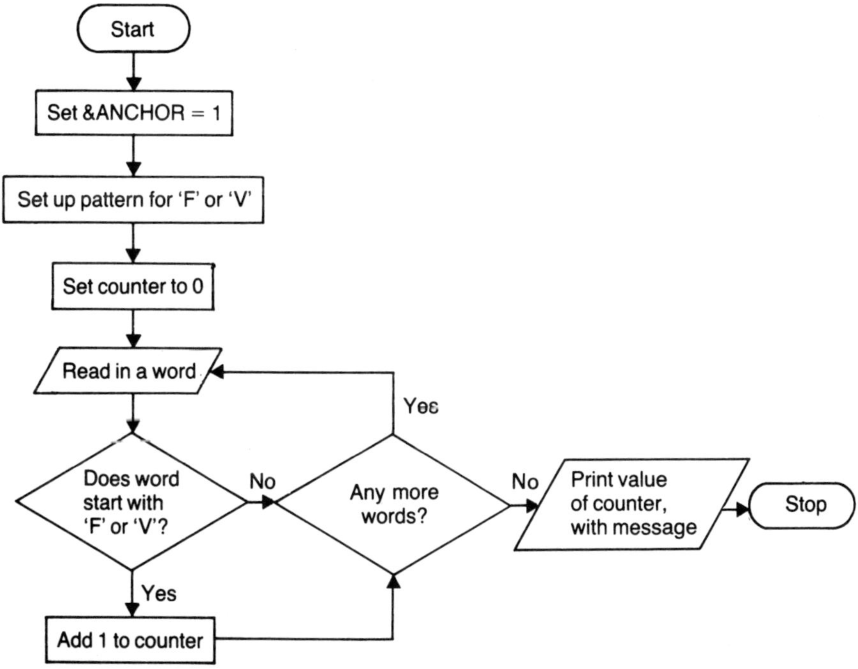

Figure E7.4 Flowchart for counting the number of words beginning with F or V

```
* THIS PROGRAM READS IN WORDS, ONE PER RECORD, AND COUNTS THE NUMBER
* WHICH BEGIN WITH EITHER 'F' OR 'V'.
*
* INITIALISATION
*
        &ANCHOR  =  1
        FVPAT   =  'F'  |  'V'
        COUNT   =  0
```

```
*
* PROCESSING
*
* READ IN A WORD.
*
READ     WORD  =  INPUT                          :F(PRINT)
*
* TEST FOR 'F' OR 'V' AT BEGINNING OF WORD.  IF SUCCESSFUL, ADD 1
* TO COUNT AND FETCH ANOTHER WORD; IF NOT, FETCH ANOTHER WORD
* STRAIGHT AWAY.
*
         WORD  FVPAT                             :F(READ)
         COUNT  =  COUNT  +  1                   :(READ)
*
* TERMINATION
*
* PRINT VALUE OF COUNT, WITH SUITABLE MESSAGE.
*
PRINT    OUTPUT  =  'THE NUMBER OF WORDS BEGINNING WITH '
+                   '"F" OR "V" IS '  COUNT
END
```

Exercises 8

1 (i) `'P'  LEN(1)  'R'`

(ii) `ANY('AEIOU')`

(iii) `BREAK(',')  ','  BREAK(',')  .  INTERCOM`

(iv) `SPAN('*')`

(v) `LEN(11)`

2

```
* THIS PROGRAM COUNTS THE NUMBER OF WORDS IN A TEXT WHICH ARE
* MORE THAN 4 LETTERS LONG.  THE HYPHEN AND APOSTROPHE ARE
* COUNTED AS LETTERS.
*
* INITIALISATION
*
         &ANCHOR  =  1
         LETTERS  =  "ABCDEFGHIJKLMNOPQRSTUVWXYZ'-"
         WPAT  =  BREAK(LETTERS)  SPAN(LETTERS)  .  WORD
         COUNT  =  0
*
* PROCESSING
*
* READ IN A LINE; ISOLATE AND DELETE A WORD.
*
READ     LINE  =  INPUT                          :F(PRINT)
GETWD    LINE  WPAT  =                           :F(READ)
*
* TEST IF WORD IS LONGER THAN 4 LETTERS.  IF SO, ADD 1 TO COUNT
* AND THEN FETCH ANOTHER WORD; IF NOT, FETCH ANOTHER WORD STRAIGHT
* AWAY.
*
         WORD  LEN(5)                            :F(GETWD)
         COUNT  =  COUNT  +  1                   :(GETWD)
*
* TERMINATION
*
* PRINT OUT THE COUNT WITH A MESSAGE.
*
PRINT    OUTPUT  =  'THE NUMBER OF WORDS WITH MORE THAN FOUR '
+                   'LETTERS IS '  COUNT
END
```

3

```
* THIS PROGRAM PROCESSES DATA RECORDS OF THE FORM
*      NAME*SEX(M/F)*ADDRESS
* IT PRINTS THE NAMES OF ALL THE FEMALES AND COUNTS THE NUMBERS
* OF MALES AND FEMALES.
*
* INITIALISATION
*
```

```
         &ANCHOR  =  1
         PAT  =  BREAK('*')  .  NAME  '*'  ('F'  |  'M')  .  SEX  '*'
         FCOUNT  =  0
         MCOUNT  =  0
*
* PROCESSING
*
* READ IN A LINE OF DATA, USE PATTERN 'PAT' TO ISOLATE NAME AND
* SEX.  IF PATTERN FAILS, PRINT ERROR MESSAGE.
*
READ     LINE  =  INPUT                             :F(PRINT)
         LINE  PAT                                  :F(ERROR)
*
* IF FEMALE, PRINT NAME AND ADD 1 TO FCOUNT; OTHERWISE ADD 1
* TO MCOUNT.  FETCH ANOTHER DATA RECORD.
*
         SEX  'F'                                   :F(INC.M)
         OUTPUT  =  NAME
         FCOUNT  =  FCOUNT  +  1                    :(READ)
INC.M    MCOUNT  =  MCOUNT  +  1                    :(READ)
*
* TERMINATION
*
* PRINT COUNTS.
*
PRINT    OUTPUT  =  'THE NUMBER OF FEMALES IS '  FCOUNT
         OUTPUT  =  'THE NUMBER OF MALES IS '  MCOUNT  :(END)
*
* ERROR MESSAGE
*
ERROR    OUTPUT  =  'DATA FORMAT ERROR IN LINE: '  LINE
END
```

4

```
* THIS PROGRAM ISOLATES SENTENCES FROM A TEXT AND PRINTS AND
* COUNTS THOSE WHICH BEGIN WITH 'AND'.  IT IS ASSUMED THAT AT
* LEAST ONE BLANK OCCURS BETWEEN SENTENCES, AND THAT THE TEXT
* CONSISTS OF A NUMBER OF COMPLETE SENTENCES, TERMINATED BY
* . ! OR ?
*
* INITIALISATION
*
         &ANCHOR  =  1
         &TRIM  =  1
         ANDCOUNT  =  0
*
* SET UP PATTERNS TO DETECT SENTENCE END, AND TO FIND INITIAL
* 'AND', WHICH MAY BE PRECEDED BY A QUOTATION MARK.
*
         SENTEND  =  '.!?'
         SENT  =  (BREAK(SENTEND)  ANY(SENTEND)  BREAK(' ')) . SENTENCE
         PUNCT  =  SENTEND  ',;:" '
         ANDPAT  =  SPAN(' ')  ('AND'  |  '"AND')  ANY(PUNCT)
*
* PROCESSING
*
* READ IN A LINE AND CONCATENATE A BLANK BEFORE IT, IN CASE THE FIRST
* WORD IS 'AND'.  ALSO CONCATENATE A BLANK AT THE END OF THE LINE,
* IN CASE THE END OF THE LINE COINCIDES WITH THE END OF A SENTENCE.
* IN BOTH OF THESE CASES, SENTENCE ISOLATION  WOULD FAIL IF NO BLANKS
* WERE ADDED, BECAUSE OT THE WAY 'SENT' NEEDS TO BE SET UP TO ISOLATE
* THE WHOLE SENTENCE.  THE MODIFIED INPUT LINE IS CONCATENATED WITH
* THE CURRENT CONTENTS OF 'LINE' (INITIALLY NULL).
*
READ     LINE  =  LINE  ' '  INPUT  ' '                :F(PRINT)
*
* TEST FOR SENTENCE END.  IF PRESENT, DELETE, AND TEST 'SENTENCE'
* FOR INITIAL 'AND'.  IF FOUND, ADD 1 TO ANDCOUNT, PRINT SENTENCE
* AND THEN LOOK FOR ANOTHER SENTENCE.  IF SENTENCE DOES NOT BEGIN
* WITH 'AND', LOOK FOR ANOTHER STRAIGHT AWAY.  IF THERE WAS NO
* SENTENCE DELIMITER IN 'LINE', CONCATENATE ANOTHER LINE.
*
GETSENT  LINE  SENT  =                                 :F(READ)
         SENTENCE  ANDPAT                              :F(GETSENT)
         ANDCOUNT  =  ANDCOUNT  +  1
         OUTPUT  =  SENTENCE
         OUTPUT  =                                     :(GETSENT)
```

```
*
* TERMINATION
*
* PRINT COUNT WITH MESSAGE.
*
PRINT    OUTPUT  =  "THE NUMBER OF SENTENCES BEGINNING WITH "
+                   "'AND' IS "  ANDCOUNT
END
```

Exercises 9

1 (i) `(N ! 3) + (5 * P) - (Q / 10)`
(ii) `S + (2 * T) - (M ! 2)`
(iii) `(0.5 * (X ! 2)) - (Y / 5.0)`

2 (i) `(L + 4) ! 2 / N + 100`
(ii) `X * Y / 100 + Z / 4`
(iii) `24 * (W - (N * (N + 1) / 4)) ! 2 / (N * (N + 1) * (2 * N + 1))`

3 (i) Succeeds: both are equal to 8.
(ii) Succeeds: both are equal to 17.8.
(iii) Fails: 3 / 2 is 1 in integer arithmetic.
(iv) Fails: the two strings are not identical.
(v) Fails: RABBIT comes *before* RABID in an alphabetical list.
(vi) Succeeds: COMPUTER comes before CONFUCIUS in an alphabetical list.

4

```
* THIS PROGRAM READS IN A TEXT ONE LINE AT A TIME, ISOLATES THE
* FIRST 100 WORDS, AND CALCULATES THE MEAN LENGTH OF THESE 100 WORDS.
*
* INITIALISATION
*
         &ANCHOR  =  1
         &TRIM  =  1
         LETTERCOUNT  =  0.0
         WORDCOUNT  =  0
         LETTERS  =  "ABCDEFGHIJKLMNOPQRSTUVWXYZ'-"
         WPAT  =  BREAK(LETTERS)  SPAN(LETTERS)  .  WORD
*
* PROCESSING
*
* READ IN A LINE, ISOLATE A WORD AND DELETE IT, ADD LENGTH TO
* 'LETTERCOUNT' AND 1 TO 'WORDCOUNT' (LETTERCOUNT IS A REAL NUMBER SO
* THAT AN ACCURATE VALUE OF THE MEAN LENGTH CAN BE CALCULATED
* LATER).
*
READ     LINE  =  INPUT                         :F(NODATA)
GETWD    LINE  WPAT  =                          :F(READ)
         LETTERCOUNT  =  LETTERCOUNT  +  SIZE(WORD)
         WORDCOUNT  =  WORDCOUNT  +  1
*
* IF 100 WORDS HAVE BEEN PROCESSED, CALCULATE AND PRINT MEAN LENGTH,
* OTHERWISE FETCH ANOTHER WORD.
*
         LT(WORDCOUNT,100)                      :S(GETWD)
*
* TERMINATION
*
         OUTPUT  =  'THE MEAN LENGTH OF THE FIRST 100 WORDS IS '
+                   LETTERCOUNT  /  WORDCOUNT  ' LETTERS'  :(END)
*
* ERROR MESSAGE FOR THE CASE WHERE THERE ARE FEWER THAN 100 WORDS
* IN THE TEXT.
*
NODATA   OUTPUT  =  'THERE ARE FEWER THAN 100 WORDS IN THE TEXT'
         WORDCOUNT  =  CONVERT(WORDCOUNT,'INTEGER')
```

```
         OUTPUT  =  'THE MEAN LENGTH OF THE '  WORDCOUNT
+                   ' WORDS PRESENT IS '  LETTERCOUNT  /  WORDCOUNT
+                   ' LETTERS'
END
```

5

```
* THIS PROGRAM READS IN NUMBERS, ONE PER DATA RECORD, AND CALCULATES
* AND PRINTS THEIR VARIANCE.
*
* INITIALISATION
*
         &TRIM  =  1
         SUM  =  0.0
         SUMSQ  =  0
         N  =  0
*
* PROCESSING
*
* READ IN A NUMBER, ADD ITS VALUE TO 'SUM', AND ITS SQUARE TO 'SUMSQ'.
* ALSO INCREMENT COUNTER.
*
READ     X  =  INPUT                        :F(CALC)
         SUM  =  SUM  +  X
         SUMSQ  =  SUMSQ  +  X ! 2
         N  =  N  +  1                      :(READ)
*
* TERMINATION
*
* CALCULATE AND PRINT VARIANCE.
*
CALC     OUTPUT  =  'THE VARIANCE OF THE '  N  ' NUMBERS IS '
+                   (SUMSQ  -  SUM ! 2  / N)  /  (N - 1)
END
```

Exercises 10

1 (i) The string NO PEACE (with an initial blank) is assigned to INTER.
(ii) Fails: when the F has been matched, the cursor has already gone past position 12.
(iii) The string O PEACE FOR THE WICKED is assigned to LAST.
(iv) Succeeds: there is an R immediately after position 3.
(v) Fails: the first E is not followed by a D. (Note that the pattern would succeed if BREAKX were used in SPITBOL.)
(vi) The string EA is assigned as the value of VLS.
(vii) The strong ON EARTH is assigned as the value of a variable named PEACE.

2 (i)
```
STRING  TAB(3)  'P'
```
or
```
&ANCHOR  =  0
STRING  POS(3)  'P'
```

(ii)
```
WORD  RTAB(3)  'ISH'
```
or
```
&ANCHOR  =  0
WORD  RPOS(3)  'ISH'
```
or
```
&ANCHOR  =  0
WORD  'ISH'  RPOS(0)
```

(iii)
```
WORD  RTAB(2) LEN(2)  .  LAST
```
or
```
&ANCHOR  =  0
WORD  RPOS(2)  LEN(2)  .  LAST
```

(iv)
```
OUTPUT  =  DUPL(' ',(132  - SIZE(HEADING)) / 2)  HEADING
```

(v)
```
CODE  RTAB(1)  ANY('0123456789')
```

3

```
* THIS PROGRAM TAKES DATA RECORDS CONTAINING THE NAME, SEX (M/F)
* AGE AND SOCIAL CLASS (1-5) OF AN INFORMANT, AND THE
* INFORMANT'S SCORE ON A LINGUISTIC TEST.  THE FORMAT IS AS FOLLOWS:
*
*          SMITH,JEAN*F*51*3*38
*
* THE PROGRAM PRODUCES A FORMATTED DATA LIST, COUNTS AND PRINTS
* THE NUMBER OF INFORMANTS IN EACH OF THE AGE RANGES <20, 21-30,
* 31-40, 41-50, 50-60, AND CALCULATES THE MEAN SCORE FOR INFORMANTS
* IN EACH AGE GROUP.
*
* INITIALISATION
*
         ANCHOR  =  1
         &TRIM   =  1
         DATAPAT  =  BREAK('*')  .  NAME  '*'  BREAK('*')  .  SEX
+                     '*'  BREAK('*')  .  AGE  '*'  BREAK('*')  .  CLASS
+                     '*'  REM  .  SCORE
*
* PROCESSING
*
* PRINT HEADING AND UNDERLINE IT.
*
         OUTPUT  =  'NAME'  DUPL(' ',36)  'SEX'  DUPL(' ',17)
+                   'AGE'  DUPL(' ',17)  'CLASS'  DUPL(' ',15)
+                   'SCORE'
         OUTPUT  =  DUPL('-',4)  DUPL(' ',36)  DUPL('-',3)
+                   DUPL(' ',17)  DUPL('-',3)  DUPL(' ',17)
+                   DUPL('-',5)  DUPL(' ',15)  DUPL('-',5)
*
* READ IN A DATA LINE AND ISOLATE ITS PARTS.
*
READ     LINE  =  INPUT                              :F(PRINT)
         LINE DATAPAT                                :F(ERROR)
*
* PRINT THE REFORMATTED LINE.
*
         OUTPUT  =  NAME  DUPL(' ',41 - SIZE(NAME))  SEX
+                   DUPL(' ',19)  AGE  DUPL(' ',19)  CLASS
+                   DUPL(' ',19)  SCORE
*
* CREATE SUITABLE AGE GROUP AND SCORE VARIABLES BY INDIRECT
* REFERENCE, USING A COUNTER WHICH INCREASES IN STEPS OF 10.
* ADD 1 TO APPROPRIATE AGE GROUP VARIABLE, AND VALUE OF 'SCORE'
* TO SCORE VARIABLE FOR THAT GROUP.
*
         N  =  10
INC.N1   N  =  LE(N,50)  N + 10
         LE(AGE,N)                                   :F(INC.N1)
         $('AGE' N)  =  $('AGE' N)  +  1
         $('SCORE' N)  =  $('SCORE' N)  +  SCORE  :(READ)
*
* TERMINATION
*
* PRINT HEADINGS AND RESULTS, AGAIN USING INDIRECT REFERENCE TO
* CREATE APPROPRIATE VARIABLES.
*
PRINT    OUTPUT  =  'UPPER BOUND OF AGE GROUP'  DUPL(' ',10)
+                   'FREQUENCY'  DUPL(' ',10)  'MEAN'
         OUTPUT  =  DUPL('-',24)  DUPL(' ',10)  DUPL('-',9)
+                   DUPL(' ',10)  DUPL('-',4)
         N  =  10
INC.N2   N  =  LE(N,50)  N  +  10                    :F(END)
         AGEGRP  =  $('AGE' N)
*
* THE FOLLOWING TEST PREVENTS DIVISION BY ZERO IF THERE
* ARE NO INFORMANTS IN A PARTICULAR AGE GROUP.
*
         GT(AGEGRP,0)                                :F(INC.N2)
         OUTPUT  =  DUPL(' ',11)  N  DUPL(' ',25)  AGEGRP
```

```
+                    DUPL(' ',13)  $('SCORE' N)  /
+                    CONVERT(AGEGRP,'REAL')          :(INC.N2)
*
* ERROR MESSAGE
*
ERROR    OUTPUT  =  'ERROR IN DATA FORMAT IN LINE: '  LINE
END
```

4

```
* THIS PROGRAM READS IN A TEXT LINE BY LINE, ISOLATES WORDS, AND
* PRINTS AND COUNTS THOSE WHICH BEGIN AND END WITH THE SAME LETTER.
*
* INITIALISATION
*
         &ANCHOR  =  1
         &TRIM  =  1
         WDCOUNT  =  0
         LETTERS  =  "ABCDEFGHIJKLMNOPQRSTUVWXYZ'-"
         WPAT  =  BREAK(LETTERS)  SPAN(LETTERS)  .  WORD
*
* THE FOLLOWING PATTERN RECOGNISES STRINGS WHICH BEGIN AND END WITH
* THE SAME CHARACTER.
*
         BEGINEND  =  LEN(1)  $  CH  RTAB(1)  *CH
*
* PROCESSING
*
* READ IN A LINE, ISOLATE AND DELETE A WORD.
*
READ     LINE  =  INPUT                         :F(PRINT)
GETWD    LINE WPAT  =                           :F(READ)
*
* TEST WORD FOR REQUIRED PATTERN.  IF PATTERN FOUND, PRINT WORD
* AND INCREMENT COUNTER.  FETCH ANOTHER WORD.
*
         WORD BEGINEND                          :F(GETWD)
         OUTPUT  =  WORD
         WDCOUNT  = WDCOUNT  +  1               :(GETWD)
*
* TERMINATION
*
PRINT    OUTPUT  =  'THE NUMBER OF WORDS BEGINNING AND ENDING '
+                   'WITH THE SAME LETTER IS '  WDCOUNT
END
```

Exercises 11

1 (i)

```
         DEFINE('LASTC(STRING)')
.
.
.
* FUNCTION 'LASTC' RETURNS THE LAST CHARACTER IN A STRING.
*
LASTC    STRING  RTAB(1)  LEN(1)  .  LASTC      :(RETURN)
LASTC.END
```

(ii)

```
         DEFINE('DELV1(STRING)')
.
.
.
* FUNCTION 'DELV1' DELETES ALL VOWELS FROM A STRING.  THIS VERSION
* CAN ONLY BE USED WHEN THE ANCHOR IS OFF.
*
DELV1    STRING  ANY(VOWEL)  =                  :S(DELV1)
         DELV1  =  STRING                       :(RETURN)
DELV1.END
```

```
         DEFINE('DELV2(STRING)')
.
.
.
```

```
* FUNCTION 'DELV2' ALSO DELETES ALL VOWELS FROM A STRING.  THIS
* VERSION CAN BE USED WHETHER THE ANCHOR IS ON OR OFF.
*
DELV2    STRING BREAK(VOWEL) . UPTOV SPAN(VOWEL) = UPTOV  :S(DELV2)
         DELV2  =  STRING                                 :(RETURN)
DELV2.END
```

(iii)

```
         DEFINE('STARS(STRING)')
.
.
.
* FUNCTION 'STARS' REPLACES ALL NON-VOWEL CHARACTERS IN A STRING
* BY ASTERISKS.  IT CAN BE USED ONLY WHEN THE ANCHOR IS OFF.
*
STARS    STRING  NOTANY(VOWEL '*')  =  '*'          :S(STARS)
         STARS  =  STRING                           :(RETURN)
STARS.END
```

(iv)

```
         DEFINE('THREES(STRING)')
.
.
.
* FUNCTION 'THREES' RETURNS THE FIRST THREE-LETTER WORD IN A STRING.
*
THREES   STRING  WPAT  =                            :F(FRETURN)
         THREES  =  EQ(SIZE(WORD),3)  WORD     :S(RETURN)F(THREES)
THREES.END
```

(v)

```
         DEFINE('FIVEWD(STRING)COUNT')
.
.
.
* FUNCTION 'FIVEWD' SUCCEEDS IF THE STRING ACTING AS ITS ARGUMENT
* CONTAINS JUST 5 WORDS, BUT FAILS OTHERWISE.
*
FIVEWD   STRING  WPAT  =                         :F(FIVEWD.1)
         COUNT  =  LT(COUNT,5)  COUNT  +  1      :S(FIVEWD)F(FRETURN)
FIVEWD.1 EQ(COUNT,5)                             :S(RETURN)F(FRETURN)
FIVEWD.END
```

```
         DEFINE('RPAD(STRING,LENGTH,CHAR)N')
.
.
.
* THE FUNCTION 'RPAD' PADS OUT A STRING ON THE RIGHT, WITH ANY
* CHOSEN CHARACTER, TO A SPECIFIED LENGTH.
*
RPAD     CHAR  =  IDENT(CHAR)  ' '
         N  =  SIZE(STRING)
         RPAD  =  GE(N,LENGTH) STRING               :S(RETURN)
         RPAD  =  STRING  DUPL(CHAR,LENGTH - N)     :(RETURN)
RPAD.END
```

```
         DEFINE('LPAD(STRING,LENGTH,CHAR)N')
.
.
.
* THE FUNCTION 'LPAD' PADS OUT A STRING ON THE LEFT, WITH ANY
* CHOSEN CHARACTER, TO A SPECIFIED LENGTH.
*
LPAD     CHAR  =  IDENT(CHAR)  ' '
         N  =  SIZE(STRING)
         LPAD  =  GE(N,LENGTH)  STRING              :S(RETURN)
         LPAD  =  DUPL(CHAR,LENGTH - N)  STRING     :(RETURN)
LPAD.END
```

(Note that if RPAD or LPAD is called with only two arguments, this is equivalent to giving a null third argument. The first statement in each function ensures that in this 'default' case, the padding character is a blank. Note also that if the string is longer than the specified length, it will be returned unaltered as a result of the third statement in each function.)

3

```
* THIS PROGRAM COUNTS, AND PRINTS IN A TABLE WITH 5 COLUMNS,
* ALL THE WORDS IN A TEXT WHICH CONTAIN THE LETTER 'E'.  IT
* COULD EASILY BE ALTERED TO FIND WORDS CONTAINING ANY OTHER
* CHARACTER, SINCE THE ISOLATION OF WORDS, THE SEARCH FOR THE
* REQUIRED CHARACTER, AND THE PRINTING OF A SUITABLE HEADING,
* ARE ALL PERFORMED BY MEANS OF FUNCTIONS.
*
* INITIALISATION
*
         &ANCHOR  =  1
         &TRIM  =  1
         DEFINE('GETWORD()')
         LETTERS  =  "ABCDEFGHIJKLMNOPQRSTUVWXYZ'-"
         WPAT  =  BREAK(LETTERS)  SPAN(LETTERS)  .  GETWORD
         DEFINE('FINDCHAR(STRING,CHAR)')
         DEFINE('HEAD(HEADING,LINEWIDTH)X,Y')
         CH  =  'E'
         COLWIDTH  =  25
         COUNT  =  0
*
* PROCESSING
*
* PRINT HEADING FOR TABLE, USING FUNCTION 'HEAD'.
*
HEAD('WORDS CONTAINING THE LETTER "'  CH  '"',132)
*
* USE FUNCTION 'GETWORD' TO ISOLATE NEXT WORD.
*
GETWD    WORD  =  GETWORD()                      :F(REST)
*
* USE FUNCTION 'FINDCHAR' TO TEST FOR REQUIRED CHARACTER IN WORD.
* IF FOUND, INCREMENT COUNTER.
*
         FINDCHAR(WORD,CH)                       :F(GETWD)
         COUNT  =  COUNT  +  1
*
* IF WORD DOES CONTAIN REQUIRED CHARACTER, APPEND FORMATTED
* WORD TO THE LINE ('OUTLINE') BEING COLLECTED FOR EVENTUAL
* OUTPUT.  TEST WHETHER 'OUTLINE' CONTAINS 5 ITEMS.  IF SO,
* PRINT IT, CLEAR 'OUTLINE' AND FETCH ANOTHER WORD.  IF NOT, GET
* ANOTHER WORD STRAIGHT AWAY.  'N' COUNTS THE NUMBER OF WORDS
* CURRENTLY IN 'OUTLINE'.
*
         OUTLINE  =  OUTLINE  WORD  DUPL(' ',COLWIDTH - SIZE(WORD))
         N  =  LT(N,5)  N  +  1                  :S(GETWD)
         OUTPUT  =  OUTLINE
         OUTLINE  =
         N  =  1                                 :(GETWD)
*
* PRINT ANYTHING REMAINING IN 'OUTLINE' WHEN ALL WORDS HAVE BEEN
* PROCESSED (THERE MAY BE AN INCOMPLETE LINE OF WORDS NOT YET
* PRINTED).
*
REST     OUTPUT  =  OUTLINE
         OUTPUT  =
*
* TERMINATION
*
* PRINT THE NUMBER OF WORDS SELECTED.
*
         OUTPUT  =  'THE NUMBER OF WORDS CONTAINING THE CHARACTER "'
+                   CH  '" IS '  COUNT           :(END)
*
* FUNCTIONS
*
* FUNCTION 'GETWORD'
*
* THIS FUNCTION RETURNS THE NEXT WORD IN THE TEXT.  IT FAILS ONLY
* WHEN THERE IS NO MORE TEXT.  IT AUTOMATICALLY READS IN A NEW LINE
* WHEN NECESSARY.  'LINE' IS A GLOBAL VARIABLE.
```

```
*
GETWORD  LINE  WPAT  =                              :S(RETURN)
         LINE  =  INPUT                             :S(GETWORD)F(FRETURN)
GETWORD.END
*
* FUNCTION 'FINDCHAR'
*
* THIS FUNCTION TESTS FOR THE PRESENCE OF A GIVEN CHARACTER IN
* A STRING.
*
FINDCHAR STRING  BREAK(CHAR)  CHAR                  :S(RETURN)F(FRETURN)
FINDCHAR.END
*
* FUNCTION 'HEAD'
*
* THIS FUNCTION PRINTS AND UNDERLINES A HEADING CENTRALLY ON A LINE.
*
HEAD     Y  =  SIZE(HEADING)
         X  =  (LINEWIDTH - Y)  /  2
         OUTPUT  =  DUPL(' ',X)  HEADING
         OUTPUT  =  DUPL(' ',X)  DUPL('-',Y)        :(RETURN)
HEAD.END
*
* END OF FUNCTIONS
*
END
```

Exercises 12

1

```
* THIS PROGRAM READS IN POETRY (OR ANY OTHER TEXT) FROM A FILE,
* AND PRINTS A TABLE GIVING THE NUMBER OF LINES CONTAINING
* 0, 1, 2, 3, ETC. PUNCTUATION MARKS.  IT ASSUMES THAT ONLY
* ,.;:?! OCCUR IN THE TEXT, AND THAT NO LINE CONTAINS MORE THAN
* 8 PUNCTUATION MARKS.
*
* INITIALISATION
*
         &ANCHOR  =  1
         &TRIM  =  1
         PUNCT  =  ',.;:?!'
         PUNCPAT  =  BREAK(PUNCT)  ANY(PUNCT)
         PMARKS  =  ARRAY(9)
*
* NOTE THAT PMARKS<1> WILL COUNT THE NUMBER OF LINES WITH 0
* PUNCTUATION MARKS, AND IN GENERAL PMARKS<N + 1> WILL COUNT
* THE NUMBER OF LINES WITH N PUNCTUATION MARKS.  AN ALTERNATIVE
* WOULD BE TO DECLARE PMARKS WITH THE BOUNDS 0 TO 8.
*
         DEFINE('PCOUNT(TEXT)')
*
* PROCESSING
*
* READ IN A LINE AND USE FUNCTION 'PCOUNT' TO COUNT NUMBER OF
* PUNCTUATION MARKS IN IT.
*
READ     LINE  =  INPUT                          :F(PRINT)
         N  =  PCOUNT(LINE)
*
* INCREMENT APPROPRIATE ELEMENT OF ARRAY 'PMARKS'.  PRINT ERROR
* MESSAGE IF N > 8 AND ARRAY BOUNDS ARE THUS EXCEEDED.
*
         PMARKS<N + 1>  =  PMARKS<N + 1>  +  1   :S(READ)F(ERROR)
*
* TERMINATION
*
* PRINT TABLE.
*
PRINT    OUTPUT  =  'NO. OF PUNCTUATION MARKS'  DUPL(' ',10)
+                   'NO. OF LINES'
         OUTPUT  =  DUPL('-',24)  DUPL(' ',10)  DUPL('-',12)
INC.I    I  =  I  +  1
         OUTPUT  =  DUPL(' ',11)  I - 1  DUPL(' ',28)  PMARKS<I>
+                                                  :S(INC.I)F(END)
*
```

```
* FUNCTION 'PCOUNT'
*
* THIS FUNCTION COUNTS THE NUMBER OF PUNCTUATION MARKS IN A STRING.
*
PCOUNT   TEXT  PUNCPAT  =                           :F(RETURN)
         PCOUNT  =  PCOUNT  +  1                    :(PCOUNT)
PCOUNT.END
*
* ERROR MESSAGE
*
ERROR    OUTPUT  =  'TOO MANY PUNCTUATION MARKS'   :(READ)
*
END
```

2

```
* THIS PROGRAM PRINTS A LIST, WITH FREQUENCIES, OF ALL CHARACTERS
* AND COMBINATIONS OF CHARACTERS IN A TEXT WHICH ARE NOT
* UPPER CASE LETTERS, NUMBERS OR BLANKS.
*
* INITIALISATION
*
         &ANCHOR  =  1
         &TRIM  =  1
         ALPHANUM  =  'ABCDEFGHIJKLMNOPQRSTUVWXYZ0123456789 '
         LETNOPAT  =  BREAK(ALPHANUM)  .  CHARS  SPAN(ALPHANUM)
         OTHERCHARS  =  TABLE()
*
* PROCESSING
*
* READ IN A LINE, APPENDING A BLANK BECAUSE OTHERWISE NON-
* ALPHANUMERIC CHARACTERS AT THE END OF A LINE WILL NOT BE FOUND
* BY LETNOPAT.  ISOLATE NON-ALPHANUMERIC, NON-BLANK CHARACTERS.
*
READ     LINE  =  INPUT  ' '                        :F(CONV)
GETCHARS LINE  LETNOPAT  =                          :F(READ)
*
* TEST TO SEE IF 'CHARS' IS NULL (THIS WILL HAPPEN WHERE AN
* ALPHANUMERIC CHARACTER OR BLANK BEGINS A LINE, SO THAT 'BREAK'
* SUCCEEDS BUT ASSIGNS THE NULL STRING TO 'CHARS').
*
         IDENT(CHARS)                               :S(GETCHARS)
*
* INCREMENT APPROPRIATE ELEMENT OF TABLE 'OTHERCHARS'.
*
         OTHERCHARS<CHARS>  =  OTHERCHARS<CHARS>  +  1  :(GETCHARS)
*
* TERMINATION
*
* CONVERT TABLE TO ARRAY.
*
CONV     OTHERCHARS  =  CONVERT(OTHERCHARS,'ARRAY')   :F(ERROR)
*
* PRINT RESULTS, WITH HEADING.
*
         OUTPUT  =  'CHARACTER(S)'  DUPL(' ',10)  'FREQUENCY'
         OUTPUT  =  DUPL('-',12)  DUPL(' ',10)  DUPL('-',9)
INC.I    I  =  I  +  1
         OUTPUT  =  DUPL(' ',5)  OTHERCHARS<I,1>
+                   DUPL(' ',21 - SIZE(OTHERCHARS<I,1>))
+                   OTHERCHARS<I,2>            :S(INC.I)F(END)
*
* ERROR MESSAGE
*
ERROR    OUTPUT  =  'TABLE CONVERSION FAILED'
*
END
```

3

```
* THIS PROGRAM PRINTS THE WORDS WHICH OCCUR ONLY ONCE IN A TEXT.
* THE OUTPUT IS IN THE FORM OF A 5-COLUMN TABLE.  THE NUMBER OF
* WORDS IS ALSO PRINTED.
*
* INITIALISATION
*
         &ANCHOR  =  1
         &TRIM  =  1
         WDS  =  TABLE()
         DEFINE('GETWORD()')
         LETTERS  =  "ABCDEFGHIJKLMNOPQRSTUVWXYZ'-"
         WPAT  =  BREAK(LETTERS)  SPAN(LETTERS)  .  GETWORD
         DEFINE('HEAD(HEADING,LINEWIDTH)X,Y')
*
* PROCESSING
*
* ISOLATE WORDS USING FUNCTION 'GETWORD'.  ACCUMULATE WORD
* FREQUENCIES IN TABLE 'WDS'.
*
GETWD    WORD  =  GETWORD()                      :F(CONV)
         WDS<WORD>  =  WDS<WORD>  +  1           :(GETWD)
*
* TERMINATION
*
* CONVERT TABLE TO ARRAY AND FIND NUMBER OF ELEMENTS USING
* 'PROTOTYPE'.
*
CONV     WDS  =  CONVERT(WDS,'ARRAY')            :F(ERROR)
         PROTOTYPE(WDS)  BREAK(',')  .  N  ',2'  RPOS(0)
*
* USE FUNCTION 'HEAD' TO PRINT HEADINGS.
*
         HEAD('WORDS OCCURRING ONCE ONLY',125)
*
* PRINT TABLE OF RESULTS.
*
PRINT    J  =  1
INC.I    I  =  LT(I,N)  I  +  1                  :F(REST)
         EQ(WDS<I,2>,1)                          :F(INC.I)
         ONES  =  ONES  +  1
         OUTLINE  =  OUTLINE  WDS<I,1>  DUPL(' ',25 - SIZE(WDS<I,1>))
         J  =  LT(J,5)  J  +  1                  :S(INC.I)
         OUTPUT  =  OUTLINE
         OUTLINE  =                              :(PRINT)
REST     OUTPUT  =  OUTLINE
         OUTPUT =  ;  OUTPUT  =
         OUTPUT  =  'THE NUMBER OF WORDS OCCURRING ONCE ONLY IS '
+                   ONES                         :(END)
*
* FUNCTIONS
*
* FUNCTION 'GETWORD'
*
GETWORD  LINE  WPAT  =                           :S(RETURN)
         LINE  =  INPUT                          :S(GETWORD)F(FRETURN)
GETWORD.END
*
* FUNCTION 'HEAD'
*
HEAD     Y  =  SIZE(HEADING)
         X  =  (LINEWIDTH - Y)  /  2
         OUTPUT  =  DUPL(' ',X)  HEADING
         OUTPUT  =  DUPL(' ',X)  DUPL('-',Y)     :(RETURN)
HEAD.END
*
* END OF FUNCTIONS
*
* ERROR MESSAGE
*
ERROR    OUTPUT  =  'TABLE CONVERSION FAILED'
*
END
```

4

```
* THIS PROGRAM READS EACH WORD IN A TEXT, TOGETHER WITH ANY
* FOLLOWING BLANKS OR PUNCTUATION MARKS, INTO A LINKED LIST.
* IT THEN READS THROUGH THE LIST AND PRINTS ALL OCCURRENCES OF
* THE WORD 'AND' FOLLOWED BY THE NEXT WORD IN THE TEXT, BOTH
* WORDS BEING ACCOMPANIED BY ANY PUNCTUATION WHICH MAY FOLLOW THEM.
* FINALLY, IT READS THE LIST AGAIN AND PRINTS ALL OCCURRENCES OF
* 'BUT' WITH THE FOLLOWING WORD.  THE LIST CAN BE PROCESSED AS
* MANY TIMES AS REQUIRED, TO EXTRACT ANY ADDITIONAL ITEMS, IF
* EXTRA CALLS OF THE FUNCTION 'PROCESS' ARE MADE.
*
* INITIALISATION
*
         &ANCHOR  =  1
         &TRIM  =  1
         PUNCT  =  '.,;:!? '
         DATA('WD(FORM,NEXT)')
         DEFINE('FETCHWD()')
         LETTERS  =  "ABCDEFGHIJKLMNOPQRSTUVWXYZ'-"
         WORDPUNC  =  BREAK(LETTERS)  (SPAN(LETTERS)  SPAN(PUNCT))
+                  .  FETCHWD
         DEFINE('PROCESS(STRING)')
*
* PROCESSING
*
* USE FUNCTION 'FETCHWD' TO FETCH THE FIRST WORD, PLUS ANY BLANKS
* OR PUNCTUATION MARKS AFTER IT.  CREATE A DATA OBJECT OF TYPE
* 'WD', WITH THE WORD FORM AS THE VALUE OF THE 'FORM' FIELD, AND
* THE 'NEXT' FIELD NULL (AS YET).  ASSIGN THIS DATA OBJECT AS THE
* VALUE OF 'FIRST'.
*
         FIRST  =  WD(FETCHWD())                    :F(ERROR)
*
* 'CURRENT' HOLDS THE WORD CURRENTLY BEING PROCESSED, TOGETHER
* WITH ITS PROPERTIES.
*
         CURRENT  =  FIRST
*
* FETCH THE NEXT WORD.  CREATE A DATA OBJECT OF TYPE 'WD'
* CORRESPONDING TO THIS NEW WORD, AND ASSIGN THE OBJECT AS THE
* VALUE OF THE 'NEXT' FIELD OF 'CURRENT', SO CREATING A POINTER
* FROM ONE WORD TO THE NEXT.  IF THERE ARE NO MORE WORDS TO BE
* FOUND, SKIP TO THE LIST PROCESSING PART OF THE PROGRAM.
*
NEXT     NEXT(CURRENT)  =  WD(FETCHWD())            :F(FIND)
*
* NOW ASSIGN THE VALUE OF THE 'NEXT' FIELD OF 'CURRENT' AS THE
* NEW VALUE OF 'CURRENT'.  THAT IS, THE NEW VALUE OF 'CURRENT'
* IS THE DATA OBJECT CORRESPONDING TO THE WORD JUST ISOLATED.
* THE LINKING PROCESS IS THEN REPEATED .
*
         CURRENT  =  NEXT(CURRENT)                  :(NEXT)
*
* USE FUNCTION 'PROCESS' TO READ THROUGH THE LIST, ISOLATING
* AND PRINTING THE REQUIRED ITEMS TOGETHER WITH THE NEXT ITEM IN
* THE TEXT, FOR EACH OCCURRENCE.
*
FIND     PROCESS('AND')
         PROCESS('BUT')                             :(END)
*
* FUNCTIONS
*
* FUNCTION 'FETCHWD' FETCHES THE NEXT WORD IN THE TEXT, TOGETHER
* WITH THE FOLLOWING BLANK(S) OR PUNCTUATION.  A  BLANK IS ADDED
* AT THE END OF EACH INPUT LINE IN CASE A WORD GOES RIGHT UP
* TO THE END POSITION.  THE FUNCTION FAILS ONLY WHEN THERE IS NO
* MORE TEXT TO BE READ.  'LINE' IS A GLOBAL VARIABLE.
*
FETCHWD  LINE WORDPUNC  =                           :S(RETURN)
         LINE  =  INPUT  ' '                :S(FETCHWD)F(FRETURN)
FETCHWD.END
*
* FUNCTION 'PROCESS'
*
* FUNCTION 'PROCESS' READS THROUGH A LINKED LIST, LOOKING FOR
* A PARTICULAR WORD, AND PRINTS EACH OCCURRENCE OF THE WORD
* TOGETHER WITH THE FOLLOWING WORD.
*
```

```
* PRINT HEADING.
*
PROCESS   OUTPUT  =  STRING
          OUTPUT  =  DUPL('-',SIZE(STRING))
*
* ASSIGN FIRST OBJECT IN LIST TO 'CURRENT'.
*
          CURRENT  =  FIRST
*
* TEST FOR THE REQUIRED STRING PLUS BLANKS OR PUNCTUATION.
*
PROCESS.1 FORM(CURRENT) STRING SPAN(PUNCT) RPOS(0) :F(PROCESS.2)
*
* IF REQUIRED STRING FOUND, PRINT ITEM AND NEXT ITEM IF THERE IS ONE
* (THAT IS, IF THE END OF THE LIST HAS NOT BEEN REACHED).
*
          OUTPUT  =  DIFFER(NEXT(CURRENT))  FORM(CURRENT)  ' '
+                    FORM(NEXT(CURRENT))              :F(PROCESS.3)
*
* USE POINTER TO MOVE TO NEXT WORD IN LIST.
*
PROCESS.2 CURRENT  =  DIFFER(NEXT(CURRENT))  NEXT(CURRENT)
+                                  :S(PROCESS.1)F(PROCESS.4)
*
* IF LIST EXHAUSTED (THAT IS, IF DATA OBJECT FOR LAST WORD ISOLATED
* HAS NULL 'NEXT' FIELD) PRINT FINAL WORD (WHICH IS THE REQUIRED
* STRING) TOGETHER WITH ANY PUNCTUATION.
*
PROCESS.3 OUTPUT  =  FORM(CURRENT)
PROCESS.4 OUTPUT  = ; OUTPUT  =        :(RETURN)
PROCESS.END
*
* END OF FUNCTIONS
*
* ERROR MESSAGE
*
ERROR     OUTPUT  =  'NO TEXT TO READ'
*
END
```

Exercises 13

1 (i)
```
          AV  =  TOTAL / COUNT
```
(no blanks round operator).

(ii)
```
PRINT     OUTPUT  =  'THE AVERAGE WORD LENGTH IS '  AV
```
(label may not begin with $; quotes round string not balanced).

(iii)
```
          LINE  BREAK('!.,;:')  .  UPTOPUNCT
```
(argument of BREAK must be a string, not a pattern).

(iv)
```
          OUTPUT  =  'THE NUMBER OF WORDS BEGINNING '
+                    'WITH E IS '  ECOUNT
```
(string quote must be closed on first line and re-opened on second).

(v)
```
          OUTPUT  =  'THE TOTAL NUMBER OF WORDS IS '
+                    TOTAL                            :(NEXT.3)
```
(a statement may not be split in the middle of a variable name; a label may not contain a semicolon).

(vi)
```
          N  =  (SIZE(WORD) - 1)  /  2)  *  X
```
(WORD presumably contains a string, so WORD – 1 is senseless: a bracket is clearly intended to go after WORD).

2 (i) *Errors*

(a) No semicolon in multi-statement line (first statement).
(b) & omitted before TRIM.
(c) No failure go-to on READ statement.
(d) Argument of BREAK is a pattern: it must be a string.
(e) Brackets omitted round label in penultimate line.
(f) BREAK takes us only up to the *first* occurrence of a punctuation mark, and if this is not at the end of the line, the pattern will fail even if there is also a punctuation mark at the end of the line. We need to use simply PUNC with the anchor off.

3 *Correct version (with improved comments)*

```
* THIS PROGRAM READS IN LINES OF POETRY AND PRINTS OUT THOSE
* ENDING WITH A PUNCTUATION MARK OTHER THAN QUOTATION MARKS.
*
* INITIALISATION
*
        &ANCHOR  =  0;   &TRIM  =  1
        PUNC  =  ANY('.,;:!?')
*
* PROCESSING
*
* READ IN A LINE AND TEST FOR REQUIRED PATTERN.  PRINT LINE IF
* PATTERN FOUND.
*
READ    LINE  =  INPUT                        :F(END)
        LINE  PUNC  RPOS(0)                   :F(READ)
        OUTPUT  =  LINE                       :(READ)
END
```

(ii) *Errors*

(a) Asterisk omitted at start of second comment line.
(b) &TRIM follows immediately after the semi-colon, and so will be interpreted as a label.
(c) No blanks round = in first line.
(d) The pattern for word-forming characters is assigned to a variable LETTERS, but the variable name used in WPAT is LETTER.
(e) The failure go-to on the READ statement is to a statement labelled PRINTOUT, but no such statement exists: the correct label is PRINT.
(f) Words are not deleted as they are found by WPAT.
(g) No blank to left of = in COUNT= COUNT + 1.
(h) In PRINT statement, no blank left after IS, and no + sign to indicate a continuation line.

Correct version

```
* THIS PROGRAM COUNTS THE NUMBER OF THREE-LETTER WORDS IN A TEXT.
*
* INITIALISATION
*
        &ANCHOR  =  1;      &TRIM  =  1
        LETTERS  =  "ABCDEFGHIJKLMNOPQRSTUVWXYZ'-"
        WPAT  =  BREAK(LETTERS)  SPAN(LETTERS)  .  WORD
*
* PROCESSING
*
```

```
* READ IN A LINE, ISOLATE A WORD, TEST LENGTH, INCREMENT
* COUNTER IF WORD IS THREE LETTERS LONG.
*
READ      LINE  =  INPUT                        :F(PRINT)
GETWD     LINE  WPAT  =                         :F(READ)
          EQ(SIZE(WORD),3)                      :F(GETWD)
          COUNT  =  COUNT  +  1                 :(GETWD)
*
* TERMINATION
*
* PRINT COUNT.
*
PRINT     OUTPUT  =  'THE NUMBER OF THREE LETTER WORDS IS '
+                    COUNT
END
```

(iii) *Errors*

(a) The pattern to test whether words begin with A and end with -ING is assigned to the variable PATT2, but this is mistyped as PATT.2 when the pattern is used later in the program.

(b) Since the anchor is on, we must use RTAB in PATT2, not RPOS.

(c) The failure go-to in the statement labelled GETWD should be :(READ), not :(GETWD).

(d) There is no END statement.

Correct version

```
* THIS PROGRAM PRINTS ALL THE WORDS IN A TEXT WHICH START WITH
* 'A' AND END WITH 'ING'.
*
* INITIALISATION
*
          &ANCHOR  =  1;     &TRIM  =  1
          LETTERS  =  "ABCDEFGHIJKLMNOPQRSTUVWXYZ'-"
          PATT1  =  BREAK(LETTERS)  SPAN(LETTERS)  .  WORD
          PATT2  =  'A'  RTAB(3)  'ING'
*
* PROCESSING
*
* READ IN A LINE, ISOLATE A WORD, TEST FOR REQUIRED PATTERN,
* PRINT WORD IF PATTERN FOUND.
*
READ      LINE  =  INPUT                        :F(END)
GETWD     LINE  PATT1  =                        :F(READ)
          WORD  PATT2                           :F(GETWD)
          OUTPUT  =  WORD                       :(GETWD)
END
```

(iv) *Errors*

(a) The function procedure is 'flowed into' from above, because a go-to :(GETWD) has been omitted from the line OUTPUT = WORD.

(b) X is a global variable. When a string is read in, X acquires that string as its value. But when the function is called, X is assigned a numerical value, and at the end of the function procedure X will have as its value the number of letters in the word. When the function returns, the line originally stored in X will have been lost, and the statement

```
X  WPAT  =
```

will fail because X now has a numerical value. The problem can be solved by declaring X as a local variable in the function definition. The X in the function will then be treated as quite separate from the global X. A neater solution is to rewrite the function without the use of a 'storage' variable, as shown below.

(c) The first line of the function procedure should read

```
X = SIZE(STRING)
```

The function, to be general, must use the 'formal' or 'dummy' variable.

Correct version

```
* THIS PROGRAM USES A FUNCTION 'LENGTH' TO COUNT THE NUMBER OF
* LETTERS, AS OPPOSED TO HYPHENS AND APOSTROPHES, IN A WORD.
* THE PROGRAM PRINTS ALL THE WORDS IN A TEXT WITH MORE THAN 8
* TRUE LETTERS.
*
* INITIALISATION
*
          &ANCHOR  =  1
          &TRIM  =  1
          LETTERS  =  "ABCDEFGHIJKLMNOPQRSTUVWXYZ'-"
          WPAT  =  BREAK(LETTERS)  SPAN(LETTERS)  .  WORD
          PUNCPAT  =  BREAK("'-")  ANY("'-")
          DEFINE('LENGTH(STRING)')
*
* PROCESSING
*
* READ IN A LINE, ISOLATE WORDS.
*
READ      X  =  INPUT                         :F(END)
GETWD     X  WPAT  =                          :F(READ)
*
* USE FUNCTION 'LENGTH' TO CALCULATE NUMBER OF 'TRUE' LETTERS.
* TEST WHETHER THIS IS GREATER THAN 8.  IF SO, PRINT WORD.
*
          GT(LENGTH(WORD),8)                  :F(GETWD)
          OUTPUT  =  WORD                     :(GETWD)
*
* FUNCTION 'LENGTH'
*
LENGTH    LENGTH  =  SIZE(STRING)
LENGTH.1 STRING  PUNCPAT  =                   :F(RETURN)
          LENGTH  =  LENGTH  -  1             :(LENGTH.1)
LENGTH.END
*
END
```

Bibliography

1 Introduction to computers

Hunt, R. and Shelley, J. (1983) *Computers and Commonsense*, 3rd edn (London: Prentice-Hall International).

2 The scope of linguistic and literary computing: general references

Ager, D. E. (ed.) (1979) *Advances in Computer-aided Literary and Linguistic Research* (Birmingham: Department of Modern Languages, University of Aston in Birmingham).

Aitken, A. J., Bailey, R. W. and Hamilton-Smith, N. (eds.) (1973) *The Computer and Literary Studies* (Edinburgh: Edinburgh University Press).

Hockey, S. M. (1980) *A Guide to Computer Applications in the Humanities* (London: Duckworth).

Jones, A. and Churchhouse, R. F. (eds.) (1976) *The Computer in Literary and Linguistic Studies: Proceedings of the Third International Symposium* (Cardiff: University of Wales Press).

Lusignan, S. and North, J. S. (eds.) (1977) *Computing in the Humanities* (Waterloo, Ontario: University of Waterloo Press).

Mitchell, J. L. (ed.) (1974) *Computers in the Humanities* (Edinburgh: Edinburgh University Press).

Oakman, R. L. (1980) *Computer Methods for Literary Research* (Columbia, S.C.: University of South Carolina Press).

Patton, P. C. and Holoien, R. A. (eds.) (1981) *Computing in the Humanities* (Aldershot: Gower).

Wisbey, R. A. (ed.) (1971) *The Computer in Literary and Linguistic Research* (Cambridge and London: Cambridge University Press).

3 Concordance production

Burton, D. M. (1981a) 'Automated concordances and word indexes: the fifties', *Computers and the Humanities*, vol. 14, pp. 1–14.

Burton, D. M. (1981b) 'Automated concordances and word indexes: the early sixties and the early centres', *Computers and the Humanities*, vol. 15, pp. 83–100.

Burton, D. M. (1981c) 'Automated concordances and word indexes: the process, the programs, and the products', *Computers and the Humanities*, vol. 15, pp. 139–54.

Burton, D. M. (1982) 'Automated concordances and word-indexes: machine decisions and editorial revisions', *Computers and the Humanities*, vol. 16, pp. 195–218.

Dixon, J. E. G. (1978) 'Concordances KWIC and complete: an appraisal', *ALLC Bulletin*, vol. 6, pp. 28–33.

Ingram, W. (1974) 'Concordances in the seventies', *Computers and the Humanities*, vol. 8, pp. 273–7.

Oakman, R. L. (1973) 'Concordances from computers: a review article', *Proof*, vol. 3, pp. 411–25.

Spevack, M. (1973) 'Concordances: old and new', *Computer Studies in the Humanities and Verbal Behavior*, vol. 4, pp. 17–19.

4 Morphological analysis/lemmatisation

Bathurst, R. D. (1971) 'Automatic alphabetisation of Arabic words', in Wisbey (1971) pp. 185–90.

Boot, M. (1980) 'Homography and lemmatization in Dutch texts', *ALLC Bulletin*, vol. 8, pp. 175–89.

Dawson, J. L. (1974) 'Suffix removal and word conflation', *ALLC Bulletin*, vol. 2(3), pp. 33–46.

Hann, M. L. (1975) 'Towards an algorithmic methodology of lemmatisation', *ALLC Bulletin*, vol. 3, pp. 140–50.

Hellberg, S. (1972) 'Computerised lemmatisation without the aid of a dictionary: a case study from Swedish lexicology', *Computers and the Humanities*, vol. 6, pp. 209–12.

Krause, W. and Willée, G. (1981) 'Lemmatising German newspaper texts with the aid of an algorithm', *Computers and the Humanities*, vol. 15, pp. 110–14.

Maegaard, B. (1976) 'The recognition of finite verbs in French texts', *ALLC Bulletin*, vol. 4, pp. 49–52.

Meunier, J. G., Boisvert, S. and Denis, F. M. (1976) 'The lemmatisation of contemporary French', in Jones and Churchhouse (1976) pp. 208–14.

Price, J. D. (1969) 'An algorithm for analysing Hebrew words', *Computer Studies in the Humanities and Verbal Behavior*, vol. 2, pp. 137–65.

Sågvall, A. -L. (1973) *A System for Automatic Inflectional Analysis (Implemented for Russian)* (Stockholm: Almqvist and Wiksell).

Spraycar, R. S. (1980) 'Automatic lemmatization in Serbo-Croatian', *ALLC Journal*, vol. 1, pp. 51–9.

Venezky, R. L. (1973a) 'Computational aids to dictionary compiliation', in R. Frank and A. Cameron (eds), *A Plan for the Dictionary of Old English* (Toronto: University of Toronto Press) pp. 307–27.

Wolfart, H. C. (1979) 'An experiment in automatic inflexional analysis: Latin', in Ager (1979) pp. 73–81.

5 Stylistics

(i) General references

Enkvist, N. E. (1964) 'On defining style: an essay in applied linguistics', in J. Spencer (ed.), *Linguistics and Style* (London: Oxford University Press) pp. 1–56.

Leech, G. N. and Short M. H. (1981) *Style in Fiction: A Linguistic Introduction to English Fictional Prose* (London: Longman).

(ii) 'Pure' computational stylistics

Adamson, R. (1977) 'The style of *L'Etranger*', *ALLC Bulletin*, vol. 5, pp. 233–6.

Adamson, R. (1979) 'The colour vocabulary of *L'Etranger*', *ALLC Bulletin*, vol. 7, pp. 221–30.

Ariew, R. A. (1978) 'André Breton's "Poisson Soluble"', *ALLC Bulletin*, vol. 6, pp. 34–41.

Burton, D. M. (1968) 'Some uses of a grammatical concordance', *Computers and the Humanities*, vol. 2, pp. 145–54.

Burton, D. M. (1973) *Shakespeare's Grammatical Style* (Austin: University of Texas Press).

Butler, C. S. (1979) 'Poetry and the computer: some quantitative aspects of the style of Sylvia Plath', *Proceedings of the British Academy*, vol. LXV, pp. 291–312.

Cherubini, W. (1975) 'The 'Goldenness' of Sidney's *Astrophel and Stella*: test of a quantitative-stylistics routine', *Language and Style*, vol. 8, pp. 47–59.

Cluett, R. (1976) *Prose Style and Critical Reading* (New York: Columbia University Teachers' College Press).

Crosland, A. T. (1975) 'The concordance and the study of the novel', *ALLC Bulletin*, vol. 3, pp. 190–6.

Dengler, R. (1974) 'A General Inquirer analysis of sixteenth century and contemporary catechisms', *Computers and the Humanities*, vol. 8, pp. 5–19.

Dilligan, R. J. (1972) '*Ibant Obscvri*: Robert Bridges' experiment in English quantitative verse', *Style*, vol. 6, pp. 38–65.

Dilligan, R. J. and Bender, T. K. (1973) 'The lapses of time: a computer-assisted investigation of English prosody', in Aitken et al. (1973) pp. 239–52.

Duggan, J. J. (1973) *The Song of Roland: Formulaic Style and Poetic Craft* (Berkeley, Calif.: University of California Press).

English, C. (1977) 'A computer-assisted analysis of Russian prose', *ALLC Bulletin*, vol. 5, pp. 249–58.

Fortier, P. A. and McConnell, J. C. (1973) 'Computer-aided thematic analysis of French prose fiction', in Aitken et al. (1973) pp. 167–81.

Fortier, P. A. and McConnell, J. C. (1976) 'Computer-aided thematic analysis of French prose fiction: II', in Jones and Churchhouse (1976) pp. 215–22.

Honoré, T. (1979) 'Some simple measures of richness of vocabulary', *ALLC Bulletin*, vol. 7, pp. 172–7.

Kliman, B. W. (1973) 'Alliteration in Barbour's "Bruce": a study using SNAP programming', in Aitken et al. (1973) pp. 253–62.

Logan, H. M. (1982) 'The computer and metrical scansion', *ALLC Journal*, vol. 3, pp. 9–14.

Martin, W. (1973) 'Some quantitative aspects of a Dutch poem', in Aitken et al. (1973) pp. 61–8.

Martin, W. (1974) 'Literary computing at ITL', *ALLC Bulletin*, vol. 2, pp. 28–34.

Milic, L. T. (1967) *A Quantitative Approach to the Style of Jonathan Swift* (The Hague: Mouton).

Oakman, R. L. (1975) 'Carlyle and the machine: a quantitative analysis of syntax in prose style', *ALLC Bulletin*, vol. 3, pp. 100–14.

Pringle, M. B. and Ross, D. (1977) 'Dialogue and narration in Joyce's *Ulysses*', in Lusignan and North (1977) pp. 73–84.

Raben, J. (1964) 'A computer-aided study of literary influence: Milton to Shelley', in J. B. Bessinger Jr, S. M. Parrish and H. F. Arader (eds) *Proceedings of a Literary Data Processing Conference* (New York: Modern Language Association) pp. 230–74.

Raben, J. and Lieberman, D. (1976) 'Text comparison: principles and a program', in Jones and Churchhouse (1976) pp. 297–308.

Ross, D. (1973) 'Beyond the concordance: algorithms for description of English clauses and phrases', in Aitken et al. (1973) pp. 85–99.

Ross, D. (1974) 'An EYEBALL view of Blake's *Songs of Innocence and Experience*', in Mitchell (1974) pp. 94–108.

Ross, D. (1981) 'EYEBALL and the analysis of literary style', in Patton and Holoien (1981) pp. 85–104.

Ross, D. Jr and Rasche, R. H. (1972) 'EYEBALL: a computer program for description of style', *Computers and the Humanities*, vol. 6, pp. 213–21.

Sedelow, S. Y. (1970) 'The computer in the humanities and fine arts', *Computing Surveys*, vol. 2, pp. 93–6.

Spolsky, E. (1970) 'Computer-assisted semantic analysis of poetry', *Computer Studies in the Humanities and Verbal Behavior*, vol. 3, pp. 163–8.

Spolsky, E. (1974) 'Dictionaries and the semantic analysis of poetry', *SIGLASH Newsletter*, vol. 7(3), pp. 5–8.

Tallentire, D. R. (1976) 'Confirming intuitions about style, using concordances', in Jones and Churchhouse (1976) pp. 309–38.

Waite, S. V. (1973) 'Approaches to metrical research in Plautus', in Aitken et al. (1973) pp. 253–62.

Waite, S. V. (1977) 'Homer and IMPRESS: an application to Greek metrics of a social-science analysis package', in Lusignan and North (1977) pp. 37–48.

Wright, N. B. (1974) 'Measuring alliteration: a study in method', in Mitchell (1974) pp. 82–93.

(iii) 'Applied' computational stylistics

Austin, W. B. (1970) 'The authorship of certain Renaissance English pamphlets: an informal account of work in progress', in F. M. Burelbach Jr (ed.), *Proceedings. Computer Applications to Problems in the Humanities* (Brockport, N.Y.: SUNY College at Brockport).

Baillie, W. M. (1974) 'Authorship attribution in Jacobean dramatic texts', in Mitchell (1974) pp. 73–81.

Brainerd, B. (1980) 'The chronology of Shakespeare's plays: a statistical study', *Computers and the Humanities*, vol. 14, pp. 221–30.

Ellegård, A. (1962a) *Who was Junius?* (Stockholm: Almqvist and Wiksell).

Ellegård, A. (1962b) *A Statistical Method for Determining Authorship: The Junius Letters 1769–1772*, Gothenburg Studies in English, no. 13 (Gothenburg: University of Gothenburg Press).

Greenblatt, D. L. (1973) 'Generative metrics and the authorship of "The Expostulation"', *Centrum*, vol. 1, pp. 87–104.

Kenny, A. (1977) 'The stylometric study of Aristotle's Ethics', in Lusignan and North (1977) pp. 11–22.

Kenny, A. J. P. (1978) *The Aristotelian Ethics* (Oxford: Oxford University Press).

Kenny, A. (1979) 'A stylometric study of Aristotle's Metaphysics', *ALLC Bulletin* vol. 7, pp. 12–21.

Kjetsaa, G. (1976) 'Storms on the Quiet Don: a pilot study', *Scando-Slavica*, vol. 22, pp. 5–24.

Kjetsaa, G. (1977) 'The battle of 'the Quiet Don': another pilot study', *Computers and the Humanities*, vol. 11, pp. 341–6.

Kjetsaa, G. (1979) '*And Quiet Flows the Don* through the computer', *ALLC Bulletin*, vol. 7, pp. 248–56.

Kjetsaa, G. (1981) 'Written by Dostoevsky?', *ALLC Journal*, vol. 2, pp. 25–33.

Köster, P. (1971) 'Computer stylistics: Swift and some contemporaries', in Wisbey (1971) pp. 129–47.

Mansell, D. (1974) '*The Old Man and the Sea* and the computer', *Computers and the Humanities*, vol. 8, pp. 195–206.

Michaelson, S. and Morton, A. Q. (1972) 'Last words: a test of authorship for Greek writers', *New Testament Studies*, vol. 18, pp. 192–208.

Michaelson, S. and Morton, A. Q. (1973) 'Positional stylometry' in Aitken et al. (1973) pp. 69–83.

Michaelson, S. and Morton, A. Q. (1976) 'Things ain't what they used to be: a study of chronological change in a Greek writer', in Jones and Churchhouse (1976) pp. 78–84.

Morton, A. Q. (1965) 'The authorship of Greek prose', *Journal of the Royal Statistical Society, Series A*, vol. 128, pp. 169–224.

Morton, A. Q. (1978) *Literary Detection: How to Prove Authorship and Fraud in Literature and Documents* (New York: Bowker).

Mosteller, F. and Wallace, D. L. (1964) *Inference and Disputed Authorship: 'The Federalist'* (Reading, Mass.: Addison-Wesley).

6 Lexicography

Aitken, A. J. (1971) 'Historical dictionaries and the computer', in Wisbey (1971) pp. 3–17.

Alford, M. H. T. (1973) 'The computer and lexicography', *ALLC Bulletin*, vol. 1(1), pp. 8–9.

Allén, S. (1977) 'Text-based lexicography and algorithmic text analysis', *ALLC Bulletin*, vol. 5, pp. 126–31.

Bailey, R. W. and Robinson, J. L. (1968) 'The University of Michigan Early Modern English dictionary project', *Shakespeare Research and Opportunities*, vol. 4, pp. 120–1.

Bratley, P. and Lusignan, S. (1976) 'Information processing in dictionary making: some technical guidelines', *Computers and the Humanities*, vol. 10, pp. 133–43.

Cameron, A. (1977) 'The *Dictionary of Old English* and the computer', in Lusignan and North (1977) pp. 101–6.

de Tollenaere, F. (1973) 'The problem of context in computer-aided lexicography' in Aitken et al. (1973) pp. 25–35.

Henderson, M. M. T. (1975) 'Use of an interactive program in analysing data for a dialect dictionary', *Computers and the Humanities*, vol. 9, pp. 105–13.

Lara, L. F. (1976) 'On lexicographical computing: some aspects of the work for a Mexican Spanish dictionary', *ALLC Bulletin*, vol. 4, pp. 97–104.

Robinson, J. L. and Bailey, R. W. (1973) 'Computer-produced microfilm in lexicography: toward a dictionary of Early Modern English', in Aitken et al. (1973) pp. 3–14.

Spevack, M. and Neuhaus, H. J. (1977) 'SHAD (A Shakespeare Dictionary): toward volume one', *ALLC Bulletin*, vol. 5, pp. 15–22.

Spevack, M., Neuhaus, H. J. and Finkenstaedt, T. (1974) 'SHAD (A Shakespeare dictionary', in Mitchell (1974) pp. 111–23.

Venezky, R. L. (1973b) 'Computer applications in lexicography', in R. I. McDavid Jr and A. R. Duckert (eds), *Lexicography in English*, Annals of the New York Academy of Sciences, vol. 211, (New York) pp. 287–92.

7 Textual editing

Cabaniss, M. S. (1970) 'Using the computer for text collation', *Computer Studies in the Humanities and Verbal Behavior*, vol. 3, pp. 1–33.

Froger, J. (1967) *La Critique des Textes et son Automatisation* (Paris: Dunod).

Gilbert, P. (1973) 'Automatic collation: a technique for medieval texts', *Computers and the Humanities*, vol. 7, pp. 139–47.

Gilbert, P. (1976) 'Using the computer to collate medieval Latin manuscripts', in Jones and Churchhouse (1976) pp. 103–13.

Griffith, J. G. (1968) 'A taxonomic study of the manuscript tradition of Juvenal', *Museum Helveticum*, vol. 25, pp. 101–38.

Griffith, J. G. (1969) 'Numerical taxonomy and some primary manuscripts of the Gospels', *Journal of Theological Studies*, vol. 20, pp. 389–406.

Ott, W. (1974) 'Bibliographie: Computer in der Editionstechnik', *ALLC Bulletin*, vol. 2(1), pp. 73–80.

Petty, G. R. and Gibson, W. M. (1970) *Project OCCULT: The Ordered Computer Collation of Unprepared Literary Text* (New York: New York University Press).

Poole, E. (1974) 'The computer in determining stemmatic relationships', *Computers and the Humanities*, vol. 8, pp. 207–16.

Silva, G. and Love, H. (1969) 'The identification of text variants by computer', *Information Storage and Retrieval*, vol. 5, pp. 89–108.

Widmann, R. L. (1971) 'The computer in historical collation: use of the IBM 360/75 in collating multiple editions of *A Midsummer Night's Dream*', in Wisbey (1971) pp. 57–63.

Widmann, R. L. (1973) 'Computer collation', *Computer Studies in the Humanities and Verbal Behavior*, vol. 4, pp. 45–51.

Zarri, G. P. (1973) 'Algorithms, *stemmata codicum* and the theories of Dom H. Quentin', in Aitken et al. (1973) pp. 225–37.

Zarri, G. P. (1976) 'A computer model for textual criticism', in Jones and Churchhouse (1976) pp. 133–55.

Zarri, G. P. (1977) 'Some experiments on automated textual criticism', *ALLC Bulletin*, vol. 5, pp. 266–90.

8 Language teaching and learning

Ahmad, K., Colenso, M. and Corbett, G. (1978) 'On the teaching of Russian numerals by using an online computer', *ALLC Bulletin*, vol. 6, pp. 235–41.

Brookman, W. R., Hockfield, G. and Patton, P. C. (1981) 'Sumerian: an experiment in CAI Language Learning', in Patton and Holoien (1981) pp. 235–51.

Burnett-Hall, D. G. and Stupples, P. (1971) 'The use of word frequency in language course writing', in Wisbey (1971) pp. 103–14.

Butler, C. S. (1974) 'German for chemists', *CILT Reports and Papers 11* (London: CILT) pp. 50–3.

Decker, H. W. (1976) 'Computer-aided instruction in French syntax', *Modern Language Journal*, vol. 60, pp. 263–7.

Decker, K. W., Schaden, O. L., Patton, P. C. and Thornton, K. C. (1981) 'A computer-based course in Ancient Egyptian hieroglyphics', in Patton and Holoien (1981) pp. 253–62.

Dudrap, C. and Emery, G. (1971) 'Sorting the French vocabulary according to word endings', in Wisbey (1971) pp. 87–92.

Gear, D. V. (1981) 'A small-computer CAI course in Classical Greek', in Patton and Holoien (1981) pp. 263–78.

Higgins, J. (1983) 'Computer-assisted language learning', *Linguistics and Language Teaching: Abstracts*, vol. 16, pp. 102–23.

Higgins, J. and Johns, T. (1984) *Computers in Language Learning* (London and Glasgow: Collins).

Holmes, G. (1980) 'A contextualised vocabulary learning drill for French', *Computers and the Humanities*, vol. 14, pp. 105–12.

Kanocz, S. and Wolff, A. (1971) 'The role of the computer in selecting contemporary German prose for a beginners' (second stage) course', in Wisbey (1971) pp. 93–102.

Kenning, M. J. and Kenning, M. -M. (1983) *An Introduction to Computer Assisted Language Teaching* (Oxford: Oxford University Press).

Last, R. W. (1979) 'The role of computer-assisted learning in modern language teaching', *ALLC Bulletin*, vol. 7, pp. 165–71.

Packard, D. W. (1975) 'Teaching Ancient Greek (with the help of a computer)', *ALLC Bulletin*, vol. 3, 45–51.

Peckett, C. W. E. (1975) 'The use of a computer in devising a beginners' Latin course', *ALLC Bulletin*, vol. 3, pp. 158–60.

Vellios, G., Erickson, G. M. and Gulino, R. (1981) 'A Latin course on a small computer', in Patton and Holoien (1981) pp. 279–86.

Wyatt, D. H. (ed.) (1984) *Computer-assisted Language Instruction* (Oxford: Pergamon).

9 Simulation of human language processing

(i) General reference

Hendrix, G. G. and Sacerdoti, E. (1981) 'Natural language processing: the field in perspective', *Byte*, September, pp. 304–52.

(ii) Generating and understanding discourse

Brady, M. and Berwick, R. C. (eds) (1983) *Computer Models of Discourse* (Cambridge, Mass.: MIT Press).

Davey, A. (1978) *Discourse Production: A Computer Model of Some Aspects of a Speaker* (Edinburgh: Edinburgh University Press).

McDonald, D. D. (1980) 'Natural language production as a process of decision-making under constraints', PhD thesis, Massachusetts Institute of Technology.

McKeown, K. R. (1982) 'Generating natural language text in response to questions about database structure', PhD thesis, University of Pennysylvania.

Mann, W. C. and Matthiessen, C. M. I. M. (1983) *Nigel: A Systemic Grammar for Text Generation*, Report no. ISI/RR-83-105, Information Sciences Institute, University of Southern California, Marina del Rey, California.

Winograd, T. (1972) *Understanding Natural Language* (Edinburgh: Edinburgh University Press).

(iii) Machine translation

CEC (Commission of the European Communities) (1978) *Overcoming the Language Barrier: 3rd European Congress on Information Systems and Networks, Luxembourg 3–6 May 1977* (London, Paris and New York: Saur) 2 vols.

Hutchins, W. J. (1978) 'Machine translation and machine-aided translation', *Journal of Documentation*, vol. 34, pp. 119–59.

King, M. and Perschke, S. (1982) 'EUROTRA and its objectives', *Multilingua*, vol. 1, pp. 27–32.

Loh, S. -C. (1976) 'Machine translation: past, present and future', *ALLC Bulletin*, vol. 4, pp. 105–14.

Loh, S. -C., Hing-Sum, H. and Kong, L. (1979) 'A dual language translator', in Ager (1979) pp. 107–16.

Loh, S. -C. and Kong, L. (1978) 'Computer translation of Chinese scientific journals', in CEC (1978) vol. 1, pp. 631–45.

Macdonald, R. R. (1979) 'The problem of machine translation', in B. Henisz-Dostert, R. R. Macdonald and M. Zarechnak, *Machine Translation*, Trends in Linguistics, Studies and Monographs, no. 11 (The Hague: Mouton) pp. 91–145.

Rolling, L. (1978) 'The facts about automatic translation', in P. J. Taylor (ed.), *New Trends in Documentation and Information: Proceedings of the 39th FID Congress, University of Edinburgh, 25–28 September 1978* (London: Aslib).

Snell, B. M. (ed.) (1979) *Translating and the Computer* (Amsterdam: North Holland).

TAUM (1973) 'Le système de traduction automatique de l'Université de Montréal (TAUM)', *META*, vol. 18, pp. 227–89.

Toma, P. (1976a) 'An operational machine translation system', in R. W. Brislin (ed.), *Translation: Applications and Research* (New York: Gardner Press) pp. 247–59.

Toma, P. (1976b) 'Systran, in FBIS Seminar on Machine Translation', *American Journal of Computational Linguistics*, vol. 46, pp. 40–5.

Toma, P. (1978) 'Systran as a multilingual machine translation system', in CEC (1978) vol. 1, pp. 569–81.

Zachary, W. (1979) 'A survey of approaches and issues in machine translation systems', *Computers and the Humanities* vol. 13, pp. 17–28.

(iv) Speech synthesis

Atmar, W. (1977) 'The time has come to talk', in D. H. Ahl and C. T. Helmers Jr (eds), *The Best of Byte* (Morristown, N.J.: Creative Computing Press) vol. 1, pp. 231–7.

Cater, J. P. (1983) *Electronically Speaking: Computer Speech Generation* (Indianapolis: Howard W. Sams).

Rice, D. L. (1977) 'Friends, humans, and countryrobots: lend me your ears', in D. H. Ahl and C. T. Helmers Jr (eds), *The Best of Byte* (Morristown, N.J.: Creative Computing Press) vol. 1, pp. 36–43.

Sclater, N. (1983) *Introduction to Electronic Speech Synthesis* (Indianapolis: Howard W. Sams).

10 Corpus-based descriptive linguistics

Akkerman, E. (1984) 'Verb and particle combinations: particle frequency ratings and idiomaticity', *ICAME News* 8(2), 60–70.

Atwell, E. S. (1983) 'Constituent-likelihood grammar', *ICAME News* 7, 34–66.

Coates, J. (1982) *The Semantics of the Modal Auxiliaries*. (London: Croom Helm).

Coates, J. and Leech, G. (1980) 'The meanings of the modals in Modern British and American English', *York Papers in Linguistics* 8, 23–34.

de Haan, P. (1984) 'Relative clauses compared', *ICAME News* 8(2), 47–59.

Elsness, J. (1982) '*That* v. zero connective in English nominal clauses', *ICAME News* 6, 1–45.

Greenbaum, S., Leech, G. and Svartvik, J. (eds) (1980) *Studies in English Linguistics for Randolph Quirk*. (London: Longman).

Gustafsson, M. (1982) 'Textual aspects of topicalisation in a corpus of English', *ICAME News* 6, 46–73.

Hermerén, L. (1978) *On Modality in English: A Study of the Semantics of the Modals*. Lund Studies in English 53. (Lund: C. W. K. Gleerup).

Hofland, K. and Johansson, S. (1982) *Word Frequencies in British and American English*. (Bergen: Norwegian Computing Centre for the Humanities).

Johansson, S. (ed.) (1982) *Computer Corpora in English Language Research*. (Bergen: Norwegian Computing Centre for the Humanities).

Krogvig, I. (1981) '*Shall, will, should* and *would* in present-day American and British English. With special reference to *shall* and *should* in British English'. Unpublished thesis, Department of English, University of Oslo.

Krogvig, I. and Johansson, S. (1981) '*Shall, will, should and would* in British and American English', *ICAME News* 5, 32–56.

Kučera, H. and Francis, W. N. (1967) *Computational Analysis of Present-Day American English*. (Providence: Brown University Press).

Leech, G. and Coates, J. (1980) 'Semantic indeterminacy and the modals', in Greenbaum et al. 1980, 79–90.

Leech, G., Garside, R. and Atwell, E. (1983) 'The automatic grammatical tagging of the LOB Corpus', *ICAME News* 7, 13–33.

Svartvik, J. (1980) '*Well* in conversation', in Greenbaum et al. 1980, 167–77.

Svartvik, J., Eeg-Olofsson, M., Forsheden, O., Oreström, B. and Thavenius, C. (1982) *Survey of Spoken English: Report on Research 1975–81*. Lund Studies in English 63. (Lund: C. W. K. Gleerup).

Svartvik, J. and Quirk, R. (eds) (1980) *A Corpus of English Conversation*. Lund Studies in English 56. (Lund: Liber).

11 Package programs

Burnard, L. (1976) *OXEYE: A Text Processing Package for the 1906A* (Oxford: Oxford University Computing Laboratory).

Burnard, L. D. (1980) 'Software review: CLOC', *Computers and the Humanities*, vol. 14, pp. 259–60.

Butler, C. S. (1985) *Statistics in Linguistics* (Oxford: Blackwell).

Hockey, S. and Marriott, I. (1979a) 'The Oxford Concordance Project (OCP)–Part 1', *ALLC Bulletin*, vol. 7, pp. 35–43.

Hockey, S. and Marriott, I. (1979b) 'The Oxford Concordance Project (OCP)–Part 2', *ALLC Bulletin*, vol. 7, pp. 155–64.

Hockey, S. and Marriott, I. (1979c) 'The Oxford Concordance Project–Part 3', *ALLC Bulletin*, vol. 7, pp. 268–75.

Hockey, S. and Marriott, I. (1980a) *Oxford Concordance Program: Users' Manual* (Oxford: Oxford University Computing Service).

Hockey, S. and Marriott, I. (1980b) 'The Oxford Concordance Project (OCP)–Part 4', *ALLC Bulletin*, vol. 8, pp. 28–35.

Norušis, M. J. (1982) *SPSS Introductory Guide: Basic Statistics and Operations* (New York: McGraw-Hill).

Reed, A. (1977) 'CLOC: a collocation package', *ALLC Bulletin*, vol. 5, pp. 168–73.

Reed, A. (1982) *CLOC Users' Guide* (Birmingham: University of Birmingham Computer Centre).

Reed, A. (1984) 'Anatomy of a text analysis package', *Computer Languages*, vol. 9(2), pp. 89–96.

Reed, A. and Schonfelder, J. L. (1979) 'CLOC: a general purpose concordance and collocations generator', in Ager (1979) pp. 59–72.

Ryan, T. A. Jr, Joiner, B. L. and Ryan, B. F. (1976) *Minitab Student Handbook* (Boston, Mass.: Duxbury Press).

12 SNOBOL4 and its uses

Butler, C. S. (1979) 'Poetry and the computer: some quantitative aspects of the style of Sylvia Plath', *Proceedings of the British Academy*, vol. LXV, pp. 291–312.

Gimpel, J. F. (1976) *Algorithms in SNOBOL4* (New York: Wiley).

Griswold, R. E., Poage, J. F. and Polonsky, I. P. (1971) *The SNOBOL4 Programming Language*, 2nd edn (Englewood Cliffs, N.J.: Prentice-Hall).

Griswold, R. E. (1975) *String and List Processing in SNOBOL4* (Englewood Cliffs, N.J.: Prentice-Hall).

Stubbs, M. W. (forthcoming) *Language and Language Use* (Oxford: Blackwell).

Index